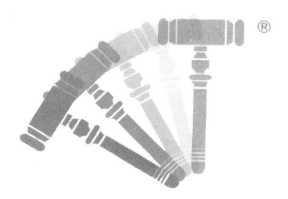

Casenote™ Legal Briefs

COMMERCIAL LAW

Keyed to **Whaley's Commercial Law,** Seventh Edition
Including his books on **Sales, Leases, and Licenses;**
Payment Law; and **Secured Transactions**

ASPEN

PUBLISHERS

1185 Avenue of the Americas, New York, NY 10036
www.aspenpublishers.com

© 2003 Aspen Publishers, Inc.
www.aspenpublishers.com

Permissions
Aspen Publishers
1185 Avenue of the Americas
New York, NY 10036

Printed in the United States of America.

ISBN 0-7355-4354-2

1 2 3 4 5 6 7 8 9 0

About Aspen Publishers

Aspen Publishers, headquartered in New York City, is a leading information provider for attorneys, business professionals, and law students. Written by preeminent authorities, our products consist of analytical and practical information covering both U.S. and international topics. We publish in the full range of formats, including updated manuals, books, periodicals, CDs, and online products.

Our proprietary content is complemented by 2,500 legal databases, containing over 11 million documents, available through our Loislaw division. Aspen Publishers also offers a wide range of topical legal and business databases linked to Loislaw's primary material. Our mission is to provide accurate, timely, and authoritative content in easily accessible formats, supported by unmatched customer care.

To order any Aspen Publishers title, go to *www.aspenpublishers.com* or call 1-800-638-8437.

For more information on Loislaw products, go to *www.loislaw.com* or call 1-800-364-2512.

For Customer Care issues, e-mail CustomerCare@aspenpublishers.com; call 1-800-234-1660; or fax 1-800-901-9075.

Aspen Publishers
A Wolters Kluwer Company

FORMAT FOR THE CASENOTE LEGAL BRIEF

PARTY ID: Quick identification of the relationship between the parties.

NATURE OF CASE: This section identifies the form of action (e.g., breach of contract, negligence, battery), the type of proceeding (e.g., demurrer, appeal from trial court's jury instructions) or the relief sought (e.g., damages, injunction, criminal sanctions).

FACT SUMMARY: This is included to refresh the student's memory and can be used as a quick reminder of the facts.

CONCISE RULE OF LAW: Summarizes the general principle of law that the case illustrates. It may be used for instant recall of the court's holding and for classroom discussion or home review.

FACTS: This section contains all relevant facts of the case, including the contentions of the parties and the lower court holdings. It is written in a logical order to give the student a clear understanding of the case. The plaintiff and defendant are identified by their proper names throughout and are always labeled with a (P) or (D).

ISSUE: The issue is a concise question that brings out the essence of the opinion as it relates to the section of the casebook in which the case appears. Both substantive and procedural issues are included if relevant to the decision.

HOLDING AND DECISION: This section offers a clear and in-depth discussion of the rule of the case and the court's rationale. It is written in easy-to-understand language and answers the issue(s) presented by applying the law to the facts of the case. When relevant, it includes a thorough discussion of the exceptions to the case as listed by the court, any major cites to other cases on point, and the names of the judges who wrote the decisions.

CONCURRENCE / DISSENT: All concurrences and dissents are briefed whenever they are included by the casebook editor.

EDITOR'S ANALYSIS: This last paragraph gives the student a broad understanding of where the case "fits in" with other cases in the section of the book and with the entire course. It is a hornbook-style discussion indicating whether the case is a majority or minority opinion and comparing the principal case with other cases in the casebook. It may also provide analysis from restatements, uniform codes, and law review articles. The editor's analysis will prove to be invaluable to classroom discussion.

QUICKNOTES: Conveniently defines legal terms found in the case and summarizes the nature of any statutes, codes, or rules referred to in the text.

PALSGRAF v. LONG ISLAND R.R. CO.
Injured bystander (P) v. Railroad company (D)
N.Y. Ct. App., 248 N.Y. 339, 162 N.E. 99 (1928).

NATURE OF CASE: Appeal from judgment affirming verdict for plaintiff seeking damages for personal injury.

FACT SUMMARY: Helen Palsgraf (P) was injured on R.R.'s (D) train platform when R.R.'s (D) guard helped a passenger aboard a moving train, causing his package to fall on the tracks. The package contained fireworks which exploded, creating a shock that tipped a scale onto Palsgraf (P).

CONCISE RULE OF LAW: The risk reasonably to be perceived defines the duty to be obeyed.

FACTS: Helen Palsgraf (P) purchased a ticket to Rockaway Beach from R.R. (D) and was waiting on the train platform. As she waited, two men ran to catch a train that was pulling out from the platform. The first man jumped aboard, but the second man, who appeared as if he might fall, was helped aboard by the guard on the train who had kept the door open so they could jump aboard. A guard on the platform also helped by pushing him onto the train. The man was carrying a package wrapped in newspaper. In the process, the man dropped his package, which fell on the tracks. The package contained fireworks and exploded. The shock of the explosion was apparently of great enough strength to tip over some scales at the other end of the platform, which fell on Palsgraf (P) and injured her. A jury awarded her damages, and R.R. (D) appealed.

ISSUE: Does the risk reasonably to be perceived define the duty to be obeyed?

HOLDING AND DECISION: (Cardozo, C.J.) Yes. The risk reasonably to be perceived defines the duty to be obeyed. If there is no foreseeable hazard to the injured party as the result of a seemingly innocent act, the act does not become a tort because it happened to be a wrong as to another. If the wrong was not willful, the plaintiff must show that the act as to her had such great and apparent possibilities of danger as to entitle her to protection. Negligence in the abstract is not enough upon which to base liability. Negligence is a relative concept, evolving out of the common law doctrine of trespass on the case. To establish liability, the defendant must owe a legal duty of reasonable care to the injured party. A cause of action in tort will lie where harm, though unintended, could have been averted or avoided by observance of such a duty. The scope of the duty is limited by the range of danger that a reasonable person could foresee. In this case, there was nothing to suggest from the appearance of the parcel or otherwise that the parcel contained fireworks. The guard could not reasonably have had any warning of a threat to Palsgraf (P), and R.R. (D) therefore cannot be held liable. Judgment is reversed in favor of R.R. (D).

DISSENT: (Andrews, J.) The concept that there is no negligence unless R.R. (D) owes a legal duty to take care as to Palsgraf (P) herself is too narrow. Everyone owes to the world at large the duty of refraining from those acts that may unreasonably threaten the safety of others. If the guard's action was negligent as to those nearby, it was also negligent as to those outside what might be termed the "danger zone." For Palsgraf (P) to recover, R.R.'s (D) negligence must have been the proximate cause of her injury, a question of fact for the jury.

EDITOR'S ANALYSIS: The majority defined the limit of the defendant's liability in terms of the danger that a reasonable person in defendant's situation would have perceived. The dissent argued that the limitation should not be placed on liability, but rather on damages. Judge Andrews suggested that only injuries that would not have happened but for R.R.'s (D) negligence should be compensable. Both the majority and dissent recognized the policy-driven need to limit liability for negligent acts, seeking, in the words of Judge Andrews, to define a framework "that will be practical and in keeping with the general understanding of mankind." The Restatement (Second) of Torts has accepted Judge Cardozo's view.

QUICKNOTES

FORESEEABILITY – The reasonable anticipation that damage is a likely result from certain acts or omissions.

NEGLIGENCE - Failure to exercise that degree of care which a person of ordinary prudence would exercise under similar circumstances.

PROXIMATE CAUSE – Something which in natural and continuous sequence, unbroken by any new intervening cause, produces an event, and without which the injury would not have occurred.

NOTE TO STUDENTS

Aspen Publishers is proud to offer *Casenote Legal Briefs*–continuing thirty years of publishing America's best-selling legal briefs.

Casenote Legal Briefs are designed to help you save time when briefing assigned cases. Organized under convenient headings, they show you how to abstract the basic facts and holdings from the text of the actual opinions handed down by the courts. Used as part of a rigorous study regime, they can help you spend more time analyzing and critiquing points of law than on copying out bits and pieces of judicial opinions into your notebook or outline.

Casenote Legal Briefs should never be used as a substitute for assigned casebook readings. They work best when read as a follow-up to reviewing the underlying opinions themselves. Students who try to avoid reading and digesting the judicial opinions in their casebooks or on-line sources will end up shortchanging themselves in the long run. The ability to absorb, critique, and restate the dynamic and complex elements of case law decisions is crucial to your success in law school and beyond. It cannot be developed vicariously.

Casenote Legal Briefs represent but one of the many offerings in Aspen's Study Aid Timeline, which includes:

- Casenotes *Legal Briefs*
- Emanuel *Outlines*
- *Examples & Explanations* Series
- *Introduction to Law* Series
- Emanuel *Law in A Flash* Flashcards
- Emanuel *CrunchTime* Series

Each of these series is designed to provide you with easy-to-understand explanations of complex points of law. Each volume offers guidance on the principles of legal analysis and, consulted regularly, will hone your ability to spot relevant issues. We have titles that will help you prepare for class, prepare for your exams, and enhance your general comprehension of the law along the way.

To find out more about Aspen Study Aid publications, visit us on-line at www.aspenpublishers.com or e-mail us at legaledu@aspenpubl.com. We'll be happy to assist you.

Free access to Briefs and Updates on-line!

Download the cases you want in your notes or outlines using the full cut-and-paste feature accompanying our on-line briefs. On-line briefs will also contain the latest updates. Please fill out this form for full access to these useful features. No photocopies of this form will be accepted.

① **Name:** _____ **Phone:** (____) _____

Address: _____ **Apt.:** _____

City: _____ **State:** _____ **ZIP Code:** _____

Law School: _____ **Year (circle one):** 1st 2nd 3rd

② **Cut out the UPC found on the lower left-hand corner of the back cover of this book. Staple the UPC inside this box. Only the original UPC from the book cover will be accepted. (No photocopies or store stickers are allowed.)**

> **Attach UPC inside this box.**

③ **E-mail:** _____ **(Print LEGIBLY or you may not get access!)**

④ **Title (course subject) of this book** _____

⑤ **Used with which casebook (provide author's name):** _____

⑥ **Mail the completed form to:**   Aspen Publishers, Inc.
Legal Education Division
Casenote On-line Access
1185 Avenue of the Americas
New York, NY 10036

I understand that on-line access is granted solely to the purchaser of this book for the academic year in which it was purchased. Any other usage is not authorized and will result in immediate termination of access. Sharing of codes is strictly prohibited.

_____
Signature

Upon receipt of this completed form, you will be e-mailed codes so that you may access the Briefs and Updates for this Casenote Legal Brief. On-line Briefs and Updates may not be available for all titles. For a full list of available titles please check www.aspenpublishers.com/casenotes.

HOW TO BRIEF A CASE

A. DECIDE ON A FORMAT AND STICK TO IT

Structure is essential to a good brief. It enables you to arrange systematically the related parts that are scattered throughout most cases, thus making manageable and understandable what might otherwise seem to be an endless and unfathomable sea of information. There are, of course, an unlimited number of formats that can be utilized. However, it is best to find one that suits your needs and stick to it. Consistency breeds both efficiency and the security that when called upon you will know where to look in your brief for the information you are asked to give.

Any format, as long as it presents the essential elements of a case in an organized fashion, can be used. Experience, however, has led *Casenotes* to develop and utilize the following format because of its logical flow and universal applicability.

NATURE OF CASE: This is a brief statement of the legal character and procedural status of the case (e.g., "Appeal of a burglary conviction").

There are many different alternatives open to a litigant dissatisfied with a court ruling. The key to determining which one has been used is to discover *who is asking this court for what.*

This first entry in the brief should be kept as *short as possible.* The student should use the court's terminology if the student understands it. But since jurisdictions vary as to the titles of pleadings, the best entry is the one that apprises the student of who wants what in this proceeding, not the one that sounds most like the court's language.

CONCISE RULE OF LAW: A statement of the general principle of law that the case illustrates (e.g., "An acceptance that varies any term of the offer is considered a rejection and counteroffer").

Determining the rule of law of a case is a procedure similar to determining the issue of the case. Avoid being fooled by red herrings; there may be a few rules of law mentioned in the case excerpt, but usually only one is *the* rule with which the casebook editor is concerned. The techniques used to locate the issue, described below, may also be utilized to find the rule of law. Generally, your best guide is simply the chapter heading. It is a clue to the point the casebook editor seeks to make and should be kept in mind when reading every case in the respective section.

FACTS: A synopsis of only the essential facts of the case, i.e., those bearing upon or leading up to the issue.

The facts entry should be a short statement of the events and transactions that led one party to initiate legal proceedings against another in the first place. While some cases conveniently state the salient facts at the beginning of the decision, in other instances they will have to be culled from hiding places throughout the text, even from concurring and dissenting opinions. Some of the "facts" will often be in dispute and should be so noted. Conflicting evidence may be briefly pointed up. "Hard" facts must be included. Both must be *relevant* in order to be listed in the facts entry. It is impossible to tell what is relevant until the entire case is read, as the ultimate determination of the rights and liabilities of the parties may turn on something buried deep in the opinion.

The facts entry should never be longer than one to three *short* sentences.

It is often helpful to identify the role played by a party in a given context. For example, in a construction contract case the identification of a party as the "contractor" or "builder" alleviates the need to tell that that party was the one who was supposed to have built the house.

It is always helpful, and a good general practice, to identify the "plaintiff" and the "defendant." This may seem elementary and uncomplicated, but, especially in view of the creative editing practiced by some casebook editors, it is sometimes a difficult or even impossible task. Bear in mind that the *party presently* seeking something from this court may not be the plaintiff, and that sometimes only the cross-claim of a defendant is treated in the excerpt. Confusing or misaligning the parties can ruin your analysis and understanding of the case.

ISSUE: A statement of the general legal question answered by or illustrated in the case. For clarity, the issue is best put in the form of a question capable of a "yes" or "no" answer. In reality, the issue is simply the Concise Rule of Law put in the form of a question (e.g., "May an offer be accepted by performance?").

The major problem presented in discerning what is *the* issue in the case is that an opinion usually purports to raise and answer several questions. However, except for rare cases, only one such question is really the issue in the case. Collateral issues not necessary to the resolution of the matter in controversy are handled by the court by language known as *"obiter dictum"* or merely *"dictum."* While dicta may be included later in the brief, it has no place under the issue heading.

To find the issue, the student again asks *who wants what* and then goes on to ask *why did that party succeed or fail in getting it.* Once this is determined, the "why" should be turned into a question.

The complexity of the issues in the cases will vary, but in all cases a single-sentence question should sum up the issue. *In a few cases,* there will be two, or even more rarely, three issues of equal importance to the resolution of the case. Each should be expressed in a single-sentence question.

Since many issues are resolved by a court in coming to a final disposition of a case, the casebook editor will reproduce the portion of the opinion containing the issue or issues most relevant to the area of law under scrutiny. A noted law professor gave this advice: "Close the book; look at the title on the cover." Chances are, if it is Property, the student need not concern himself with whether, for example, the federal government's treatment of the plaintiff's land really raises a federal question sufficient to support jurisdiction on this ground in federal court.

The same rule applies to chapter headings designating sub-areas within the subjects. They tip the student off as to what the text is designed to teach. The cases are arranged in a casebook to show a progression or development of the law, so that the preceding cases may also help.

It is also most important to remember to *read the notes and questions* at the end of a case to determine what the editors wanted the student to have gleaned from it.

HOLDING AND DECISION: This section should succinctly explain the rationale of the court in arriving at its decision. In capsulizing the "reasoning" of the court, it should always include an application of the general rule or rules of law to the specific facts of the case. Hidden justifications come to light in this entry; the reasons for the state of the law, the public policies, the biases and prejudices, those considerations that influence the justices' thinking and, ultimately, the outcome of the case. At the end, there should be a short indication of the disposition or procedural resolution of the case (e.g., "Decision of the trial court for Mr. Smith (P) reversed").

The foregoing format is designed to help you "digest" the reams of case material with which you will be faced in your law school career. Once mastered by practice, it will place at your fingertips the information the authors of your casebooks have sought to impart to you in case-by-case illustration and analysis.

B. BE AS ECONOMICAL AS POSSIBLE IN BRIEFING CASES

Once armed with a format that encourages succinctness, it is as important to be economical with regard to the time spent on the actual reading of the case as it is to be economical in the writing of the brief itself. This does not mean "skimming" a case. Rather, it means reading the case with an "eye" trained to recognize into which "section" of your brief a particular passage or line fits and having a system for quickly and precisely marking the case so that the passages fitting any one particular part of the brief can be easily identified and brought together in a concise and accurate manner when the brief is actually written.

It is of no use to simply repeat everything in the opinion of the court; the student should only record enough information to trigger his or her recollection of what the court said. Nevertheless, an accurate statement of the "law of the case," i.e., the legal principle applied to the facts, is absolutely essential to class preparation and to learning the law under the case method.

To that end, it is important to develop a "shorthand" that you can use to make margin notations. These notations will tell you at a glance in which section of the brief you will be placing that particular passage or portion of the opinion.

Some students prefer to underline all the salient portions of the opinion (with a pencil or colored underliner marker), making marginal notations as they go along. Others prefer the color-coded method of underlining, utilizing different colors of markers to underline the salient portions of the case, each separate color being used to represent a different section of the brief. For example, blue underlining could be used for passages relating to the concise rule of law, yellow for those relating to the issue, and green for those relating to the holding and decision, etc. While it has its advocates, the color-coded method can be confusing and time-consuming (all that time spent on changing colored markers). Furthermore, it can interfere with the continuity and concentration many students deem essential to the reading of a case for maximum comprehension. In the end, however, it is a matter of personal preference and style. Just remember, whatever method you use, underlining must be used sparingly or its value is lost.

For those who take the marginal notation route, an efficient and easy method is to go along underlining the key portions of the case and placing in the margin alongside them the following "markers" to indicate where a particular passage or line "belongs" in the brief you will write:

N   (NATURE OF CASE)
CR   (CONCISE RULE OF LAW)
I   (ISSUE)
HC   (HOLDING AND DECISION, relates to the CONCISE RULE OF LAW behind the decision)
HR   (HOLDING AND DECISION, gives the RATIONALE or reasoning behind the decision)
HA   (HOLDING AND DECISION, APPLIES the general principle(s) of law to the facts of the case to arrive at the decision)

Remember that a particular passage may well contain information necessary to more than one part of your brief, in which case you simply note that in the margin. If you are using the color-coded underlining method instead of margin notation, simply make asterisks or checks in the margin next to the passage in question in the colors that indicate the additional sections of the brief where it might be utilized.

The economy of utilizing "shorthand" in marking cases for briefing can be maintained in the actual brief writing process itself by utilizing "law student shorthand" within the brief. There are many commonly used words and phrases for which abbreviations can be substituted in your briefs (and in your class notes also). You can develop abbreviations that are personal to you and which will save you a lot of time. A reference list of briefing abbreviations will be found elsewhere in this book.

C. USE BOTH THE BRIEFING PROCESS AND THE BRIEF AS A LEARNING TOOL

Now that you have a format and the tools for briefing cases efficiently, the most important thing is to make the time spent in briefing profitable to you and to make the most advantageous use of the briefs you create. Of course, the briefs are invaluable for classroom reference when you are called upon to explain or analyze a particular case. However, they are also useful in reviewing for exams. A quick glance at the fact summary should bring the case to mind, and a rereading of the concise rule of law should enable you to go over the underlying legal concept in your mind, how it was applied in that particular case, and how it might apply in other factual settings.

As to the value to be derived from engaging in the briefing process itself, there is an immediate benefit that arises from being forced to sift through the essential facts and reasoning from the court's opinion and to succinctly express them in your own words in your brief. The process ensures that you understand the case and the point that it illustrates, and that means you will be ready to absorb further analysis and information brought forth in class. It also ensures you will have something to say when called upon in class. The briefing process helps develop a mental agility for getting to the *gist* of a case and for identifying, expounding on, and applying the legal concepts and issues found there. Of most immediate concern, that is the mental process on which you must rely in taking law school examinations. Of more lasting concern, it is also the mental process upon which a lawyer relies in serving his clients and in making his living.

ABBREVIATIONS FOR BRIEFING

acceptance	acp	offer	O
affirmed	aff	offeree	OE
answer	ans	offeror	OR
assumption of risk	a/r	ordinance	ord
attorney	atty	pain and suffering	p/s
beyond a reasonable doubt	b/r/d	parol evidence	p/e
bona fide purchaser	BFP	plaintiff	P
breach of contract	br/k	prima facie	p/f
cause of action	c/a	probable cause	p/c
common law	c/l	proximate cause	px/c
Constitution	Con	real property	r/p
constitutional	con	reasonable doubt	r/d
contract	K	reasonable man	r/m
contributory negligence	c/n	rebuttable presumption	rb/p
cross	x	remanded	rem
cross-complaint	x/c	res ipsa loquitur	RIL
cross-examination	x/ex	respondeat superior	r/s
cruel and unusual punishment	c/u/p	Restatement	RS
defendant	D	reversed	rev
dismissed	dis	Rule Against Perpetuities	RAP
double jeopardy	d/j	search and seizure	s/s
due process	d/p	search warrant	s/w
equal protection	e/p	self-defense	s/d
equity	eq	specific performance	s/p
evidence	ev	statute of limitations	S/L
exclude	exc	statute of frauds	S/F
exclusionary rule	exc/r	statute	S
felony	f/n	summary judgment	s/j
freedom of speech	f/s	tenancy in common	t/c
good faith	g/f	tenancy at will	t/w
habeas corpus	h/c	tenant	t
hearsay	hr	third party	TP
husband	H	third party beneficiary	TPB
in loco parentis	ILP	transferred intent	TI
injunction	inj	unconscionable	uncon
inter vivos	I/v	unconstitutional	unconst
joint tenancy	j/t	undue influence	u/e
judgment	judgt	Uniform Commercial Code	UCC
jurisdiction	jur	unilateral	uni
last clear chance	LCC	vendee	VE
long-arm statute	LAS	vendor	VR
majority view	maj	versus	v
meeting of minds	MOM	void for vagueness	VFV
minority view	min	weight of the evidence	w/e
Miranda warnings	Mir/w	weight of authority	w/a
Miranda rule	Mir/r	wife	W
negligence	neg	with	w/
notice	ntc	within	w/i
nuisance	nus	without prejudice	w/o/p
obligation	ob	without	w/o
obscene	obs	wrongful death	wr/d

TABLE OF CASES

1

CHAPTER 1
BASIC CONCEPTS

QUICK REFERENCE RULES OF LAW

1. **Transactions in Goods.** The reasonable care and competence owed generally by practitioners in a particular trade or profession defines the limits of an injured party's justifiable demands. (Milau Associates, Inc. v. North Avenue Development Corp.)

2. **Transactions in Goods.** A contract for a computerized reordering system is a transaction in goods subject to the U.C.C. (Analysts Intl. Corp. v. Recycled Paper Products, Inc.)

3. **Transactions in Goods.** Where one sells consumer goods which retain their character as consumer goods after completion of performance, the provisions of the U.C.C. dealing with implied warranties apply, even if the transaction is predominantly one for the rendering of consumer services. (Anthony Pools v. Sheehan)

4. **Merchants.** A person making an isolated sale of goods is not a merchant within the scope of Article 2 of the U.C.C. (Siemen v. Alden)

MILAU ASSOCIATES, INC. v.
NORTH AVENUE DEVELOPMENT CORP.
Contractors (D) v. Plaintiff (P)
N.Y. Ct. App., 42 N.Y.2d 482, 368 N.E.2d 1247, 398 N.Y.S.2d 882 (1977).

NATURE OF CASE: Appeal from denial of damages for breach of implied warranty.

FACT SUMMARY: After an underground section of pipe connecting a sprinkler system to the city's water line burst, causing substantial damage to textiles stored in a warehouse, the textile companies whose bolts of textiles were damaged filed suit against Milau (D), the general contractor which built the warehouse, and Higgins Fire Protection Inc. (D), the subcontractor which designed and installed the sprinkler system.

CONCISE RULE OF LAW: The reasonable care and competence owed generally by practitioners in a particular trade or profession defines the limits of an injured party's justifiable demands.

FACTS: When an underground section of pipe, connecting a sprinkler system to the city water line, burst, it caused substantial water damage to bolts of textiles stored in a warehouse. The commercial tenants of the building sought recovery against both Milau Associates (D), the general contractor which built the warehouse, and Higgins Fire Protection Inc. (D), the subcontractor which designed and installed the sprinkler system. The suit was brought on the alternative theories of negligence and breach of implied warranty of fitness for a particular purpose. Expert testimony suggested that a pressure phenomenon known as a "water hammer" caused a crack to develop at the root of a V-shaped notch discovered toward the end of the conduit. The "stress-raising" notch was alleged to have been produced by a dull tooth on the hydraulic squeeze cutter used by Higgins (D) to cut sections of the commercially marketed pipe furnished by the subcontractor. The textile companies alleged that only a few months of use had caused enough rusting at the base of the notch to affect the integrity of the entire system. Milau (D) and Higgins (D) produced offsetting expert opinion that the pipe itself was neither defective as manufactured nor improperly installed. The case was submitted to the jury on the sole question of negligent installation, and the jury returned a verdict in favor of Milau (D) and Higgins (D). The appellate division found no evidence that the pipe installed by Higgins (D) was unfit for its intended purpose and concluded that neither the U.C.C. nor the case law could be invoked to grant the extension of warranty protection sought by the textile companies. This appeal followed. [North Avenue Development Corp. is not identified in the casebook excerpt.]

ISSUE: Does the reasonable care and competence owed generally by practitioners in a particular trade or profession define the limits of an injured party's justifiable demands?

HOLDING AND DECISION: (Wachtler, J.) Yes. The reasonable care and competence owed generally by practitioners in a particular trade or profession defines the limits of an injured party's justifiable demands. Reasonable expectations, not perfect results in the face of any and all contingencies, will be ensured under a traditional negligence standard of conduct. U.C.C. § 2-313 requires that a seller's affirmation of fact to a buyer be made as part of the basis of the bargain, that is, the contract for the sale of goods. The express warranty section would therefore be no more applicable to a service contract than the U.C.C.'s implied warranty provisions. Of course, where the party rendering services can be shown to have expressly bound itself to the accomplishment of a particular result, the courts will enforce that promise. Both the subcontract and the agreement between Milau (D) and the owner were no more than a series of performance undertakings, plans, schedules, and specifications for the incorporation of the specialized system during the erection of a building — a predominantly labor-intensive endeavor. Thus, neither the U.C.C. nor New York common law can be read to imply an undertaking to guard against economic loss stemming from nonnegligent performance by a construction firm which has not contractually bound itself to provide perfect results. Affirmed.

EDITOR'S ANALYSIS: The court noted that where courts in other jurisdictions have purported to apply an implied warranty of fitness to transactions which in essence contemplated the rendition of services, what was actually imposed was no more than a "warranty that the performer would not act negligently," or a "warranty of workmanlike performance" imposing only the degree of care and skill that a reasonably prudent, skilled, and qualified person would have exercised under the circumstances, or an "implied warranty of competence and ability ordinarily possessed by those in the profession." The court found that the performance of Higgins (D) and Milau (D) had been tested under precisely this standard and was free from any actionable departure. In the words of the court, those who hire experts for the predominant purpose of rendering services, relying on their special skills, cannot expect infallibility.

NOTES:

ANALYSTS INTL. CORP. v. RECYCLED PAPER PRODUCTS, INC.

Corporation (P) v. Corporation (D)
1987 WL 12917 (N.D. Ill. 1987).

NATURE OF CASE: Motion for summary judgment on a counterclaim of breach of contract and warranty.

FACT SUMMARY: Recycled Paper Products, Inc. (RPP) (D) contracted with Analysts International Corporation (AIC) (P) for a computerized reordering system known as a computer-assisted merchandising program (CAMP). After CAMP was implemented, it failed to perform and, instead, disrupted RPP's business. AIC (P) attempted to fix the program, but eventually RPP (D) refused to pay and AIC (P) sued under breach of contract to recover the unpaid balance. RPP (D) countersued for breach of contract and warranty.

CONCISE RULE OF LAW: A contract for a computerized reordering system is a transaction in goods subject to the U.C.C.

FACTS: RPP (D) entered into a contract with AIC (P) whereby AIC (P) would create a custom-made computerized reordering system known as a computer-assisted merchandising program (CAMP). The parties disagreed about the material terms of their agreement. RPP (D) claimed that AIC (P) agreed to provide the system within 36 months, by October 1984, and for a set price. AIC (P) claimed that the price was only a rough estimate and that RPP (D) had agreed to pay on an hourly basis. In October 1984, AIC (P) announced CAMP would not be completed on time, and when CAMP was implemented in December, it did not perform any of its intended functions. Instead, RPP's (D) business was severely disrupted from January to June 1985. Throughout this period, AIC (P) tried to fix the program, and RPP (D) continued to pay AIC's (P) invoices. Outside auditors concluded that the system would have to be replaced, and in October 1985, despite AIC's (P) claim that the system was substantially operational, RPP (D) refused to pay an outstanding bill of $330, 386. AIC (P) sued in federal district court for breach of contract and fraud. RPP (D) countersued for, among other things, breach of contract and breach of an express warranty, implied warranty of merchantability, and warranty of fitness for a particular purpose. AIC (P) moved for summary judgment on these counterclaims.

ISSUE: Is a contract for a computerized reordering system a transaction in goods subject to the U.C.C.?

HOLDING AND DECISION: (Grady, C. J.) Yes. The claims for breach of implied warranty, brought under Sections 2-314 and 2-315 of the U.C.C., apply only to sales of goods. AIC (P) argues that the contract called for performance of services, not the sale of goods. Although RPP (D) concedes that the contract called for substantial design and programming services to be rendered by AIC (P), this alone does not entitle AIC (P) to judgment as a matter of law. The legal issue is whether the U.C.C. applies to CAMP, and that, in turn, depends on whether the agreement is for a "transaction in goods." The reasoning in cases holding that the subject of computer program contracts is the skill of programmers is unpersuasive. Software has both tangible and intangible elements; focusing on the intangible elements (as those cases do) to the exclusion of the tangible aspects, loses sight of the whole of the contract. The knowledge of the programmer is important, but only to the extent that it enables production of the contracted-for software. Here, the contract, which was not altogether explicit on this point, called for "system delivery." Where an agreement involves both goods and services, state law requires use of the "dominant purpose" test to determine whether the agreement is one for goods. Here, under this test, the dominant factor of the contract was the provision of a good—a computerized recording system. But for this end product, the contract would have had no purpose. Accordingly, RPP's (D) agreement with AIC (P) was a transaction in goods and is therefore within the U.C.C.'s purview. Summary judgment is denied.

EDITOR'S ANALYSIS: The issue of whether transactions involving the creation and sale of software are transactions in goods has been a vexing one for the courts, and has produced all sorts of stands as to the applicability of U.C.C. Article 2. The majority of courts, like the majority in this case, have found that Article 2 is applicable.

NOTES:

3

ANTHONY POOLS v. SHEEHAN
Contractor (D) v. Diver (P)
Md. Ct. App., 295 Md. 285, 455 A.2d 434 (1983).

NATURE OF CASE: Appeal from remand for new trial, reversing a denial of damages for breach of implied warranty and for strict liability in tort.

FACT SUMMARY: After he injured himself when he slipped on the diving board installed by Anthony (D), a builder of swimming pools, Sheehan (P) filed suit based on the theories of implied warranty of merchantability and strict liability in tort.

CONCISE RULE OF LAW: Where one sells consumer goods which retain their character as consumer goods after completion of performance, the provisions of the U.C.C. dealing with implied warranties apply, even if the transaction is predominantly one for the rendering of consumer services.

FACTS: After Anthony Pools (D) installed a swimming pool and diving board for the Sheehans (P), Sheehan (P) sustained bodily injuries when, walking toward the pool end of the diving board, he slipped and fell from the right side of the board and struck the coping of the pool. Sheehan (P) filed two causes of action for damages: (1) breach of an implied warranty of merchantability because the skid-resistant material built into the surface of the top of the diving board did not extend to the very edge on each side and (2) strict liability in tort because use of the "defective" diving board, particularly as positioned in the alcove of the pool, was unreasonably dangerous. The trial court directed a verdict for Anthony (D) as to liability founded on warranty because the contract between the parties contained express warranties which superseded any other warranties, express or implied. The jury verdict on the strict liability issue was also in favor of Anthony (D). The court of special appeals reversed and remanded for a new trial on the ground that the swimming pool package constituted consumer goods, rendering ineffective Anthony's (D) attempt to limit the implied warranty of merchantability. Anthony (D) petitioned the Maryland Supreme Court for certiorari.

ISSUE: Where one sells consumer goods which retain their character as consumer goods after completion of the promised performance, do the provisions of the U.C.C. dealing with implied warranties apply, even if the transaction is predominantly one for the rendering of consumer services?

HOLDING AND DECISION: (Rodowsky, J.) Yes. Where one sells consumer goods which retain their character as consumer goods after completion of the promised performance, the provisions of the U.C.C. dealing with implied warranties apply, even if the transaction is predominantly one for the rendering of consumer services. The subject contract presents a mixed or hybrid transaction. It is in part a contract for the rendering of services and in part a contract for the sale of goods. To determine the applicability of the U.C.C. in such a contract, the predominant purpose test has generally been applied. Were that test to be mechanically applied to the facts of this case, there would be no quality warranty implied as to the diving board. However, the diving board itself is not structurally integrated into the swimming pool. Anthony (D) offered the board as an optional accessory. Thus, the diving board, considered alone, is goods. Had it been purchased by the Sheehans (P) in a transaction distinct from the pool construction agreement with Anthony (D), there would have been an implied warranty of merchantability. In addition, C.L. § 2-316.1 declares that a seller of consumer services may not contractually disclaim implied warranties. An all-or-nothing classification of the instant transaction under the predominant purpose test would be contrary to the legislative policy implicit in § 2-316.1. Therefore, the better test to apply is the gravamen test, focusing on whether the gravamen of the action involves goods or services. Using that test, the diving board carried an implied warranty of merchantability. Anthony's (D) contractual disclaimer of that warranty was ineffective under C.L. § 2-316.1. As a result, the trial court erred in relying on the disclaimer as a basis for directing a verdict in favor of Anthony (D) on the warranty count. Affirmed.

EDITOR'S ANALYSIS: The court observed that a number of commentators advocated a more policy-oriented approach to determining whether warranties of quality and fitness were implied with respect to goods sold as part of a hybrid transaction in which service predominated. The gravamen test enunciated by the court was formulated by W. Hawkland in Uniform Commercial Code Series (1982), § 2-102:04, at Art. 2, p. 12. Another commentator, R. Anderson, had previously noted that: "It is probable that a goods-service transaction will come to be subjected to Article 2 of the Code insofar as the contractor's obligations with respect to the goods themselves are involved."

QUICKNOTES

IMPLIED WARRANTY OF MERCHANTABILITY - An implied promise made by a merchant in a contract for the sale of goods that such goods are suitable for the purpose for which they are purchased.

STRICT LIABILITY - Liability for all injuries proximately caused by a party's conducting of certain inherently dangerous activities without regard to negligence or fault.

SIEMEN v. ALDEN
Operator of sawmill (P) v. Manufacturer of saws (D)
Ill. Ct. App., 34 Ill. App. 3d 961, 341 N.E.2d 713 (1975).

NATURE OF CASE: Appeal from summary judgment denying damages for strict liability and breach of warranty.

FACT SUMMARY: After he was injured while using an automated multirip saw manufactured by Alden (D) and purchased from Korleski (D), Siemen (P) sought damages based on theories of strict tort liability for sale of a defective product, breach of warranties, and negligence.

CONCISE RULE OF LAW: A person making an isolated sale of goods is not a merchant within the scope of Article 2 of the U.C.C.

FACTS: When Siemen (P), owner and operator of a sawmill, tried to purchase a multirip saw from Alden (D), manufacturer of the saws, he was told that a new saw could not be delivered in less than six months. However, Alden (D) suggested that Siemen (P) contact Korleski (D), who owned two of the Alden (D) saws. Korleski (D) used one of the saws, while the other older saw sat partially dismantled and covered with boards and sawdust. After Korleski (D) informed Siemen (P) that he would have to supply and install various parts in order to use the saw, the parties agreed on a purchase price. Siemen (P) was later injured while operating the saw. He sought damages against both Alden (D) and Korleski (D) in strict tort liability for sale of a defective product, breach of warranties, and negligence. Alden (D) argued that it was not a merchant under the U.C.C. The trial court granted Alden's (D) motion for summary judgment on counts one and two. Siemen (P) filed this appeal against Korleski (D) only, contending that summary judgment in Korleski's (D) favor should be reversed because Korleski (D) had sufficient relationship to the saw to subject Korleski (D) to strict liability for sale of the defective product and, under the U.C.C., for breach of implied warranties.

ISSUE: Is a person making an isolated sale of goods a merchant within the scope of Article 2 of the U.C.C.?

HOLDING AND DECISION: (Moran, J.) No. A person making an isolated sale of goods is not a merchant within the scope of Article 2 of the U.C.C. U.C.C. § 2-314 states in pertinent part, "Unless excluded or modified . . . a warranty that the goods shall be merchantable is implied in a contract for their sale if the seller is a merchant with respect to goods of that kind." Korleski (D) was engaged in the sawmill business. The sale in the instant case was an isolated transaction and therefore did not come within the terms of § 2-314. In addition, U.C.C. § 2-315 provides that, where the seller has reason to know any particular purpose for which the goods are required and that the buyer is relying on the seller's skill or judgment to select or furnish suitable goods, there is an implied warranty that the goods shall be fit for such purpose. Here, the first

requirement was met, in that it was undisputed that Korleski (D) knew Siemen's (P) purpose for buying the saw. As to the second requirement, Siemen (P) failed to show sufficiently that he relied on Korleski's (D) skill and expertise in making the decision to purchase the saw. Rather, the uncontroverted facts established that Siemen (P) had decided to purchase an Alden (D) saw prior to his initial contact with Korleski (D). Therefore, the trial court properly granted Korleski's (D) motion for summary judgment. Affirmed.

EDITOR'S ANALYSIS: U.C.C. § 2-104 defines a merchant as: "A person who deals in goods of the kind or otherwise by his occupation holds himself out as having knowledge or skill peculiar to the practices or goods involved in the transaction or to whom such knowledge or skill may be attributed by his employment of an agent or broker or other intermediary who by his occupation holds himself out as having such knowledge or skill." However, the court noted that the comments to § 2-314 make clear that the definition of a merchant within that section is a narrow one and that the warranty of merchantability is applicable only to a person who, in a professional status, sells the particular kind of goods giving rise to the warranty. Clearly, this narrow interpretation of the definition of a merchant does not apply to sawmill owner Korleski (D).

QUICKNOTES

NEGLIGENCE - Conduct falling below the standard of care that a reasonable person would demonstrate under similar conditions.

STRICT LIABILITY - Liability for all injuries proximately caused by a party's conducting of certain inherently dangerous activities without regard to negligence or fault.

SUMMARY JUDGMENT - Judgment rendered by a court in response to a motion by one of the parties, claiming that the lack of a question of material fact in respect to an issue warrants disposition of the issue without consideration by the jury.

NOTES:

2

CHAPTER 2
CONTRACT FORMATION

QUICK REFERENCE RULES OF LAW

1. **Statute of Frauds.** For the purposes of an exception to the statute of frauds, a delay in the delivery of a written confirmation of an oral contract of over a month is not unreasonable as a matter of law where the sale price is large and the market is volatile but where the parties have developed a custom and practice of delaying written confirmation. (St. Ansgar Mils, Inc. v. Streit)

2. **The Parol Evidence Rule.** Even if the court finds a sales contract to be intended by the parties as a complete and exclusive statement of the terms of the agreement, those terms may still be explained or interpreted by evidence as to the course of dealing, usage of the trade, or course of performance. (Columbia Nitrogen Corp. v. Royster Co.)

3. **Offer and Acceptance.** Under U.C.C. § 2-207, when the offeree conditions its acceptance on assent to additional terms, the offeror must give specific assent, or the provisions of § 2-207(3) will supply the terms of the contract. (Diamond Fruit Growers, Inc. v. Krack Corp.)

4. **Offer and Acceptance.** In a "battle of the forms" case, the party opposing the inclusion of an additional term bears the burden of proving that the term works a material alteration of the contract. (Bayway Refining Co. v. Oxygenated Marketing and Trading A.G.)

5. **Offer and Acceptance.** Where an oral agreement has been reached, followed by one or both of the parties sending formal memoranda embodying the terms agreed upon and adding terms not discussed, the additional terms will become part of the agreement unless they materially alter it. (Leonard Pevar Co. v. Evans Products Co.)

6. **Offer and Acceptance.** Terms shipped with a computer do not become part of the sales contract where the vendor does not expressly make its acceptance conditional on the buyer's assent to the additional, shipped, terms and where the buyer does not expressly agree to the terms. (Klocek v. Gateway, Inc.)

ST. ANSGAR MILLS, INC. v. STREIT
Grain dealer (P) v. Livestock farmer (D)
Iowa Sup. Ct., 613 N.W.2d 289 (2000).

NATURE OF CASE: Appeal from an order of summary judgment in action to enforce an oral contract.

FACT SUMMARY: Duane Streit (Duane) (D) entered into an oral contract with St. Ansgar Mills, Inc. (St. Ansgar Mills) (P), a grain dealer, for 60,000 bushels of corn. Despite Duane's (D) longstanding custom of accepting delivery of grain from St. Ansgar Mills (P), notwithstanding the absence of, or long delay in obtaining, written confirmation of the parties' oral contracts, Duane (D) refused delivery in this instance because the market price of corn had plummeted between the time he placed his order and the delivery date. St. Ansgar Mills (P) sued for contract damages, and Duane (D) moved for summary judgment under the statute of frauds.

CONCISE RULE OF LAW: For purposes of an exception to the statute of frauds, a delay in the delivery of a written confirmation of an oral contract of over a month is not unreasonable as a matter of law where the sale price is large and the market is volatile but where the parties have developed a custom and practice of delaying written confirmation.

FACTS: Duane (D), a livestock farmer, and his father, John, who helped with the farming operations, called St. Ansgar Mills (P), a grain dealer, via telephone on July 1, 1996, to place two orders for 60,000 bushels of corn to be delivered in December 1996 and May 1997. Duane (D) later refused delivery of the corn that had been orally purchased. The custom between the parties for many years had been that Duane (D) would enter into an oral contract with St. Ansgar Mills (P). St. Ansgar Mills (P) would prepare a written confirmation of the sale and then would either mail it to Duane (D) to sign and return or wait for Duane (D) or John to sign the confirmation when they would stop into the business, which they regularly did on a monthly basis. Sometimes the confirmation would not be signed for a very long time, or it would never be returned, but in any event, Duane (D) had never before refused delivery. Departing from their monthly routine, the Streits did not come to the business in July and did not receive the written confirmation until John stopped by on August 10, 1996. St. Ansgar Mills did not have an explanation for why it did not send the confirmation to Duane (D) immediately after John failed to make his July stop at the business. Between July and December, the market price of corn plummeted. St. Ansgar Mills (P) brought an action for contract damages of $152,100 (the difference between the contract price and the market price at the time of delivery refusal), and Duane (D) moved for summary judgment, claiming the oral contract was unenforceable as a matter of law under the U.C.C.'s statute of frauds. The trial court granted the motion on the ground that St. Ansgar Mills' (P) delay of getting

written confirmation to Duane until August 10 was, as a matter of law, unreasonable.

ISSUE: For purposes of an exception to the statute of frauds, is a delay in the delivery of a written confirmation of an oral contract of over a month unreasonable as a matter of law where the sale price is large and the market is volatile but where the parties have developed a custom and practice of delaying written confirmation?

HOLDING AND DECISION: (Cady, J.) No. The statute of frauds, which is codified in the U.C.C. (Iowa Code § 554.2201), requires certain types of contracts for the sale of goods for $500 or more to be in writing. One statutory exception to the writing requirement applies to merchants where written confirmation of an oral contract is received within a reasonable time. The standard of reasonableness to establish the time in which the confirmation must be received is a flexible one and is defined in relationship to the "nature, purpose and circumstances" of the action. The "circumstances" include the custom and practice—course of dealings—of the parties and must be considered in determining what constitutes a reasonable time. Generally, the question of reasonableness of conduct is a jury question, and usually the question of what constitutes a reasonable time under the written confirmation exception of the U.C.C. is a jury question unless the evidence is so one-sided that one party should prevail as a matter of law. As demonstrated by a host of cases, the resolution of each case depends on the particular facts and circumstances. Here, the trial court relied on the large amount of the sale, volatile market conditions, and lack of an explanation by St. Ansgar Mills (P) for failing to send the written confirmation to Duane to determine that St. Ansgar Mills (P) acted unreasonably as a matter of law. However, other relevant factors that must be considered are the custom and practice of the parties to delay delivery of the confirmation and that the parties had engaged in many other similar transactions without incident. The evidence also supports an inference that St. Ansgar Mills (P) did not suspect John's failure to follow his customary practice in July of stopping by the business was a concern at the time. Accordingly, there is a genuine dispute over the reasonableness of the delay in delivering the written confirmation, and the resolution of this issue is appropriate for a jury. Reversed and remanded.

EDITOR'S ANALYSIS: Merchant confirmation letters are one of four of the exceptions to the written contract requirement under the statute of frauds, along with special manufacture, part performance, and admission in legal proceedings. As this case

Continued on next page.

demonstrates, many issues can arise with regard to each exception. For example, in this case, in addition to the issue on appeal, an issue that had come before the trial court was whether Duane (D) was a merchant. Unlike its decision with regard to written confirmation, the trial court's decision on the "merchant" issue was that a jury question was presented.

NOTES:

COLUMBIA NITROGEN CORP. v. ROYSTER CO.
Purchaser (D) v. Manufacturer (P)
451 F.2d 3 (4th Cir. 1971).

NATURE OF CASE: Appeal in action on breach of sales contract.

FACT SUMMARY: Following a drastic drop in the price of phosphate, Columbia (D) insisted that evidence of the course of dealing and trade usage should be admitted into evidence to show that Columbia (D) was not obliged to purchase a yearly minimum quantity of phosphate from Royster (P) at the original contract price.

CONCISE RULE OF LAW: Even if the court finds a sales contract to be intended by the parties as a complete and exclusive statement of the terms of the agreement, those terms may still be explained or interpreted by evidence as to the course of dealing, usage of the trade, or course of performance.

FACTS: Royster (P), a manufacturer and seller of mixed fertilizers, had for many years been a major purchaser of nitrogen from Columbia (D), although, previous to the contract in question, Columbia (D) had never been a significant customer of Royster (P). However, in 1966 both companies contracted for Royster (P) to sell a minimum of 31,000 tons of phosphate yearly to Columbia (D) at a stated price. Soon thereafter, phosphate prices dropped so steeply that Columbia (D) was unable to resell the phosphate at a competitive price. Although Royster (P) made some concessions, it came to the point where Columbia (D) finally refused to accept delivery. Royster (P), therefore, sold the unaccepted phosphate for Columbia's (D) account at a price substantially below the contract price and brought this suit for the balance. During the trial, Columbia (D) had offered evidence: (1) that due to numerous factors (weather, farming practices, etc.), it was the practice of the trade to regard express price and quantity terms of this type of contract to be a mere projection subject to adjustment according to market forces; (2) that during the six years' course of dealing in which Columbia (D) had sold to Royster (P), there had been a pattern of repeated and substantial deviation from the contract price, and there were four instances in which Royster (P) had taken none of the goods for which it had contracted. However, the district court excluded this evidence on the grounds that "custom and usage or course of dealing are not admissible to contradict the express, plain, and unambiguous language of a valid written contract which, by virtue of its detail, negates the proposition that the contract is open to variances in its terms." Columbia (D) cited this as error and appealed the judgment in the amount of $75,000 for Royster (P).

ISSUE: Is evidence of custom, usage of the trade, and course of dealing between the parties admissible to explain or supplement terms intended by the parties as a final expression of their agreement?

HOLDING AND DECISION: (Butzner, J.) Yes. Even if the court finds a sales contract to be intended by the parties as a complete and exclusive statement of the terms of their agreement, still those terms may be explained or interpreted by evidence as to the course of dealing, usage of the trade or course of performance. This is in accord with U.C.C. § 1-102, which speaks of expanding "commercial practices through custom, usage, and agreement of the parties." Also, U.C.C. § 2-202 explicitly authorizes evidence of the usage of the trade and course of dealing between the parties to explain or supplement a contract. The official comment states that the latter section rejects the old rule that such evidence may be introduced only when the contract is ambiguous. A finding of ambiguity is not necessary for the admission of such evidence. Royster's (P) next argument was based on the premise that the evidence should be excluded because this contract was complete on its face. However, reading U.C.C. § 2-202 in the light of U.C.C. § 1-205(4), the test of admissibility is not whether the contract appears on its face to be complete in every detail but whether the proffered evidence of the course of dealing and usage of the trade can reasonably be construed as consistent with the express terms of the contract. But the evidence offered here — indicating that dealers usually adjust prices due to various factors — is consistent with the terms of this contract since (1) the contract does not exclude the use of such evidence; (2) the contract is silent or neutral about adjusting prices and quantities to reflect a declining market; (3) the contract's description for minimum tonnages and additional quantities is consistent with what the proffered testimony purports to show; and (4) the default clause in the contract refers only to the buyer's failure to pay, whereas this default is based on Columbia's (D) failure to take delivery. Further, the problem cannot be solved by applying general contract law, as Royster (P) insisted. Before a court can reach the point of allowing damages under contract law, it must determine if there has been a default. This requires interpreting the agreement by such evidence as is here offered. Finally, Royster (P) argued that the contract excludes "verbal misunderstandings." However, according to U.C.C. § 2-202, the course of dealing and usage of the trade are not synonymous with verbal misunderstandings and can be used to modify a complete statement unless carefully negated. Therefore, Columbia's (D) evidence about course of dealing and usage of the trade should have been admitted. Remanded.

Continued on next page.

EDITOR'S ANALYSIS: In non-U.C.C. transactions, the parol evidence rule generally operates both as a rule of evidence and of substantive law, excluding evidence of verbal representations or understandings which would alter or vary the terms of the written document. The basic assumption is that if the parties have executed a written statement, they intended it to be a complete and final statement of the agreed-upon terms. However, as to sales contracts, the Code rejects the assumption that because a writing has been worked out which is final on some matters, it is to be taken as including all matters agreed upon. Instead, before the writing can operate to exclude parol evidence, the court must find that the parties intended the writing to be the complete and exclusive statement of the terms of the agreement. As indicated above, even those terms may be explained or interpreted by parol evidence as to course of dealing, usage of trade, or course of performance.

QUICKNOTES

COURSE OF DEALING - Previous conduct between two parties to a contact which may be relied upon to interpret their actions.

COURSE OF PERFORMANCE - Previous conduct between two parties to a contact which may be relied upon to interpret their actions.

USAGE OF TRADE - A course of dealing or practice commonly used in a particular trade.

NOTES:

DIAMOND FRUIT GROWERS, INC. v. KRACK CORP.

Buyer (P) v. Manufacturer (D)

794 F.2d 1440 (9th Cir. 1986).

NATURE OF CASE: Appeal from award of consequential damages for breach of warranty.

FACT SUMMARY: Krack (D) and Metal Matic (D) disputed the effectiveness of a disclaimer of consequential damages that Metal Matic (D) included on order acknowledgment forms.

CONCISE RULE OF LAW: Under U.C.C. § 2-207, when the offeree conditions its acceptance on assent to additional terms, the offeror must give specific assent, or the provisions of § 2-207(3) will supply the terms of the contract.

FACTS: Metal Matic (D) sold tubing to Krack (D) for use in the cooling systems that Krack (D) manufactured. Krack (D) sent a blanket purchase order to Metal Matic (D) at the beginning of the year for its tubing requirements for that year. As the tubing was needed, Krack (D) sent release purchase orders requesting that the tubing be delivered. Metal Matic (D) returned an acknowledgment form and shipped the tubing. Metal Matic's (D) acknowledgment made its acceptance conditional on the purchaser's assent to the terms of the acknowledgment. It also contained a provision that disclaimed all liability for consequential damages. Krack's (D) purchase orders did not contain this provision. In previous dealings, Krack (D) had attempted to have the disclaimer eliminated but Metal Matic (D) refused. Diamond Fruit Growers (P) purchased a cooling system from Krack (D) which failed due to defective tubing. Diamond (P) filed suit against Krack (D), which in turn filed a third-party complaint against Metal Matic (D), seeking contribution. At trial, the jury ruled for Diamond (P) and that Krack (D) was entitled to contribution from Metal Matic (D). Metal Matic (D) appealed, contending that the disclaimer of consequential damages prevented contribution liability.

ISSUE: Are the offeree's additional terms part of the contract when the acceptance is conditioned on assent to the additional terms?

HOLDING AND DECISION: (Wiggins, J.) No. The offeror must give specific assent to the offeree's additional terms for those terms to control even when acceptance is conditioned on assent. If specific assent is not given by the offeror, the provisions of U.C.C. § 2-207(3) control the agreement. U.C.C. § 2-207 replaces the last shot doctrine of common law. Under the last shot rule, the terms contained in the last form to which no objection is made control the contract. Under § 2-207, the terms on which the parties disagree drop out, and the U.C.C. supplies the missing terms. If the offeror fails to give specific assent to a different term in the offeree's form, that term is eliminated. Metal Matic's (D)

acknowledgment form contained a consequential damages disclaimer not contained on Krack's (D) purchase order. Although Krack (D) accepted delivery of the tubing, this was not sufficient to show that Krack (D) assented to the different term. Therefore, the disclaimer was ineffective, and the U.C.C. supplies the contract's warranty terms. The U.C.C. allows for consequential damages unless disclaimed, so Krack (D) is entitled to those damages since the disclaimer was ineffective. Affirmed.

EDITOR'S ANALYSIS: The decision is in accord with the White and Summer viewpoint. They acknowledge that when § 2-207(3) supplies the contract's terms, it often works to the disadvantage of the seller. This is due to the fact that sellers typically desire to limit their liability when the U.C.C. seeks to hold them liable.

QUICKNOTES

CONSEQUENTIAL DAMAGES - Monetary compensation that may be recovered in order to compensate for injuries or losses sustained as a result of damages that are not the direct or foreseeable result of the act of a party, but that nevertheless are the consequence of such act and which must be specifically pled and demonstrated.

CONTRIBUTION - The right of a person or party who has compensated a victim for his injury to seek reimbursement from others who are equally responsible for the injury in proportional amounts.

NOTES:

BAYWAY REFINING CO. v. OXYGENATED MARKETING AND TRADING A.G.
Seller (P) v. Buyer (D)
215 F.3d 219 (2d Cir. 2000).

NATURE OF CASE: Appeal from summary judgment order finding that, as a matter of law, an additional term to a contract did not materially alter the contract.

FACT SUMMARY: Bayway Refining Co. (Bayway) (P) sold to Oxygenated Marketing and Trading, A.G. (OMT) (D) a petroleum product, and, as required by federal law, paid an excise tax on the transaction. Bayway's (P) acceptance confirmation incorporated by reference the company's general terms and conditions, which included a provision that shifted responsibility of any excise taxes in a transaction to the buyer. OMT (D) did not object to the acceptance and accepted delivery. Bayway (P) demanded payment of the excise tax in addition to the purchase price. OMT (D) argued it had not agreed to make the tax payment and refused to pay it. Bayway (P) sued for breach of contract.

CONCISE RULE OF LAW: In a "battle of the forms" case, the party opposing the inclusion of an additional term bears the burden of proving that the term works a material alteration of the contract.

FACTS: Bayway (P) sold to OMT (D) 60,000 barrels of a gasoline blendstock known as MTBE. In response to OMT's (D) written confirmation, which served as an offer, Bayway (P) faxed its confirmation, which served as the acceptance, the next day. That acceptance incorporated by reference Bayway's (P) "General Terms and Conditions," which had not been transmitted with the confirming fax. Those terms and conditions contained a clause (the Tax Clause) that shifted to the buyer the responsibility of paying any non-income taxes related to a certain transaction. Federal law imposes an excise tax, payable by the seller, on the sale of gasoline blendstocks to any buyer who is not registered under federal law for a tax exemption. After delivery, Bayway (P) learned that OMT (D) was not registered for the exemption and that, therefore, the transaction created a tax liability of $464,035.12, which Bayway (P) paid. Invoking the Tax Clause, Bayway (P) demanded payment by OMT (D) of the tax. OMT (D) denied it had agreed to pay the tax and refused to pay it. Bayway (P) filed suit in federal district court for breach of contract. The district court held that the Tax Clause had been properly incorporated into the contract, and granted summary judgment in favor of Bayway (P), concluding that OMT (D) had failed to carry its burden of proving that the Tax Clause materially altered the contract.

ISSUE: In a "battle of the forms" case, does the party opposing the inclusion of an additional term bear the burden of proving that the term works a material alteration of the contract?

HOLDING AND DECISION: (Jacobs, J.) Yes. Bayway's (P) confirming fax was effective to form a contract even though it referenced additional terms, such as the Tax Clause. Therefore, under the U.C.C., the Tax Clause is a proposal for an addition to the contract, and (as between two merchants, as here) is presumed to become part of the contract unless one of three exceptions applies. Here, OMT (D) invokes the "material alteration" exception. Because the general provision provides that the additional term becomes part of the contract, it is a presumption of the intent of the contracting parties. To implement that presumption, the burden of proving the materiality of the alteration must fall on the party that opposes inclusion. Here, OMT (D) has failed to carry that burden. A material alteration is one that would "result in surprise or hardship if incorporated without express awareness by the other party." Certain terms are deemed material per se. Here, the Tax Clause is not per se material because it does not provide for open-ended tax liability, but merely allocates responsibility for a tax payable on one specific transaction; it is limited, discrete, and the subject of no special protection. Therefore, OMT (D) must prove that the Tax Clause resulted in surprise or hardship. With regard to surprise, OMT (D) must show not only that it was subjectively surprised, but also that it was objectively surprised, i.e., what it should have known. OMT (D) established that it was subjectively surprised—the company truly felt ambushed—but it failed to show that a reasonable petroleum merchant would have been surprised by the Tax Clause. Moreover, Bayway (P) introduced evidence that the Tax Clause reflected custom and practice in the petroleum industry. OMT (D) challenged this evidence as raising a genuine issue of fact. A review of the evidence shows that shifting tax liability to a buyer is the custom and practice in the petroleum industry. Expert opinions and other contracts from the industry support that conclusion, as does common sense, because it is the buyer who controls whether any tax liability will be incurred in a transaction, since it is within the buyer's control as to whether it will be registered for a tax exemption. Because allocating tax liability to the buyer is the custom and practice in the petroleum industry, OMT (D) could not objectively be surprised by the incorporation of the Tax Clause, which merely reflected that practice. As to hardship, OMT (D) failed to raise a genuine issue of material fact. Its only evidence on this issue was that it is a small business that would suffer a loss it cannot afford by having to shoulder the tax liability. This does not amount to hardship. Typically, hardship comes about from an additional contract term that creates open-ended or prolonged liability. Here, any loss that

Continued on next page.

the Tax Clause imposed on OMT (D) would be limited, routine, and self-inflicted (because OMT (D) could have avoided the liability by registering for the exemption). Affirmed.

EDITOR'S ANALYSIS: The result of this case, like the result of many "battle of the forms" cases under U.C.C. §2-207, should serve as a warning to merchants to carefully read the boilerplate on standard preprinted purchase order and acknowledgment forms that they receive. Had OMT (D) read Bayway's acceptance fax, it could at the very least have requested and reviewed Bayway's General Terms and Conditions and could have objected to Bayway's acceptance or to the incorporation of the Terms and Conditions if it so chose.

NOTES:

LEONARD PEVAR CO. v. EVANS PRODUCTS CO.

Purchaser (P) v. Seller (D)
524 F. Supp. 546 (D. Del. 1981).

NATURE OF CASE: Cross-motions for summary judgment in action for breach of express and implied warranties.

FACT SUMMARY: When plywood delivered by Evans (D) to Pevar (P) proved unacceptable, Pevar (P) filed suit for an alleged breach of express and implied warranties which Evans (D) denied, claiming that its acknowledgment of Pevar's (P) confirmatory memorandum expressly disclaimed any warranties and limited its liability in its contract with Pevar (P).

CONCISE RULE OF LAW: Where an oral agreement has been reached, followed by one or both of the parties sending formal memoranda embodying the terms agreed upon and adding terms not discussed, the additional terms will become part of the agreement unless they materially alter it.

FACTS: In a telephone conversation with Evans (D), Pevar (P) obtained price quotations for the purchase of plywood. Pevar (P) claimed that it called Evans (D) two days later and ordered the plywood, entering into an oral contract of sale. Evans (D) admitted that Pevar (P) called but denied acceptance of that order. Pevar (P) then sent a written purchase order which did not make any reference to warranties or remedies but simply ordered the lumber, specifying the price, quantity, and shipping instructions. The acknowledgment Evans (D) sent to Pevar (P) included boilerplate language that the contract of sale would be expressly contingent upon Pevar's (P) acceptance of all terms contained in the document, and one of those terms disclaimed most warranties, while another limited the "buyer's remedy" by restricting liability if the plywood proved to be defective. Pevar (P) filed suit when the ordered plywood was unacceptable. Evans (D) denied liability, claiming that it expressly disclaimed warranties and limited its liability in its contract with Pevar (P). Evans (D) also contended that if Pevar (P) and Evans (D) entered into an oral contract, it would be unenforceable because it would be in violation of the Statute of Frauds. Both parties filed cross motions for summary judgment.

ISSUE: Where an oral agreement has been reached, followed by one or both of the parties sending formal memoranda embodying the terms agreed upon and adding terms not discussed, will the additional terms become part of the agreement unless they materially alter it?

HOLDING AND DECISION: (Latchum, J.) Yes. Where an oral agreement has been reached, followed by one or both of the parties sending formal memoranda embodying the terms agreed upon and adding terms not discussed, the additional terms will become part of the agreement unless they materially alter it. This rule is embodied in U.C.C. § 2-207 and was intended to eliminate the mirror rule of common law, under which the terms of an acceptance or confirmation were required to be identical to the terms of the offer or oral agreement. Section 2-207 recognizes that a buyer and seller can enter into a contract by agreeing orally and then sending confirmatory memoranda, § 2-207(1), by exchanging writings, without oral agreement, which do not contain identical terms but nevertheless constitute a seasonable acceptance, § 2-207(2); or, the conduct of the parties may recognize the existence of a contract, despite their previous failure to agree orally or in writing, § 2-207(3). Pevar's (P) written purchase order constituted a confirmatory memorandum, and Evans' (D) acknowledgment did not expressly deny the existence of the purported contract but merely asserted additional terms. Generally, disclaimers of warranties and limits on liability "materially alter" the agreement. However, the question of material alteration rests upon the facts of each case. If the trier of fact determines that the acknowledgment includes additional terms which do not materially alter the oral agreement, then the terms will be incorporated into the agreement. If they materially alter it, however, the terms will not be included in the agreement. Here, the parties' conduct indicated that they recognized the existence of a contract. If this court finds after trial that Pevar (P) and Evans (D) did not enter into an oral agreement, then § 2-207(3) will apply. The terms of the contract will include those terms to which Pevar's (P) purchase order and Evans' (D) acknowledgment agree. For those terms where the writings do not agree, the standardized "gap filler" provisions of Article 2 will provide the terms of the contract. Motions for summary judgment denied.

EDITOR'S ANALYSIS: U.C.C. § 2-201 generally provides that an oral contract for the sale of goods in excess of $500 is unenforceable. However, § 2-201(2) provides an exception where, if the receiving party does not object to the written confirmation within 10 days, the oral agreement may be enforceable, despite the Statute of Frauds. The instant case presents an example of what is referred to as the "battle of the forms," which the drafters of the U.C.C. addressed in § 2-207 in an attempt to conform contract law to modern-day business transactions.

QUICKNOTES

SUMMARY JUDGMENT - Judgment rendered by a court in response to a motion by one of the parties, claiming that the lack of a question of material fact in respect to an issue warrants disposition of the issue without consideration by the jury.

KLOCEK v. GATEWAY, INC.

Consumer (P) v. Computer vendor (D)

104 F. Supp. 2d 1332 (D. Kan. 2000).

NATURE OF CASE: Motion to dismiss on the ground that claims brought by the purchaser of a computer must be arbitrated pursuant to the vendor's standard agreement included with the computer.

FACT SUMMARY: William Klocek (Klocek) (P) purchased a computer from Gateway, Inc. (Gateway) (D), which included a copy of its Standard Terms and Conditions Agreement (Standard Terms) with the computer. The Standard Terms provided that they would be accepted by the purchaser if the computer was kept beyond five days and also provided for arbitration of any claims arising from the agreement. Klocek (P) sued Gateway (D) for breach of contract and of warranty. Gateway (D) moved to dismiss, asserting that the claims had to be arbitrated under the Standard Terms agreement.

CONCISE RULE OF LAW: Terms shipped with a computer do not become part of the sales contract where the vendor does not expressly make its acceptance conditional on the buyer's assent to the additional, shipped, terms and where the buyer does not expressly agree to the terms.

FACTS: Klocek (P) purchased a computer from Gateway (D), which included a copy of its Standard Terms and Conditions Agreement (Standard Terms) in the box that contained the computer battery power cables and instruction manuals. The Standard Terms provided in bold type that they would be accepted by the purchaser if the computer was kept beyond five days. Paragraph 10 of the Standard Terms provided for arbitration of any claims arising from the agreement. Klocek (P) sued Gateway (D) for breach of contract and of warranty, and Gateway (D) moved to dismiss, asserting that the claims had to be arbitrated under the Standard Terms agreement.

ISSUE: Do terms shipped with a computer become part of the sales contract where the vendor does not expressly make its acceptance conditional on the buyer's assent to the additional, shipped, terms, and where the buyer does not expressly agree to the terms?

HOLDING AND DECISION: (Vratil, J.) No. Gateway (D) bears an initial burden of showing that it is entitled to arbitration. To do so, it must demonstrate that an enforceable agreement to arbitrate exists. When deciding if such an agreement exists, the court applies state law contract formation principles. Here, the U.C.C. governs the parties' transaction under both Kansas and Missouri law. The fact that Klocek (P) paid for and received a computer is evidence of a contract for the sale of a computer. Here, the issue is whether terms received with a product become part of the parties' agreement—an issue not decided by either Kansas or Missouri state courts. Authority from other courts is split, and seems to depend on whether the court finds that the parties formed their contract before or after the vendor communicated its terms to the purchaser. Gateway (D) urges following the approach taken by the Seventh Circuit, which enforced an arbitration clause in a situation similar to the one in this case. The Seventh Circuit reasoned that by including the license with the software, the vendor proposed a contract that the buyer could accept by using the software after having an opportunity to read the license. The Seventh Circuit, however, concluded, without support, that U.C.C. § 2-207 was irrelevant because the case involved only one written form, and that the vendor was the master of the offer. The Missouri or Kansas courts would not follow this reasoning because nothing in the language of § 2-207 precludes its application in a case that involves only one form. By its terms, § 2-207 applies to an acceptance or written confirmation. Therefore, the state courts would apply § 2-207 to the facts of this case. In addition, in typical consumer transactions, it is the purchaser who is the offeror, and the vendor is the offeree. Here, Gateway (D) has provided no evidence that would support a finding that it was the offeror—and therefore could propose limitations on the kind of conduct that constituted acceptance. Instead, the court assumes that plaintiff offered to purchase the computer and that Gateway (D) accepted plaintiff's offer. Under § 2-207, the Standard Terms are either an expression of acceptance or written confirmation. As an expression of acceptance, they would constitute a counteroffer only if Gateway (D) expressly made its acceptance conditional on Klocek's (P) assent to the additional or different terms, but here, Gateway (D) has not shown that its mere shipment of the Standard Terms with the computer communicated to the plaintiff that the sale was conditioned on his acceptance of the Standard Terms. Because Klocek (P) was not a merchant, any additional or different terms contained in the Standard Terms did not become part of the parties' agreement unless Klocek (P) expressly agreed to them. Gateway (D) has not shown that Klocek (P) expressly agreed to the Standard Terms. It provided no evidence that it informed Klocek (P) of the five-day review-and-return period as a condition of the sales transaction, or that the parties contemplated additional terms to the agreement. The fact that Klocek (P) kept the computer past five days was insufficient to demonstrate that he expressly agreed to the Standard Terms. Therefore, Gateway (D) has not shown that Klocek (P) agreed to the arbitration provision, and its motion to dismiss is overruled.

Continued on next page.

EDITOR'S ANALYSIS: The decision in this case would find support from legal commentators who have found that software shrinkwrap agreements are a form of adhesion contracts and who have criticized the line of cases that support such agreements, such as those in the Seventh Circuit, on the ground that they ignore the issue of informed consumer consent. Nonetheless, several courts have followed the Seventh Circuit line of cases.

NOTES:

3

CHAPTER 3
WARRANTIES

QUICK REFERENCE RULES OF LAW

1. **Merchantability.** The serving for value of food or drink to be consumed either on the premises or elsewhere is a sale, and such food and drink must be adequately contained, packaged, and labeled as the agreement may require. (Shaffer v. Victoria Station, Inc.)

2. **Merchantability.** Where a particular use of the trunk compartment of an automobile is unforeseeable, the manufacturer has no duty to design an internal release or opening mechanism that might have prevented injury or to warn of the danger of such unforeseeable use. (Daniell v. Ford Motor Co.)

3. **Fitness for a Particular Purpose.** The possible presence of fish bones in fish chowder is so well known that it can be reasonably anticipated and guarded against by anyone eating such fish chowder, thus precluding a breach of implied warranty under the Uniform Commercial Code. (Webster v. Blue Ship Tea Room Inc.)

4. **Warranty Disclaimers and Limitations.** (1) An express warranty that arises from textual representations that are not labeled as such may not be disclaimed under U.C.C. § 2-313. (2) A finding of breach of express warranty is not inconsistent with a finding of no negligence. (Bell Sports, Inc. v. Yarusso)

5. **Warranty Disclaimers and Limitations.** A disclaimer of the implied warranty of merchantability is ineffective unless it is conspicuous or the party has actual knowledge of the disclaimer. (Cate v. Dover Corp.)

6. **Warranty Disclaimers and Limitations.** A manufacturer may disclaim the implied warranties of merchantability and fitness provided that the disclaimer is in writing, is conspicuous, and is part of the parties' bargain. (Bowdoin v. Showell Growers, Inc.)

7. **Warranty Disclaimers and Limitations.** A disclaimer of the warranty of merchantability that is otherwise conspicuous and that is contained inside the packaging of a product is sufficiently conspicuous to be effective. (Rinaldi v. Iomega Corp.)

8. **Warranty Disclaimers and Limitations.** A buyer who accepts goods has a reasonable time after he discovers or should have discovered a breach to notify the seller of such breach. (Wilson Trading Corp. v. David Ferguson, Ltd.)

9. **Warranty Disclaimers and Limitations.** Where a limited warranty is breached in bad faith, consequential damages are available despite an express disclaimer in the warranty that excludes such damages. (Pierce v. Catalina Yachts, Inc.)

10. **A Note on Strict Products Liability.** If a defective product causes only damage to itself and purely economic loss, a cause of action is stated under contract warranty law and not products liability. (East River Steamship Corp. v. Transamerica Delaval, Inc.)

11. **U.C.C. Warranties and the Magnuson-Moss Act.** If a supplier of consumer products provides a written limited warranty with respect to the goods to the consumer, it may not completely disclaim implied warranties. (Ventura v. Ford Motor Corp.)

12. **Warranties and Article 2A.** A "hell-or-high-water" clause does not insulate a lessor's assignee from a claim of fraud where an agency relationship can be established between the assignee and the perpetrators of the alleged fraud. (Colonial Pacific Leasing Corp. v. McNatt Datronic Rental Corp.)

SHAFFER v. VICTORIA STATION, INC.
Wine drinker (P) v. Restaurant (D)
Wash. Sup. Ct., 91 Wash. 2d 295, 588 P.2d 233 (1978).

NATURE OF CASE: Appeal from dismissal of action for damages for negligence, breach of implied warranty, and strict liability.

FACT SUMMARY: After Shaffer's (P) hand was permanently injured when the glass containing wine he had ordered in Victoria Station's (D) restaurant broke, Shaffer (P) sought damages for negligence, breach of implied warranty, and strict liability.

CONCISE RULE OF LAW: The serving for value of food or drink to be consumed either on the premises or elsewhere is a sale, and such food and drink must be adequately contained, packaged, and labeled as the agreement may require.

FACTS: Shaffer (P) ordered a glass of wine at the "Victoria Station" restaurant operated by Victoria Station, Inc. (D). While drinking the wine, the wine glass broke in Shaffer's (P) hand, resulting in permanent injury. Shaffer (P) sued Victoria Station, Inc. (D), seeking damages for negligence, breach of implied warranty under the U.C.C., and strict liability under the Restatement (Second) of Torts § 402A. [Prior to trial, Shaffer's (P) attorney, indicating he could not prove negligence, took a voluntary nonsuit on the negligence issue.] Victoria Station (D) argued that the U.C.C. did not apply since it was not a merchant with respect to wine glasses. Shaffer (P), however, argued that U.C.C. § 2-314 was controlling. The trial court, ruling that the case sounded in negligence alone, granted Victoria Station's (D) motion for dismissal. The court of appeals affirmed, and Shaffer (P) appealed.

ISSUE: Is the serving for value of food or drink to be consumed either on the premises or elsewhere a sale such that the food and drink must be adequately contained, packaged, and labeled as the agreement may require?

HOLDING AND DECISION: (Dolliver, J.) Yes. The serving for value of food or drink to be consumed either on the premises or elsewhere is a sale, and such food and drink must be adequately contained, packaged, and labeled as the agreement may require. Section 2-314 embodies the rule stated above. The wine could not be served as a drink or consumed without an adequate container. The drink sold thus includes the wine and the container, both of which must be fit for the ordinary purpose for which used. Shaffer (P) has a cause of action both on the face of the statute and under the principles of prior case law. An action also lies under the strict liability theory of Restatement (Second) of Torts § 402A. Confirmation of the applicability of § 402A to this case is given in comment h, which says in pertinent part: "No

reason is apparent for distinguishing between the product itself and the container in which it is supplied, and the two are purchased by the user or consumer as an integrated whole. Where the container is itself dangerous, the product is sold in a defective condition. The container cannot logically be separated from the contents when the two are sold as a unit." Shaffer (P) has thus also stated a cause of action under the theories of implied warranty of fitness and strict liability. Reversed.

EDITOR'S ANALYSIS: Victoria Station (D) contended that the restaurant was not a merchant with respect to wine glasses as defined in § 2-104, and, since the glass itself was not sold, there was no passing of title as required under § 2-106. The court of appeals expressed concern over an uncontrollable broadening of the doctrine of strict liability, stating that the argument could be made that numerous aspects of a restaurant's operation were integral to each sale. Thus, to ignore the fact that this allegedly defective glass was never sold would create great uncertainty as to the limits of strict liability. However, in finding that U.C.C. § 2-314 controlled here, the Washington State Supreme Court declared that if the court of appeals' predictions as to future lawsuits came to pass, it would deal with the situation at that time.

QUICKNOTES

BREACH OF CONTRACT - Unlawful failure by a party to perform its obligations pursuant to contract.

NEGLIGENCE - Conduct falling below the standard of care that a reasonable person would demonstrate under similar conditions.

STRICT LIABILITY - Liability for all injuries proximately caused by a party's conducting of certain inherently dangerous activities without regard to negligence or fault.

NOTES:

DANIELL v. FORD MOTOR CO.
Attempted suicide victim (P) v. Manufacturer (D)
581 F. Supp. 728 (D.N.M. 1984).

NATURE OF CASE: Defense motion for summary judgment in action for damages for strict liability, negligence, and breach of express and implied warranties of merchantability.

FACT SUMMARY: After Daniell (P) was injured when she locked herself in the trunk of her automobile while attempting suicide, remaining there for nine days, she filed this action against Ford (D) based on strict products liability, negligence, and breach of express and implied warranties of merchantability.

CONCISE RULE OF LAW: Where a particular use of the trunk compartment of an automobile is unforeseeable, the manufacturer has no duty to design an internal release or opening mechanism that might have prevented injury or to warn of the danger of such unforeseeable use.

FACTS: Daniell (P) became locked inside the trunk of a Ford (D) automobile when she attempted to commit suicide. She remained in the trunk for nine days. After being rescued, she sought to recover for psychological and physical injuries arising from that occurrence. Daniell (P) contended that the automobile had a design defect in that the trunk lock or latch lacked an internal release or opening mechanism. Daniell (P) also maintained that Ford (D) was liable based on a failure to warn of this condition. Her suit was based on strict products liability under the Restatement (Second) of Torts § 402A, negligence, and breach of express warranty and implied warranties of merchantability and fitness for a particular purpose. Ford (D) moved for summary judgment.

ISSUE: Where a particular use of the trunk compartment of an automobile is unforeseeable, does the manufacturer have a duty to design an internal release or opening mechanism that might have prevented injury or to warn of the danger of such unforeseeable use?

HOLDING AND DECISION: (Baldock, J.) No. Where a particular use of the trunk compartment of an automobile is unforeseeable, the manufacturer has no duty to design an internal release or opening mechanism that might have prevented injury or to warn of the danger of such unforeseeable use. As a general principle, a design defect is actionable only where the condition of the product is unreasonably dangerous to the user or consumer. Further, under strict products liability or negligence, a manufacturer has a duty to consider only those risks of injury which are foreseeable. A risk is not foreseeable by a manufacturer where a product is used in a manner which could not reasonably be anticipated by the manufacturer and that use

causes injury to a plaintiff. Daniell's (P) use of the trunk compartment as a means to attempt suicide was an unforeseeable use as a matter of law. Moreover, there is no duty to warn of known dangers in strict products liability or tort. In addition, Daniell (P) has not come forward with any evidence of an express warranty regarding exit from the inside of the trunk. Any implied warranty of merchantability in this case requires that the product must be fit for the ordinary purposes for which such goods are used. Daniell's (P) use of the trunk was highly extraordinary, and there is no evidence that the trunk was not fit for the ordinary purpose for which it was intended. Daniell (P) admitted that, at the time she purchased the automobile, neither she nor her husband gave any particular thought to the trunk mechanism or even thought about getting out from inside the trunk. She did not rely on the seller's skill or judgment to select or furnish an automobile suitable for the unfortunate purpose for which she used it. Therefore, no breach of any implied warranties of merchantability occurred. The overriding factor barring Daniell's (P) recovery is that she intentionally sought to end her life by crawling into an automobile trunk from which she could not escape. Daniell (P) was aware of the natural and probable consequences of her perilous conduct, and she, not Ford (D), is responsible for her injuries. Motion for summary judgment is granted.

EDITOR'S ANALYSIS: The court noted several times that the purposes of an automobile trunk are to transport, stow, and secure a spare tire, luggage, and other items and to protect those items from the elements. Moreover, the potential efficacy of any warning, given a plaintiff's use of an automobile trunk compartment for a deliberate suicide attempt, was questionable. Because the court held that Daniell's (P) conception of the manufacturer's duty was in error, it did not reach the issues of the effect of comparative negligence or other defenses such as assumption of the risk on the products liability claim. The court did not reach the comparative negligence defense on the negligence claim for the same reason.

QUICKNOTES
FORESEEABILITY - A reasonable expectation that an act or omission would result in injury.

NEGLIGENCE - Conduct falling below the standard of care that a reasonable person would demonstrate under similar conditions.

STRICT LIABILITY - Liability for all injuries proximately caused by a party's conducting of certain inherently dangerous activities without regard to negligence or fault.

WEBSTER v. BLUE SHIP TEA ROOM, INC.
Customer (P) v. Restaurant (D)
Mass. Sup. Jud. Ct., 347 Mass. 421, 198 N.E.2d 309 (1964).

NATURE OF CASE: Appeal of award of damages for breach of an implied warranty.

FACT SUMMARY: After a fish bone became lodged in Webster's (P) esophagus while she was eating a bowl of fish chowder at the Blue Ship Tea Room (D), she sought damages for breach of an implied warranty of food served in the restaurant.

CONCISE RULE OF LAW: The possible presence of fish bones in fish chowder is so well known that it can be reasonably anticipated and guarded against by anyone eating such fish chowder, thus precluding a breach of implied warranty under the Uniform Commercial Code.

FACTS: While eating a bowl of New England fish chowder in the Blue Ship Tea Room (D), Webster (P), a native New Englander, felt something lodge in her throat preventing her from swallowing and/or clearing her throat by gulping. During the second of two esophagoscopies at Massachusetts General Hospital, a fish bone was found and removed. As a result of her injuries, Webster (P) sought damages, under applicable provisions of the U.C.C. for breach of implied contract, of food served by the Blue Ship Tea Room (D). An auditor, whose findings of fact were not final, found for Webster (P). On a retrial in the superior court, the jury returned a verdict for Webster (P). Blue Ship (D) appealed on exceptions to the judge's refusal to strike certain portions of the auditor's report, to direct a verdict for Blue Ship (D), and to allow Blue Ship's (D) motion for the entry of a verdict in its favor under leave reserved.

ISSUE: Is the possible presence of fish bones in fish chowder so well known that it can be reasonably anticipated and guarded against by anyone eating such fish chowder, thus precluding a breach of implied warranty under the Uniform Commercial Code?

HOLDING AND DECISION: (Reardon, J.) Yes. The possible presence of fish bones in fish chowder is so well known that it can be reasonably anticipated and guarded against by anyone eating such fish chowder, thus precluding a breach of implied warranty under the Uniform Commercial Code. According to the cookbooks consulted, fish chowder has for many years been made with fish that have not been fileted. The recipes indicate that, in the preparation of chowders in New England over the years, worries about fish bones played no part whatsoever. This broad outlook on chowders persists in more modern cookbooks, and this court is not inclined to tamper with age-old recipes by any amendment reflecting Webster's (P) view of the effect of the U.C.C. upon them. The joys of life in New England include the ready availability of fresh fish chowder. Diners should be prepared to cope with the hazards of fish bones, the occasional presence of which in chowder is to be anticipated and does not impair fitness or merchantability. Thus, while this court sympathizes with Webster (P), who has suffered a peculiarly New England injury, Blue Ship's (D) exceptions must be sustained.

EDITOR'S ANALYSIS: In reaching its decision, the court cited cookbooks, a New England dictionary, and Nathaniel Hawthorne's "The House of the Seven Gables," with publication dates ranging from 1883 to 1957. The court observed that while there is a heavy body of case law involving foreign substances in food, there is a strong distinction between those cases and a fish bone in a fish chowder. Some jurisdictions make a distinction between natural and foreign objects found in food, with some denying liability for natural substances and others allowing recovery if the consumer had a "reasonable expectation" that the substance in question would have been removed.

QUICKNOTES

FORESEEABILITY - A reasonable expectation that an act or omission would result in injury.

IMPLIED WARRANTY - An implied promise made by one party to a contract that the other party may rely on a fact, relieving that party from the obligation of determining whether the fact is true and indemnifying the other party from liability if that fact is shown to be false.

NOTES:

BELL SPORTS, INC. v. YARUSSO
Manufacturer (D) v. Helmet wearer (P)
Del. Sup. Ct., 759 A.2d 582 (2000).

NATURE OF CASE: Appeal from denial of judgment as a matter of law on breach of warranty claims.

FACT SUMMARY: Although he was wearing a helmet made by Bell Sports, Inc. (Bell) (D), Yarusso (P) became a quadriplegic after he landed on his head when his off-road motorcycle hit a bump and catapulted him. Yarusso (P) claimed that the helmet's design was defective and alleged negligence, breach of express warranties, and breach of an implied warranty of merchantability.

CONCISE RULES OF LAW: (1) An express warranty that arises from textual representations that are not labeled as such may not be disclaimed under U.C.C. § 2-313. (2) A finding of breach of express warranty is not inconsistent with a finding of no negligence.

FACTS: Yarusso (P) was riding his off-road motorcycle when he hit a mogul and was catapulted off the vehicle and onto his head. He sustained a burst fracture of the C5 vertebral body, rendering him a quadriplegic. At the time, he was wearing Bell's (D) Bell Moto-5, a full-face motocross helmet designed for off-road use. Yarusso (P) filed suit, alleging negligence in the design and construction of the helmet, breach of express warranties, and breach of an implied warranty of merchantability. His express warranty claim arose from textual representations in the helmet's owner's manual, which included the statement: "the primary function of a helmet is to reduce the harmful effects of a blow to the head" and which described how the helmet would work on impact. The express warranty also attempted to limit itself to five years and warned in bold, capital letters that "no helmet can protect the wearer against all foreseeable impacts." Experts for both parties disagreed as to whether the helmet had functioned properly at the time of impact. At the close of the evidence, Bell (D) moved for judgment as a matter of law as to liability, but the court sent the claims to the jury, which ultimately found that Bell (D) had not been negligent but had breached an express or implied warranty that proximately caused Yarusso's (P) injuries (the jury was permitted to find liability under alternative theories of breach of warranty, express or implied, without differentiating between the two). Bell (D) appealed, claiming that Yarusso failed as a matter of law to establish an evidentiary basis for recovery under express or implied warranty.

ISSUES: (1) May an express warranty that arises from textual representations that are not labeled as such be disclaimed under U.C.C. § 2-313? (2) Is a finding of breach of express warranty inconsistent with a finding of no negligence?

HOLDING AND DECISION: (Walsh, J.) No as to #1. No as to #2. (1) According to the U.C.C.'s official commentary, the U.C.C.'s warranty provisions are intended to be liberally construed and applied in favor of a buyer of goods. Formal wording is not necessary to create a warranty, and a seller does not have to express any specific intention to create one. Here, the helmet's owner's manual contained textual representations of fact on which a buyer was entitled to rely, even though they were not expressly labeled as warranties. Because the U.C.C. and its state counterparts are restrictive, any effort to disclaim these express warranties is ineffective. Even though the manual contained disclaimers warning that use of the helmet could not prevent all injuries, such disclaimers are ineffective to disclaim the express warranties. Because the evidence presented to the jury by both parties was inconclusive, the jury could come to a logical conclusion that express warranties were made and that they were breached. Therefore, the trial court did not err in submitting this issue to the jury. Evidence that the helmet could have been designed to reduce certain neck injuries also provided a sufficient factual predicate for submitting the implied warranty claim to the jury. (2) Bell (D) argues that the jury's finding that it was not negligent is inconsistent with its finding of a breach of an express or implied warranty because, it argues, the jury found no product defect that could support negligence and, therefore, could not properly find a defect that would support a warranty claim. However, a claim for breach of warranty is conceptually distinct from a negligence claim because the latter focuses on the manufacturer's conduct, whereas a warranty claim focuses on the product itself. Therefore, there is no inconsistency between the jury's verdict negating negligence but finding a breach of warranty. Affirmed.

EDITOR'S ANALYSIS: The instant case demonstrates the difficulty of disclaiming any express warranties, even when they are mere statements of fact that serve to create buyer expectations or interest. Accordingly, a seller must carefully weigh the benefits of such statements (e.g., in advertising) against the potential exposure to liability they can entail.

NOTES:

CATE v. DOVER CORP.

Customer (P) v. Manufacturer (D)

Texas Sup. Ct., 790 S.W.2d 559 (1990).

NATURE OF CASE: Appeal of summary judgment denying damages for breach of warranty.

FACT SUMMARY: Cate (P) purchased lifts manufactured by Dover (D) which came with a warranty which disclaimed the implied warranty of merchantability.

CONCISE RULE OF LAW: A disclaimer of the implied warranty of merchantability is ineffective unless it is conspicuous or the party has actual knowledge of the disclaimer.

FACTS: Cate (P) purchased three lifts from Beech Tire Mart. The lifts were manufactured and designed by Dover (D). Dover's (D) warranty for the lifts contained a disclaimer of the implied warranty of merchantability. The text of the warranty appeared in regular size print. The disclaimer appeared in a separate paragraph, but in the same typeface, size, and color as the remainder of the text. Cate (P) was aware of the warranty and read it. The lifts never functioned properly and Cate (P) filed suit against Dover (D) for breach of the implied warranty of merchantability. Dover (D) contended that the claim was barred by the disclaimer in the written warranty. The trial court upheld the disclaimer and granted summary judgment to Dover (D), and Cate (P) appealed.

ISSUE: Does a disclaimer of the implied warranty of merchantability have to be conspicuous in order to be effective?

HOLDING AND DECISION: (Doggett, J.) Yes. Disclaimers of the implied warranty of merchantability must be conspicuous, or the party must have actual knowledge of it, in order to be effective. A clause is conspicuous when it is written so that a reasonable person against whom it will operate should have noticed it. Contrasting typefaces or colors are evidence that a clause is conspicuous. Although a disclaimer is not conspicuous, it will be effective if the party has actual knowledge of it at the time of purchase. Dover's (D) disclaimer clause was contained within a section outlining the terms of the warranty and was not in different typeface or color. Therefore, it failed to alert a reasonable person that an exclusion was intended. Although Cate (P) admitted to reading the warranty, the evidence did not establish that he understood the limitation which would constitute actual knowledge of the disclaimer. Thus, Dover's (D) disclaimer was ineffective. Reversed and remanded.

CONCURRENCE: (Spears, J.) The implied warranty of merchantability is designed to protect consumers who don't read limitations or understand the effect of disclaimers. Therefore, disclaimers should be prohibited by the state legislature.

DISSENT: (Ray, J.) The statute allowing disclaimers requires conspicuousness and does not provide for an actual knowledge exception, which should be irrelevant to the determination.

EDITOR'S ANALYSIS: Some commentators support the position of the dissent that actual knowledge of the buyer should not play a role in determining the validity of a disclaimer. They claim that a rule requiring conspicuousness reduces the need for courts to make difficult evaluations of actual awareness. See W. Powers, Texas Products Liability Law § 2.0723 (1989).

QUICKNOTES

IMPLIED WARRANTY OF MERCHANTABILITY - An implied promise made by a merchant in a contract for the sale of goods that such goods are suitable for the purpose for which they are purchased.

NOTES:

BOWDOIN v. SHOWELL GROWERS, INC.
Chicken growers (P) v. Chicken buyers (D)
817 F.2d 1543 (11th Cir. 1987).

NATURE OF CASE: Appeal from summary judgment denying damages for breach of implied warranties of fitness and merchantability.

FACT SUMMARY: While cleaning out their chicken house and chicken coop pallets with a spray rig lent to them by Showell Growers (D), with whom the Bowdoins (P) contracted as chicken raisers, Mrs. Bowdoin (P) suffered severe injuries when the spray rig malfunctioned.

CONCISE RULE OF LAW: A manufacturer may disclaim the implied warranties of merchantability and fitness provided that the disclaimer is in writing, is conspicuous, and is part of the parties' bargain.

FACTS: The Bowdoins (P), under their contract to raise chickens for Showell Growers, Inc. (D), were required to thoroughly clean their chicken house and chicken coop pallets once a year. To accomplish this task, Showell (D) lent the Bowdoins (P) a high-pressure spray rig Showell (D) had purchased from the manufacturers. Two weeks after Showell (D) purchased the spray rig, it was delivered with an instruction manual which included a purported warranty disclaimer on the last page. Usually, the manufacturer required its dealer and the purchaser to complete an "agriculture delivery report," containing a disclaimer of the implied warranties of fitness and merchantability, before a sale. However, the record showed that no agriculture delivery report was completed in connection with the purchase of the spray rig by Showell (D). Mrs. Bowdoin (P) was using the spray rig to clean the pallets when an article of her clothing caught in the safety shield covering the spray rig's power takeoff shaft, pulling her into the shaft and causing her to suffer severe injuries. The Bowdoins (P) filed a diversity action in federal court against Showell (D) and the manufacturers, seeking to recover on a number of counts, including one alleging breach of the implied warranties of fitness and merchantability. The manufacturers moved for summary judgment, which the district court granted, concluding that, under Alabama law, the manufacturers had effectively disclaimed the implied warranties in the instruction manual. The Bowdoins (P) appealed.

ISSUE: May a manufacturer disclaim the implied warranties of merchantability and fitness provided that the disclaimer is in writing, is conspicuous, and is part of the parties' bargain?

HOLDING AND DECISION: (Wisdom, J.) Yes. A manufacturer may disclaim the implied warranties of merchantability and fitness provided that the disclaimer is in writing, is conspicuous, and is part of the parties' bargain. This "basis of the bargain" rule protects purchasers from unexpected and coercive disclaimers.

However, Showell (D) purchased the spray rig at least two weeks before it was delivered, and the instruction manual delivered with the spray rig was never brought to Showell's (D) attention. Such a postsale disclaimer is ineffective. By definition, a disclaimer that appears for the first time after the sale in a manual supplied by the seller is not a part of the basis of the bargain and therefore is not binding on the buyer. Decisions of other courts construing U.C.C. § 2-316 have also concluded that a postsale disclaimer is not effective. Reversed [with instructions to reinstate the Bowdoins' (P) breach of implied warranties of fitness and merchantability claims against the manufacturers].

EDITOR'S ANALYSIS: The court noted that to be effective, a disclaimer must be conspicuous before the sale, for only then will the law presume that the disclaimer was part of the bargain. However, whether or not a postsale disclaimer was conspicuous was immaterial. As the court observed, by definition, a postsale disclaimer is not conspicuous in the full sense of that term because the reasonable person against whom it is intended to operate could not have noticed it before the consummation of the transaction. A postsale disclaimer is therefore not effective merely because it was otherwise conspicuous.

QUICKNOTES

IMPLIED WARRANTY OF MERCHANTABILITY - An implied promise made by a merchant in a contract for the sale of goods that such goods are suitable for the purpose for which they are purchased.

NOTES:

RINALDI v. IOMEGA CORP.
Consumer (P) v. Manufacturer (D)
Del. Super. Ct., 41 U.C.C. Rep. Serv. 2d 1143 (1999).

NATURE OF CASE: Class action for breach of implied warranty of merchantability.

FACT SUMMARY: Plaintiffs (P), as a class, purchased "Zip drives" from Iomega Corp. (Iomega) (D) that were allegedly defective and caused irreparable damage to computer data. They brought suit for breach of warranty of merchantability, negligence, fraud, and negligent failure to warn. Iomega (D) moved to dismiss the breach of warranty claim because its disclaimer, shipped with the drive, disclaimed all liability.

CONCISE RULE OF LAW: A disclaimer of the warranty of merchantability that is otherwise conspicuous and that is contained inside the packaging of a product is sufficiently conspicuous to be effective.

FACTS: Iomega (D) manufactured the Zip drive, a large capacity computer data storage drive. A class action on behalf of all persons who purchased purportedly defective Zip drives was brought against Iomega. The plaintiffs (P) alleged, inter alia, that a defect in the drive caused the "Click of Death," which caused irreparable damage to computer data, and could be transferred to other drives. Plaintiffs (P) brought suit for breach of warranty of merchantability, negligence, fraud, and negligent failure to warn. The breach of warranty count of the complaint asserted that Iomega (D) manufactured a product that was not fit for the ordinary purpose for which such products are used and that Iomega's (D) disclaimer of this implied warranty that was contained in the packaging of the drive was ineffective because it was not sufficiently "conspicuous" as required by the state counterpart to the U.C.C. Iomega (D) moved to dismiss this count of the complaint on the ground that it failed to state a claim because the disclaimer in the drive packaging was sufficiently conspicuous and effectively disclaimed all liability.

ISSUE: Is a disclaimer of the warranty of merchantability that is otherwise conspicuous and that is contained inside the packaging of a product sufficiently conspicuous to be effective?

HOLDING AND DECISION: (Cooch, J.) Yes. The state's counterpart to the U.C.C. (6 Del. C. §2-316(2)) requires that to disclaim the warranty of merchantability, the language in a writing must mention merchantability and must be conspicuous. Various aspects of "conspicuousness" are not at issue here, e.g., type size, wording, readability, location of the disclaimer in the warranty itself, etc. Instead, the only issue is whether by being located in the packaging of the product, the disclaimer could not realistically be called to the attention of the consumer until after the sale had been consummated and, therefore, was not "conspicuous" as a matter of law. To determine this issue, the purpose of the U.C.C. must be looked to. That purpose is to protect a buyer from unexpected and unbargained for language of disclaimer. An analogous case, relating to software shrinkwrap license agreements, is the Seventh Circuit's ProCD, Inc. v. Zeidenberg, 86 F.3d 1447 (1996), which reasoned that it would be impractical to print additional terms of the sales contract on the outside of the box in microscopic print. That case also reasoned that the consumer had the ability to reject the goods if it found the additional terms unacceptable. Other courts have also held that various contract terms, like arbitration clauses, are effective even though located inside the packaging of a product. Still, other courts have held that a disclaimer of the warranty of merchantability is conspicuous so long as it can be noticed and understood. Here, the sales of the Zip drives were not consummated until after each plaintiff (P) had a chance to inspect and then to reject or accept the drive with the additional terms that were enclosed along with it. The commercial practicalities of modern retail purchasing make it "eminently reasonable" for sellers to place disclaimers insider their products' packaging, and for buyers to reject the contract terms if they so choose. Therefore, the disclaimer physically placed inside the Zip drive packing was conspicuous, and Iomega's (D) motion to dismiss is granted.

EDITOR'S ANALYSIS: Other courts have held that to be effective, a disclaimer such as the one in the instant case must be conspicuous before the sale. Those courts would hold that by definition a postsale disclaimer could not be conspicuous because the buyer could not have noticed it before consummation of the transaction. It seems the court here is implying that the sale transaction is not complete until the buyer has had a chance to review the additional terms that are inside the packaging and has either rejected or accepted them by either using the product or returning it.

NOTES:

WILSON TRADING CORP. v. DAVID FERGUSON, LTD.
Yarn seller (P) v. Yarn buyer (D)
N.Y. Ct. App., 23 N.Y.2d 398, 244 N.E.2d 685 (1968).

NATURE OF CASE: Appeal from affirmance of summary judgment awarding damages for breach of contract.

FACT SUMMARY: When Ferguson (D) discovered a defect in the yarn it had purchased from Wilson (P), Ferguson (D) refused to pay for the goods, despite the fact that its notice to Wilson (P) of the defect was made after the 10-day limitation period stipulated in the contract of sale.

CONCISE RULE OF LAW: A buyer who accepts goods has a reasonable time after he discovers or should have discovered a breach to notify the seller of such breach.

FACTS: After Wilson Trading Corporation (P) sold a specified quantity of yarn to David Ferguson, Ltd. (D), the yarn was cut and knitted into sweaters, which were then washed. It was during this washing that Ferguson (D) discovered that the color of the yarn varied from piece to piece and within the pieces. Ferguson (D) claimed the defect rendered the sweaters unmarketable. The contract for sale of the yarn foreclosed claims made after weaving, knitting, or processing, or made more than 10 days after receipt of shipment. Wilson (P) sought to recover the contract price of the yarn after Ferguson (D) refused to pay for the yarn purchased. As a defense and as a counterclaim for damages, Ferguson (D) alleged that Wilson (P) delivered defective and unworkmanlike goods. Special term granted Wilson's (P) motion for summary judgment for the contract price of the yarn on the ground that notice of an alleged breach of warranty for defect in shading was not given within the time expressly limited by the contract and was not now available by way of defense or counterclaim. The appellate division affirmed, and this appeal followed.

ISSUE: Does a buyer who accepts goods have a reasonable time after he discovers or should have discovered a breach to notify the seller of such breach?

HOLDING AND DECISION: (Jasen, J.) Yes. A buyer who accepts goods has a reasonable time after he discovers or should have discovered a breach to notify the seller of such breach. However, the U.C.C. allows the parties, within limits established by it, to modify or exclude warranties and to limit remedies for breach of warranty. Under the U.C.C., parties are given broad latitude within which to fashion their own remedies for breach of contract. Nevertheless, it is clear from the official comment to § 2-719 that it is the very essence of a sale contract that at least minimum adequate remedies be available for its breach. Official comment to § 2-719 explains that "where an apparently fair and reasonable clause because of circumstances fails in its purpose or operates to deprive either party of the substantial value of the

bargain, it must give way to the general remedy provisions of this Article." Here, the time provision of the contract eliminated all remedies for defects not discoverable before knitting and processing; thus, § 2-719 applies. Ferguson's (D) affidavits alleged that sweaters manufactured from the yarn were rendered unmarketable because of latent shading defects not reasonably discoverable before knitting and processing. If these factual allegations are established at trial, the limited remedy established by the contract has failed its "essential purpose," and the buyer is, in effect, without remedy. The time limitation clause of the contract must then give way to the general code rule stated above. Ferguson's (D) affidavits are thus sufficient to create a question of fact concerning whether notice was given within a reasonable time after the shading defect should have been discovered. The order of the appellate division should be reversed, and Wilson's (P) motion for summary judgment should be denied.

CONCURRENCE: (Fuld, C.J.) There should be a reversal — but on the sole ground that a substantial question of fact has been raised as to whether the clause limiting the time in which to make a claim is "manifestly unreasonable" as applied to the type of defect of which Ferguson (D) complained, without discussing unconscionability.

EDITOR'S ANALYSIS: As noted by the concurrence, the majority also discussed unconscionability, before stating that it did not need to decide that specific issue here. In its analysis, the court noted that the contract between the parties not only limited remedies for its breach but also purported to modify the warranty of merchantability. The court declared that an attempt to both warrant and refuse to warrant goods creates an ambiguity which can only be resolved by making one term yield to the other. U.C.C. § 2-316 provides that warranty language prevails over the disclaimer if the two cannot be reasonably reconciled. Under these circumstances, the contract language creating the unlimited express warranty must prevail over the time limitation insofar as the latter modifies the warranty.

QUICKNOTES

BREACH OF CONTRACT - Unlawful failure by a party to perform its obligations pursuant to contract.

UNCONSCIONABILITY - Rule of law whereby a court may excuse performance of a contract, or of a particular contract term, if it determines that such term(s) are unduly oppressive or unfair to one party to the contract.

PIERCE v. CATALINA YACHTS, INC.
Boat purchaser (P) v. Boat manufacturer (D)
Alaska Sup. Ct., 2 P.3d 618 (1999).

FACT SUMMARY: The Pierces (P) purchased a new sailboat from Catalina Yachts, Inc. (Catalina) (D), which gave them a limited warranty for the repair of any below waterline blisters appearing in the boat's gel coat. The warranty expressly disclaimed Catalina's (D) responsibility for consequential damages. The Pierces (P) discovered blistering on the hull and promptly notified Catalina with an estimate, which Catalina refused to accept. The Pierces (P) sued, and a jury awarded them monetary damages for repair, as well as finding that Catalina had acted in bad faith. However, before trial, the trial court had ruled that their claim for consequential damages was barred by the warranty disclaimer.

CONCISE RULE OF LAW: Where a limited warranty is breached in bad faith, consequential damages are available despite an express disclaimer in the warranty that excludes such damages.

FACTS: In 1992, the Pierces (P) purchased a new sailboat from Catalina (D), which gave them a limited warranty promising to repair or pay for the repair of any below waterline blisters appearing in the boat's gel coat—an outer layer of resin on the boat's hull. The warranty expressly disclaimed Catalina's (D) responsibility for consequential damages. In 1994, the Pierces (P) discovered blistering on the hull and promptly notified Catalina with a repair estimate of $10,645, which Catalina refused to accept. Catalina insisted that the hull only needed minor patching. Six months later, the Pierces (P) sued, claiming tort and contract damages. Before trial, the trial court ruled that their claim for consequential damages was barred by the warranty disclaimer. The jury awarded them monetary damages for repair, as well as finding that Catalina had acted in bad faith. The Pierces (P) appealed, claiming that the trial court had erred in striking their consequential damages claim.

ISSUE: Where a limited warranty is breached in bad faith, are consequential damages available despite an express disclaimer in the warranty that excludes such damages?

HOLDING AND DECISION: (Bryner, J.) Yes. The issue is whether the failure of a warranty provision that creates a limited remedy requires failure of another provision that excludes consequential damages. Under the state's U.C.C. counterpart (AS 45.02.719(b)), a limited remedy is the exclusive remedy. When that limited remedy fails, the warranty's limitations are nullified and the remedy available is the remedy provided by the code. Thus, it would seem that here the gel-coat warranty failed

its essential purpose and that the Pierces (P) can pursue any remedy available under the code, including consequential damages. However, another code provision (.719(c)) separately provides that consequential damages may be limited or excluded unless the limitation or exclusion is unconscionable. Thus, there is tension between these two subsections because .719 (c) casts doubt on .719(b)'s implication that when a limited remedy fails, consequential damages may be available. The code itself does not resolve this tension. The majority of courts find that the two subsections are independent, ruling that when a warranty fails, the provision barring consequential damages survives unless it is unconscionable. Because this approach serves the purpose of the code and allows parties flexibility to contract around consequential damages, the court adopts the independent approach. However, courts applying this approach examine the totality of the circumstances surrounding the limited remedy's failure to see if there is anything unconscionable about enforcing the parties' allocation of risk. One consideration is whether the seller acted unreasonably or in bad faith. Here, Catalina's (D) actions weigh heavily against enforcing the consequential damages exclusion, and the finding by the jury that Catalina (D) acted in bad faith establishes a "circumstance resulting in failure of performance that makes it unconscionable to enforce the parties' allocation of risk." Because Catalina (D) consciously deprived the Pierces (P) of their rights, Catalina (D) cannot conscionably demand to enforce its own warranty rights. Therefore, the trial court erred in ruling that it would be conscionable to enforce the consequential damages exclusion. Vacated and remanded.

EDITOR'S ANALYSIS: In the instant case, the court found it significant that the Pierces (P) were consumers, rather than merchants, who were not sophisticated business people and who were not bargaining on equal footing with Catalina (D). In a commercial setting, where the buyer is not a consumer, the courts are more likely to uphold the consequential damages exclusion, even where the limited remedy portion of the warranty has failed.

NOTES:

EAST RIVER STEAMSHIP CORP.
v. TRANSAMERICA DELAVAL, INC.
Ship owner (P) v. Ship manufacturer (D)
476 U.S. 858 (1986).

NATURE OF CASE: Appeal from summary judgment denying damages for products liability.

FACT SUMMARY: Transamerica Delaval (D) (Delaval) built and installed four steamship engines, each of which malfunctioned during use, causing damage to itself and other economic losses.

CONCISE RULE OF LAW: If a defective product causes only damage to itself and purely economic loss, a cause of action is stated under contract warranty law and not products liability.

FACTS: Delaval (D) designed, manufactured, and supervised the installation of four steamship engines. Within a year, three of the ships developed the same problem: an engine valve disintegration, resulting in damage to the engine as a whole. The fourth ship experienced severe engine vibrations until it was discovered that a valve had been installed backwards. No persons were harmed in any of the mishaps. East River Steamship Co. (P) and three other companies which had chartered the ships brought a products liability suit, contending that Delaval's (D) defective engines or negligent installation had caused an unreasonable risk of harm to persons and property. The district court gave summary judgment to Delaval (D), holding that a products liability suit was improper on these facts, and that where a defective product harms itself and causes only economic loss, plaintiffs should pursue a contract warranty claim. The appellate court affirmed, and East River (P) appealed to the Supreme Court.

ISSUE: Will a cause of action lie in products liability where a defective product causes damage only to itself and other purely economic loss?

HOLDING AND DECISION: (Blackmun, J.) No. A cause of action will not lie in products liability where a defective product causes damage only to itself and other purely economic loss. Products liability theory permits recovery without proof of negligence because public policy requires that responsibility for hazards to life and health be taken by the entity which can most effectively reduce them, the manufacturer. Such drastic concern for safety is not warranted where the product harms only itself. The essence of East River's (P) claim was that a consumer did not receive a product of the quality expected. This was a warranty claim, requiring no additional protections. Further, the increased cost to the public which would be caused by permitting tort claims in this kind of situation is not warranted. Affirmed.

EDITOR'S ANALYSIS: Products liability theory provides extra protection for consumers over and above warranty law. It permits injured consumers to sue manufacturers directly, regardless of privity, and hold them liable for unreasonably dangerous defects in their products, regardless of fault, intent, or actual negligence. The Court rejected distinctions based on the type and degree of injury when purely economic harm comes from the use of a defection product. It does not matter whether the economic loss was suffered by a "disappointed" party, or by an "endangered" party. As long as there was no injury to the person, there is no tort—just a contract—based action.

QUICKNOTES

PRIVITY - Commonality of rights or interests between parties.

PRODUCT LIABILITY - The legal liability of manufacturers and sellers for damages and injuries suffered by buyers, users, and even bystanders because of defects in goods purchased.

STRICT LIABILITY - Liability for all injuries proximately caused by a party's conducting of certain inherently dangerous activities without regard to negligence or fault.

NOTES:

VENTURA v. FORD MOTOR CORP.

Car owner (P) v. Car manfacturer (D)

180 N.J. Super. 45, 433 A.2d 801 (1981).

NATURE OF CASE: Appeal from award of rescission of contract for breach of warranty.

FACT SUMMARY: Venura (P) bought a new car from Marino Auto Sales (D) and then sued for breach of warranty when it turned out to be a lemon.

CONCISE RULE OF LAW: If a supplier of consumer products provides a written limited warranty with respect to the goods to the consumer, it may not completely disclaim implied warranties.

FACTS: Ventura (P) bought a Mercury Marquis, manufactured by Ford (D), from an authorized dealer, Marino Auto Sales, Inc. (D). Paragraph 7 of Marino's (D) sales contract expressly stated that Marino (D) was not making any warranties regarding the car and, instead, passed Ford's (D) written warranty on to the consumer. The same paragraph stated that Marino (D) would be responsible for performing all terms and conditions of Ford's (D) owner service policy. As it turned out, the car hesitated and stalled constantly. When Marino (D) refused to fix it, Ventura (P) sued Marino (D) and Ford (D) for breach of the implied warranties of merchantability and fitness. Marino (D) cross-claimed against Ford Motor Corp. (D) for indemnification. The trial court granted Ventura (P) recision of the contract plus refund of the purchase price less an allowance for use of the car and found in favor of Marino (D) on its cross-claim against Ford (D). Ford (D) and Marino (D) appealed.

ISSUE: Can a supplier completely disclaim implied warranties for a consumer product where it has provided a written limited warranty to the consumer with respect to the goods?

HOLDING AND DECISION: (Botter, J.) No. A supplier may not completely disclaim implied warranties for a consumer product where it has provided a written limited warranty to the consumer with respect to the goods. The Magnuson-Moss Warranty Act § 2304 specifically forbids it. Among other things, paragraph 7 of the sales agreement promised that Marino (D) would perform any remedial action required by Ford's (D) warranty. This is a limited warranty within the meaning of Magnuson-Moss, and Marino's (D) disclaimer of the implied warranty of merchantability and fitness was therefore invalid. As Marino (D) clearly breached these warranties, judgment for Ventura (P) was proper. Affirmed.

EDITOR'S ANALYSIS: Title I of the Magnuson-Moss Warranty Act applies to all consumer products covered by a written warranty. 15 U.S.C. §§ 2301–2312. Magnuson-Moss divides all warranties into two categories: full and limited. Full warranties are those which give consumers the choice to receive a full refund or replacement of a defective product that is beyond repair. Anything

else is a limited warranty. Limited warranties cannot disclaim implied warranties or modify them, except to limit them in time. This is a radical departure from previous law, where the warrantor could disclaim almost anything so long as it was done with clear notice, such as a writing given to the consumer.

QUICKNOTES

IMPLIED WARRANTY OF MERCHANTABILITY - An implied promise made by a merchant in a contract for the sale of goods that such goods are suitable for the purpose for which they are purchased.

INDEMNIFICATION - Reimbursement for losses sustained or security against anticipated loss or damages.

NOTES:

COLONIAL PACIFIC LEASING CORP. v. McNATT
DATRONIC RENTAL CORP.
Lessor (D) v. Lessee (P)
Ga. Sup. Ct., 268 Ga. 265, 486 S.E.2d 804 (1997).

NATURE OF CASE: Certiorari to review breach of contract.

FACT SUMMARY: Quick-Trip (P) brought suit against the equipment supplier, manufacturer and lessors (D) of defective computer equipment it leased from Colonial and Datronic (D), seeking rescission of the leases.

CONCISE RULE OF LAW: A "hell or high water" clause does not insulate a lessor's assignee from a claim of fraud where an agency relationship can be established between the assignee and the perpetrators of the alleged fraud.

FACTS: The McNatts, sole shareholders and officers of Quick-Trip Printers, entered into negotiations with Itex for the acquisition of a computer printing system. They executed a finance agreement with Burnham, which assigned its interests to Colonial and Datronic. Quick-Trip experienced problems with the equipment and delayed payment to Itex. The lessors repossessed the equipment and Quick-Trip (P) filed suit against the equipment supplier, manufacturer and lessors seeking rescission of the leases. Colonial and Datronic (D) filed counterclaims seeking payment on the leases. The trial court granted summary judgment in favor of lessors (D) on the main claims and counterclaims. The court of appeals reversed as to the main claims and counterclaim for unpaid rent, holding that the leases' requirement that the rental payments be made even if the equipment were damaged, defective or unfit (the hell or high water clauses) could not be enforced where it was alleged that the employees of the vendor had fraudulently induced the lessee to acquire the equipment.

ISSUE: Does a "hell or high water" clause insulate a lessor's assignee from a claim of fraud where an agency relationship can be established between the assignee and the perpetrators of the alleged fraud?

HOLDING AND DECISION: (Benham, C.J.) No. A "hell-or-high-water" clause does not insulate a lessor's assignee from a claim of fraud where an agency relationship can be established between the assignee and the perpetrators of the alleged fraud. In Georgia all lease contracts for goods after 1993 are governed by the UCC Article 2A. Under pre-Article 2A law, the conduct of the parties to a lease finance transaction is governed by the terms of the lease and the law favors such bargains so long they are not the product of fraud or violative of public policy. A finance lessor's disclaimers of warranties is not expressly prohibited. A contractual requirement the lessee make its rental payments is also valid in the absence of fraud on the part of the finance lessor. Here the leases clearly exclude warranty and promissory liability

of the finance lessor and its assignees to Quick-Trip (P), stating that Quick-Trip (P) agreed to pay the full amount of the rental agreement to assignee/lessors regard of defect, damage or unfitness of the equipment, and that the lessee agreed not to assert against the assignee lessors defenses it could not assert against the original lessor. Thus, the contract precludes the lessee from asserting fraud of the original finance lessor as a defense against the assignee lessor's claim for payment. Here, however, Quick-Trip (P) sued first to rescind its lease contracts on the ground of fraudulent inducement. In order for the alleged fraud of the employees of the equipment supplier to authorize rescission of the finance lease, their actions must somehow be imputed to the assignee lessors through the finance lessor. The record indicates that the requirement supplier's employees acted only as a conduit of information between the lessee and the finance lessor and that there was no evidence that the lease was negotiated pursuant to authorization given to the employees by the lessor (i.e., there is no evidence of a relationship pursuant to which the alleged fraud of the supplier's employers could be imputed to the finance lessor so as to invalidate the contracts.) Thus the "hell or high water" clauses in the lease are viable. Affirmed in part and reversed in part.

EDITOR'S ANALYSIS: Whether or not employees of an equipment supplier are agents of the finance lessor depends upon the circumstances of the particular arrangement. While a contractual statement denying the existence of such relationship is not conclusive, the mere submission of a supplier's employee of a business/lessee's credit application to the finance lessor does not make that employee, as a matter of law, an agent of the finance lessor. However, where the supplier's employees were trained with respect to completing the leasing documents and authorized to negotiate such leases, this has been sufficient to support a finding of agency. Potomac Leasing v. Thrasher, 181 Ga. App. 833 (1987).

NOTES:

4

CHAPTER 4
TERMS OF THE CONTRACT

QUICK REFERENCE RULES OF LAW

1. **Filling in the Gaps.** Even if a contract lacks necessary terms, a valid contract may have been formed if there is a reasonably certain basis for filling them in. (Landrum v. Devenport)

2. **Delivery Terms.** Where a contract specifies shipment by a carrier, unless the contract states otherwise, risk of loss passes to the buyer as soon as the goods are delivered to the carrier. (Cook Specialty Co. v. Schrlock)

3. **Delivery Terms.** If a seller is authorized to send goods to the buyer and no particular destination is specified, seller must give prompt notice to buyer of actual shipment so that buyer may protect his interests. (Rheinberg-Kellerei GmbH v. Vineyard Wine Co.)

LANDRUM v. DEVENPORT
Automobile collector (P) v. Automobile dealer (D)
Tex. Ct. Civ. App., 616 S.W.2d 359 (1981).

NATURE OF CASE: Appeal from directed verdict denying damages for breach of contract.

FACT SUMMARY: Landrum's (P) sales contract to buy a unique car had a blank space where the price should have been.

CONCISE RULE OF LAW: Even if a contract lacks necessary terms, a valid contract may have been formed if there is a reasonably certain basis for filling them in.

FACTS: Landrum (P), a car collector, wanted to buy the limited-edition Chevrolet Corvette Z78 Indy Pace Car which was to be delivered to Devenport Chevrolet (D). Landrum's (P) son went to buy the car as his father's agent and later testified that Devenport (D) offered to sell the car upon its arrival for the sticker price, estimated at between $14,000 and $18,000. As he felt they had agreed on the price, Landrum's (P) son said nothing when the price space was left blank on his sales contract. When the car arrived, Devenport (D) demanded $22,000 for the car, threatening to sell it elsewhere if Landrum (P) refused. Reserving his rights, Landrum (P) paid $22,000 and then sued for breach of contract. The trial judge did not permit Landrum's (P) case to go to the jury, entering a direct verdict in favor of Devenport (D). The judge reasoned that a valid contract had never been formed, as the sales agreement lacked the necessary term of price. Landrum (P) appealed.

ISSUE: If a contract lacks necessary terms, can a valid contract still have been formed?

HOLDING AND DECISION: (Cornelius, J.) Yes. Even if a contract lacks necessary terms, a valid contract may have been formed if there is a reasonably certain basis for filling in the missing terms. The same result is reached whether proceeding under conventional contract law or through application of the Uniform Commercial Code. Under contract law, if a writing is obviously incomplete, it may be completed by the introduction of other proofs as to the missing terms. Under U.C.C. § 2-204(3), a missing price may be implied if there is a reasonable basis for doing so. The question of what a reasonable price actually was for this contract should have been left for the jury. Reversed.

EDITOR'S ANALYSIS: It is never the proper role of a court to guess what the parties' contract might or should have been. At common law, if necessary terms were left out of an agreement, a court would not even try to fill them in. The Uniform Commercial Code was written in direct opposition to the common law practice. Many U.C.C. provisions attempt to save a contract by letting a court add reasonable terms, consistent with the expectations of the parties, according to set guidelines.

QUICKNOTES
BREACH OF CONTRACT - Unlawful failure by a party to perform its obligations pursuant to contract.

NOTES:

COOK SPECIALTY CO. v. SCHRLOCK

Buyer (P) v. Defendant (D)

772 F. Supp. 1532 (E.D. Pa. 1991).

NATURE OF CASE: Cross-motions for summary judgment in action for damages for breach of contract.

FACT SUMMARY: Cook Specialty (P) ordered a press brake from Machinery Systems Inc. (D) (MSI) which fell from the carrier's truck and broke before delivery.

CONCISE RULE OF LAW: Where a contract specifies shipment by a carrier, unless the contract states otherwise, risk of loss passes to the buyer as soon as the goods are delivered to the carrier.

FACTS: Machinery Systems Inc. (D) sold Cook Specialty (P) an hydraulic press brake worth $28,000. The terms were F.O.B. MSI's (D) warehouse, after which a carrier would deliver the brake to Cook (P). When the brake fell off the carrier's truck and broke during transit, Cook (P) was only able to recover $5,000 from the carrier's insurer. Cook (P) sued MSI (D) for the difference, claiming that MSI's (D) delivery to an underinsured carrier was unreasonable, and as the brake was not properly delivered to a carrier, risk of loss never passed to Cook (P). Both parties moved for summary judgment.

ISSUE: Where a contract specifies shipment by a carrier, does risk of loss pass to the buyer as soon as the goods are delivered to the carrier?

HOLDING AND DECISION: (Waldman, J.) Yes. If a contract specifies shipment by a carrier, unless the contract states otherwise, risk of loss passes to the buyer as soon as the goods are delivered to the carrier. U.C.C. § 2-504 states that "F.O.B. (name of place)" means that the seller bears the risk of delivering goods to the carrier at that place. Section 2-509 states that as soon as the carrier takes possession, risk of loss shifts to the buyer. The requirement in U.C.C. § 2-504 that transportation must be arranged "as may be reasonable having regard to the nature of the goods" does not require MSI (D) to ensure adequate insurance. It imposes only a duty to choose a mode of transportation that will be suitable to the goods, such as shipping perishables in a refrigerated carrier (U.C.C. § 2-504 Official Comment 3). MSI's (D) delivery was reasonable. MSI's (D) motion for summary judgment granted; Cook's (P) motion for summary judgment denied.

EDITOR'S ANALYSIS: Cook (P) relied on the minority case of LaCasse v. Blaustein, 403 N.Y.S.2d 440 (Civ. Ct. 1979). In LaCasse, a student ordered calculators and authorized the seller to spend up to $50 for shipping and insurance. The seller shipped in two cartons by fourth-class mail; spent only $9.98; insured for only $400 when the calculators were worth in excess of $3,000; misaddressed one carton; and "inscribed a theft-tempting notation on it." Plaintiff student won breach of contract action brought against the seller. As the court noted, the facts in LaCasse are exceptionally egregious, and it is the only reported case to hold that the seller's failure to obtain insurance breached U.C.C. § 2-504.

QUICKNOTES

RISK OF LOSS - Liability for damage to or loss of property that is the subject matter of a contract for sale.

NOTES:

RHEINBERG-KELLEREI GMBH v. VINEYARD WINE CO.
Wine supplier (P) v. Wine buyer (D)
N.Y. Ct. of App., 53 N.C. App. 560, 281 S.E.2d 425 (1981).

NATURE OF CASE: Cross-appeals from order dismissing suit for breach of contract.

FACT SUMMARY: Vineyard's (D) order of German wine was lost at sea while in transit.

CONCISE RULE OF LAW: If a seller is authorized to send goods to the buyer and no particular destination is specified, seller must give prompt notice to buyer of actual shipment so that buyer may protect his interests.

FACTS: Vineyard Wine Co. ("Vineyard") (D) ordered 620 cases of wine from Rheinberg-Kellerei ("Rheinberg") (P), a West German wine company. The order was placed in the United States through Rheinberg's (P) agent and was to be shipped by sea from Germany. Vineyard (D) sent Rheinberg (P) special instructions, stating that Vineyard (D) would cover insurance and requesting notice of arrival of the shipment. Shipment was delayed, and although Vineyard (D) made several inquiries of Rheinberg's (P) agent, it received no information about shipment or arrival dates. When Rheinberg (P) finally shipped the wine, it notified its agent, who failed to pass this information on to Vineyard (D). Approximately one week later, the ship sank, together with all hands and cargo. Vineyard (D) received no information about the shipment until after it had been lost at sea. When Vineyard (D) refused to pay for the wine, Rheinberg (P) sued. When the lower court dismissed Rheinberg's (P) action on the grounds that it had failed to give Vineyard (D) notice of the shipment as required in U.C.C. § 2-504(c), both parties appealed. [The casebook excerpt does not include the grounds for Vineyard's (D) appeal.]

ISSUE: If a seller is authorized to send goods to the buyer and no particular destination is specified, must seller give prompt notice to buyer of when shipment is made?

HOLDING AND DECISION: (Wells, J.) Yes. If a seller is authorized to send goods to the buyer and no particular destination is specified, seller must give prompt notice to buyer of when shipment is made. Under U.C.C. § 2-504, risk of loss passes to the buyer upon delivery to the carrier. If buyer does not know that delivery has been made, buyer has no reasonable opportunity to protect against loss. Therefore, U.C.C. § 2-504 also requires that seller "promptly notify buyer of the shipment" so that buyer may act to guard his interests. Rheinberg's (P) failure to give notice of shipment until well after the wine was lost was not prompt notice within the meaning of U.C.C. § 2-504. Affirmed.

EDITOR'S ANALYSIS: The U.C.C. states that if the seller is a "merchant" as defined in the code, she retains risk of loss until buyer receives the goods. If she is not a "merchant," risk passes to buyer when she tenders. (See U.C.C. § 2-509). This approach is a radical departure from prior law, where risk of loss belonged to whichever party had actual title to the goods. U.C.C. § 2-401(1) specifically rejects this approach and takes great pains to allocate the risk of loss according to the various stages of a mercantile transaction. The appropriate party, knowing when risk has passed to or from him, can obtain insurance for the correct time period.

QUICKNOTES

RISK OF LOSS - Liability for damage to or loss of property that is the subject matter of a contract for sale.

NOTES:

CHAPTER 5
PERFORMANCE OF THE CONTRACT

QUICK REFERENCE RULES OF LAW

1. **Installment Sales.** A party to a sales contract may not suspend its performance for which it has already received the agreed return without reasonable grounds for insecurity as to the remainder of the other party's performance. (Cherwell-Ralli, Inc. v. Rytman Grain Co.)

2. **Cure.** The seller has the right to cure minor defects through repair rather than replacement. (Wilson v. Scampoli)

3. **Rejection and Acceptance.** Buyers have the right to reject goods which do not conform to the contract because of defects. (Ramirez v. Autosport)

4. **Rejection and Acceptance.** A buyer may be found to have accepted goods despite their known nonconformity and despite the absence of actual delivery. (Plateq Corp. of North Haven v. Machlett Laboratories, Inc.)

5. **Revocation of Acceptance.** A buyer may revoke acceptance of goods where defects substantially impair the value of the goods to that buyer. (Rester v. Morrow)

6. **Risk of Loss: Breach.** The seller of goods remains liable for the risk of their loss when the buyer receives nonconforming goods without accepting the nonconformity and the seller has not effected cure. (Jakowski v. Carole Chevrolet, Inc.)

7. **Impossibility of Performance.** Impossibility is not a defense to a contract where the event causing the impossibility was foreseeable. (Arabian Score v. Lasma Arabian Ltd.)

8. **Impossibility of Performance.** Increases in costs do not allow sellers to raise commercial impracticability as a defense to performing under the contract unless they are unreasonable and severe. (Louisiana Power & Light Co. v. Allegheny Ludlum Industries, Inc.)

CHERWELL-RALLI, INC. v. RYTMAN GRAIN CO., INC.
Seller (P) v. Buyer (D)
Conn. Sup. Ct., 433 A.2d 984 (1980).

NATURE OF CASE: Appeal from award of damages for breach of contract.

FACT SUMMARY: Rytman (D) stopped payment on a check sent to Cherwell-Ralli (P) to compensate for past deliveries made under an installment contract because an independent contractor truck driver led Rytman (D) to believe that Cherwell-Ralli (P) would be unable to complete the deliveries, while Cherwell-Ralli (P) gave assurances.

CONCISE RULE OF LAW: A party to a sales contract may not suspend its performance for which it has already received the agreed return without reasonable grounds for insecurity as to the remainder of the other party's performance.

FACTS: Cherwell-Ralli (P) entered into an installment contract for the sale of Cherco Meal and C-R-T Meal. Rytman (D), the buyer, became delinquent in payment almost immediately, but Cherwell-Ralli (P) continued to make deliveries. When the price of meal rose, Rytman (D) became concerned that Cherwell-Ralli (P) might not be able to supply all of the meal contracted for, but Cherwell-Ralli (P) assured that it would. However, when a truck driver, who did not work for Cherwell-Ralli (P), told Rytman (D) that this was his last load, Rytman (D) stopped payment on the check it had tendered for payment on previous shipments already received. Cherwell-Ralli (P) refused further deliveries and recovered $21,013.60 for payments due and owing. Rytman (D) unsuccessfully pressed a counterclaim for damages for breach of contract due to Cherwell-Ralli's (P) refusal to make the remaining installment deliveries. Rytman (D) appealed.

ISSUE: May a party to a sales contract suspend its performance for which it has already received the agreed return without reasonable grounds for insecurity as to the remainder of the other party's performance?

HOLDING AND DECISION: (Peters, J.) No. The trial court found that Rytman (D) had no reasonable grounds for doubting Cherwell-Ralli's (P) performance. Furthermore, Rytman (D) showed no accurate evidence to establish the damages it might have sustained because of the failure to deliver. Rytman (D) received all goods it ordered under the contract and could not rely upon its own nonpayments as a basis for such insecurity as would entitle Rytman (D) to demand assurances or resort to any remedy. A party to a sales contract may not suspend its performance for which it has already received the agreed return without reasonable grounds for insecurity as to the remainder of the other party's performance. The insecurity alleged by Rytman (D) was found to be inadequate by the trial court, and the record sustains this finding. Affirmed.

EDITOR'S ANALYSIS: U.C.C. § 1-609(2) states that the reasonableness of the grounds for insecurity must be determined according to "commercial standards." Note 2 of the Official Comment under that section points out that a reasonable ground for insecurity need not, however, arise from or be directly related to the contract in question. Something more than price fluctuation and a remark by a third party to the contract is required, nonetheless, as this case demonstrates.

QUICKNOTES
INSTALLMENT CONTRACT - A contract pursuant to which the parties are to render performance or payment in periodic intervals.

NOTES:

WILSON v. SCAMPOLI
(Parties not identified.)
D.C. Ct. App., 228 A.2d 848 (1967).

NATURE OF CASE: Appeal of rescission of award of contract.

FACT SUMMARY: Kolley (P), who bought a television set which arrived defective, rejected the retailer's (D) offer to repair the set and insisted on a new television.

CONCISE RULE OF LAW: The seller has the right to cure minor defects through repair rather than replacement.

FACTS: Kolley (P), representing her father, bought a color television set on November 4, 1965 from a retailer (D). The television came with a guarantee of free service for 90 days and replacement of any defective parts for one year. The set was delivered two days later, at which time it did not operate properly. A service representative came two days after that and informed Kolley (P) that the television needed to be taken to a repair shop in order to determine the problem. Kolley (P) refused this offer and insisted upon a new television set. The retailer (D) would not refund the purchase price nor give Kolley (P) a new television. Kolley (P) filed suit, seeking a rescission of the sales contract. The trial court found for Kolley (P), and the retailer (D) appealed. [The title parties were not identified and the retailer's (D) was not given in the casebook excerpt.]

ISSUE: May a seller cure minor defects by repairing the defective goods rather than replacing the merchandise?

HOLDING AND DECISION: (Myers, J.) Yes. Sellers may repair minor defects in goods in order to have them conform to the contract. U.C.C. § 2-601 retains the perfect tender rule. However, U.C.C. § 2-508 allows the seller to cure defects in the goods in a reasonable time where the seller believed that the goods were conforming at the time of performance. This cure may be effected through repair of the goods rather than replacement. Here, the retailer (D) reasonably believed that the television would conform to the contract at the time of delivery. Therefore, the retailer (D) was entitled to a reasonable time in which to repair the television so that it would conform with the contract. Kolley (P) denied the retailer (D) this opportunity and thus is not entitled to rescission of the contract. Reversed.

EDITOR'S ANALYSIS: The perfect tender rule, as preserved by U.C.C. § 2-601, allows the buyer to reject goods for any nonconformity. It protects the buyer against delivery of flawed goods. It was created for single delivery sales because the buyer does not have the same bargaining position as buyers do in installment sales.

RAMIREZ v. AUTOSPORT
Buyer (P) v. Seller (D)
N.J. Sup. Ct., 88 N.J. 277, 440 A.2d 1345 (1982).

NATURE OF CASE: Appeal from award of rescission of contract and denial of damages on counterclaim for breach of contract.

FACT SUMMARY: Ramirez (P) bought a camper from Autosport (D) which had minor defects which were not immediately repaired, causing Ramirez (P) to seek rescission of the contract.

CONCISE RULE OF LAW: Buyers have the right to reject goods which do not conform to the contract because of defects.

FACTS: The Ramirezes (P) bought a camper from Autosport (D) on July 20, 1978. The camper cost $14,100, from which $4,700 was deducted for the Ramirezes' (P) van, which was traded in to Autosport (D). Delivery of the camper was contracted to take place on August 3, 1978. On that date the camper was discovered to have many small defects, and the Ramirezes (P) chose not to accept it. On August 14, 1978, Autosport (D) told the Ramirezes (P) that the camper was ready, but again several defects were present and the Ramirezes (P) chose not to accept the camper. The next day Autosport (D) transferred title to the Ramirezes (P) without informing them. Autosport (D) and the Ramirezes (P) attempted to negotiate a settlement, but finally the Ramirezes (P) requested that the contract be canceled and their van returned. However, Autosport (D) had already sold their old van to a third party and refused to cancel the contract. The Ramirezes (P) filed suit to rescind the sales contract, and Autosport (D) counterclaimed for breach of contract. At trial, the Ramirezes (P) prevailed, and Autosport (D) appealed.

ISSUE: May buyers reject goods which do not completely conform to the contract?

HOLDING AND DECISION: (Pollock, J.) Yes. Buyers may reject goods which do not completely conform to the contract. Under U.C.C. § 2-602, a buyer may reject goods for any nonconformity to the contract and obtain cancellation. This rejection must take place within a reasonable time. The seller must prove conformity or cure the defect within a reasonable time in order to avoid cancellation. The Ramirezes (P) rejected the camper when they refused to accept it on August 14, 1978. Autosport (D) failed to demonstrate that the defects were corrected within a reasonable time. Ramirezes (P) acted rightfully and were entitled to cancellation of the contract. Since the Ramirezes (P) van was sold to a third party, they were also entitled to its fair market value as determined by the trial court. Affirmed.

EDITOR'S ANALYSIS: The definition of acceptance is found in U.C.C. § 2-606. Upon acceptance, the burden of proof on the issue of whether the goods conform to the contract shifts from the seller to the buyer. Under U.C.C. § 2-601, the perfect tender rule is preserved and mandates that the seller prove conformity as of the time of delivery.

NOTES:

PLATEQ CORP. OF NORTH HAVEN v. MACHLETT LABORATORIES

Tank constructor (P) v. Tank buyer (D)
Conn. Sup. Ct., 189 Conn. 433, 456 A.2d 786 (1983).

NATURE OF CASE: Appeal from award of damages for breach of contract.

FACT SUMMARY: Machlett (D) contended it never effectively accepted the tanks purchased from Plateq (P) and, therefore, could reject them for nonconformity.

CONCISE RULE OF LAW: A buyer may be found to have accepted goods despite their known nonconformity and despite the absence of actual delivery.

FACTS: Machlett (D) contracted to pay Plateq (P) for constructing certain lead covered steel tanks. The tanks were to be designed for the purpose of testing X-ray tubes and thus had to be radiation-proof. Plateq (P) constructed the tanks and while Machlett (D) noted several minor defects, it never indicated that the tanks did not substantially conform to the contract. On the contrary, Machlett (D) communicated its general acquiescence to the construction, Machlett (D) led Plateq (P) to believe it would pick up the tanks for transport to its premises. No trucks were sent, and Machlett (D) notified Plateq (P) that it was rejecting tender of goods. Plateq (P) sued, contending Machlett (D) had already accepted the goods and that no grounds existed for rejection or repudiation of acceptance. Machlett (D) appealed from a verdict for Plateq (P).

ISSUE: May a buyer be found to have accepted goods despite their known nonconformity and despite the absence of actual delivery?

HOLDING AND DECISION: (Peters, J.) Yes. A buyer may be found to have accepted goods despite their known nonconformity with the contract despite the absence of actual delivery. Under U.C.C. § 2-606(1), acceptance occurs where the buyer signifies that he will take the goods after he has inspected them. Clearly in this case, Machlett (D) signified its willingness to take the goods even though it was aware of the defects. Thus, acceptance occurred. As a result Machlett (D) could avoid the contract only by proving acceptance substantially impaired the value of the goods to it. Consequently, no revocation is available. Affirmed.

EDITOR'S ANALYSIS: A buyer must have been afforded a reasonable time to inspect and object to the defect in the goods. Thus, if Machlett (D) had had no such opportunity, presumably the "Perfect Tender Rule" would have allowed it to reject the tanks. However, Plateq (P) would have been afforded an opportunity to cure the nonconformity.

QUICKNOTES

PERFECT TENDER - Goods tendered pursuant to a contract for sale, which conform precisely to the contract's requirements.

NOTES:

41

RESTER v. MORROW
Car buyer (P) v. Car dealer (D)
Miss. Sup. Ct., 491 So. 2d 204 (1986).

NATURE OF CASE: Appeal of denial of award of rescission of contract.

FACT SUMMARY: Rester (P), who purchased a car which suffered persistent minor problems, sought to revoke his acceptance of the car and rescind the contract.

CONCISE RULE OF LAW: A buyer may revoke acceptance of goods where defects substantially impair the value of the goods to that buyer.

FACTS: Rester (P) purchased a used 1981 Renault from Tommy Morrow A.M.C. (D) on April 13, 1981 for $18,000. The car came with a limited warranty against defects for the first of 12,000 miles or 12 months, whichever occurred first. Rester (P) discovered a number of minor defects, including a gas odor in the car, immediately after accepting the car. Morrow (D) attempted to fix the problems and returned the Renault to Rester (P). However, the problems persisted, and this pattern was repeated numerous times over the next several months as Morrow (D) attempted without success to remedy the problems. While the Renault was in for extended service, Rester (P) was forced to buy another car to carry out his employment. Finally, Rester (P) returned the car in September 1981 after having driven it a total of 11,000 miles. Rester (P) sought to revoke his acceptance of the car and demanded rescission of the contract. Morrow (D) responded that the defects in the car when Rester (P) returned it were minor and did not substantially impair its value. At trial, Morrow (D) prevailed on this defense. Rester (P) appealed.

ISSUE: May a buyer revoke acceptance of goods the defects of which substantially impair their value to that particular buyer?

HOLDING AND DECISION: (Robertson, J.) Yes. A buyer may revoke acceptance of goods whose value is substantially impaired to that buyer due to defects. U.C.C. § 2-608, which governs revocation of acceptance, states that the value of the goods must be substantially impaired. This is to be determined by the subjective needs of the particular buyer. Additionally, the determination of substantial impairment must include the goods' performance over the entire time the buyer has held them, not only the defects which remain at the time of revocation. Rester (P) required a car which operated consistently in order to maintain his employment. The Renault's need of constant service substantially impaired its value to Rester (P). Also, the Renault's poor performance over the five-month period was relevant to this determination. The inquiry is not limited to just the minor defects which were present when Rester (P) returned the car to Morrow (D). Therefore, Rester (P) must be entitled to argue these facts at trial. Reversed and remanded.

EDITOR'S ANALYSIS: Rester (P) had a choice of remedies available. Instead of seeking rescission, he also had the option of bringing a breach of warranty claim for damages against Morrow (D) under U.C.C. §§ 2-714 and 2-715. The courts are split on whether a buyer may continue to use goods after acceptance has been revoked.

QUICKNOTES
PERFECT TENDER - Goods tendered pursuant to a contract for sale, which conform precisely to the contract's requirements.

NOTES:

95 for course installs
90 in MBuckons
50 in Payants

344
50
72000
65k
65
130k

JAKOWSKI v. CAROLE CHEVROLET, INC.
Car buyer (P) v. Car dealer (D)
N.J. Super. Ct., 433 A.2d 841 (1981).

NATURE OF CASE: Action for damages for breach of contract.

FACT SUMMARY: After Carole (D) neglected to undercoat Jakowski's (P) new car purchased from Carole (D), Jakowski (P) returned the car to Carole's (D) lot for the work, from where it was stolen.

CONCISE RULE OF LAW: The seller of goods remains liable for the risk of their loss when the buyer receives nonconforming goods without accepting the nonconformity and the seller has not effected cure.

FACTS: Jakowski (P) entered into a contract to purchase from Carole (D) a new 1980 Chevrolet Camaro. Prior to delivery, Carole (D) was instructed to apply undercoatings and a finish coating. The car was delivered without the coatings, and the next day Jakowski (P) so notified Carole (D), who agreed to cure the defect and add the coatings. The car was in Carole's (D) lot awaiting cure when it was stolen and never recovered. Carole (D) refused demands to replace the car or refund the purchase price paid. Jakowski (P) was still liable on his installment loan for that price. Jakowski (P) then brought this action for damages based on the purchase price.

ISSUE: Does the seller of goods remain liable for the risk of their loss when the buyer receives nonconforming goods without accepting the nonconformity and the seller has not cured?

HOLDING AND DECISION: (Newman, J.) Yes. The seller of goods remains liable for the risk of their loss when the buyer receives nonconforming goods without accepting the nonconformity and the seller has not effected cure. The seller contends that the risk of loss passed to Jakowski (P) under U.C.C. § 2-509(3) upon the latter's receipt of the automobile. That section goes on to provide, however, that § 2-510 governs the effect of breach upon the risk of loss. The automobile as delivered failed to conform to the contract and would have given Jakowski (P) the right to reject but for cure provision of that section passing the risk to the buyer after cure. Since no evidence of cure was interposed and no contention was made that cure had been effected, the nonconformity remained and so did Carole's (D) liability for risk of loss. It has been established that receipt of an automobile is not always an "acceptance," and in this case, Jakowski (P) did not accept the nonconforming car because he had no "reasonable opportunity to inspect" it under U.C.C. § 2-606 or to reject the goods in the face of Carole's (D) acknowledgment of the nonconformity and offer of cure. Thus, U.C.C. § 2-510(1) is applicable. The seller of goods remains liable for the risk of their loss when the buyer receives nonconforming goods without

accepting the nonconformity and the seller has not cured. Jakowski (P) is entitled here to a refund of so much of the purchase price as has been paid, including the finance charges.

EDITOR'S ANALYSIS: The Official Comment clearly states that the cure by the seller in such cases does not operate to shift the risk of loss from the seller to the buyer until such cure is completed. This is true even where delivered goods are repossessed in contemplation of a new tender after cure.

QUICKNOTES

NONCONFORMING GOODS - Goods tendered pursuant to a contract for sale that do not conform with the contract's requirements or which are otherwise defective in some way.

RISK OF LOSS - Liability for damage to or loss of property that is the subject matter of a contract for sale.

NOTES:

15   100
 x   250

100 x =

2 courses w/
              18 = 21,000 42,000

1 course 2 on 18 = 37,000
                     16000
                   ‾‾‾‾‾‾‾‾
                    53000
                    42,000

ARABIAN SCORE v. LASMA ARABIAN LTD.
Horse buyer (P) v. Horse seller (D)
814 F.2d 529 (8th Cir. 1987).

NATURE OF CASE: Appeal of grant of motion for summary judgment denying rescission of contract.

FACT SUMMARY: After Arabian (P) bought a horse from Lasma (D), who promised to promote the horse for five years, the horse died, and Arabian (P) sought to recover the amount of money which would have been spent promoting the horse.

CONCISE RULE OF LAW: Impossibility is not a defense to a contract where the event causing the impossibility was foreseeable.

FACTS: Arabian (P) purchased a horse named Score from Lasma (D) for $1 million on October 27, 1983. The price included various promotional activities for Score that Lasma (D) was to perform over a period of five years. The agreement purported to disclaim all implied warranties. Arabian (P) obtained life insurance for Score in February 1984. Score died in September 1984. Arabian (P) sought to recover the amount of money which Lasma (D) would have spent promoting Score over the next four years on the grounds of impossibility. Lasma (D) responded that Score's death was a foreseeable risk assumed by Arabian (P). Furthermore, Lasma (D) presented evidence that they often promoted dead horses. Summary judgment was granted in favor of Lasma (D), and Arabian (P) appealed.

ISSUE: May an event which is foreseeable provide the basis for defending a contract on the grounds of impossibility?

HOLDING AND DECISION: (Wollman, J.) No. When a foreseeable event occurs, it may not be the basis for an action for rescission of due to impossibility performance. The doctrine of commercial frustration applies where performance under a contract becomes impossible due to the occurrence of enforceable events beyond the control of the parties. The death of Score was a foreseeable event to Arabian (P). This was evidenced by the fact that Arabian (P) obtained life insurance for Score. In addition, despite Score's death, Lasma (D) never indicated any inability or unwillingness to complete their promotional duties. Thus, there is no evidence that performance is impossible under these circumstances. Affirmed.

EDITOR'S ANALYSIS: Events such as the changing of zoning regulations and price increases are generally ruled foreseeable to the parties and do not provide the basis for the impossibility defense. Events which do qualify as unforeseeable are usually wars, embargoes, or natural catastrophes which affect the parties' ability to perform under the contract.

QUICKNOTES

FORESEEABILITY - A reasonable expectation that an act or omission would result in injury.

IMPOSSIBILITY - A doctrine relieving the parties to a contract from liability for nonperformance of their duties thereunder, if the subject matter of the contract ceases to exist, a person essential to the performance of the contract is deceased, or the service or goods contracted for has become illegal.

RESCISSION - The canceling of an agreement and the return of the parties to their positions prior to the formation of the contract.

NOTES:

LOUISIANA POWER & LIGHT CO. v. ALLEGHENY LUDLUM INDUSTRIES, INC.

Buyer (P) v. Seller (D)

517 F. Supp. 1319 (E.D. La. 1981).

NATURE OF CASE: Motion for summary judgment for breach of contract.

FACT SUMMARY: Allegheny (D) claimed that performance under the contract by which Louisiana Power & Light (P) bought steel tubing for delivery two years after the agreement was made was impracticable when the cost of producing the tubing rose substantially during this period.

CONCISE RULE OF LAW: Increases in costs do not allow sellers to raise commercial impracticability as a defense to performing under the contract unless they are unreasonable and severe.

FACTS: Louisiana Power & Light (P) contracted with Allegheny Ludlum Industries (D) to buy condenser tubing for use at a nuclear power plant. The contract was executed on February 8, 1974 with delivery to take place during June 1976. In May 1975, Allegheny (D) wrote to Louisiana Power & Light (P) requesting an adjustment in the contract price because the costs of making the tubing had increased substantially, causing Allegheny (D) to lose money on the contract, although the plant producing the tubing would remain slightly profitable overall. Louisiana Power & Light (P) refused, and Allegheny (D) responded that they might not perform under the contract. In February 1976, Allegheny (D) informed Louisiana Power & Light (P) that it would deliver the tubing only at the price which it cost to produce, which was 38% higher than at the time of the contract. Louisiana Power & Light (P) refused this offer and contracted with another company to deliver the tubing at a higher price than was provided for in the parties' contract. Louisiana Power & Light (P) filed suit to recover these extra costs due to Allegheny's (D) refusal to perform under the contract. Allegheny (D) defended by claiming that the higher production costs made performance commercially impracticable. Louisiana Power & Light (P) moved for summary judgment.

ISSUE: May sellers raise commercial impracticability as a defense to performing under a contract where the reason for the impracticability is substantially increased production costs?

HOLDING AND DECISION: (Gordon, J.) No. Sellers may not raise commercial impracticability as a defense to performance under a contract where the reason is increased production costs. According to U.C.C. § 2-615, commercial impracticability excuses performance of the contract when it is impracticable due to the occurrence of a contingency not contemplated by the parties. In order to show impracticability, the party must show that performance would cause an unreasonable and severe loss.

Allegheny's (D) loss would not have been unreasonable because production costs increased only 38% from when the contract was executed. Other cases, including Iowa Electric Light and Power Co. v. Atlas Corp., 467 F. Supp. 129 (N.D. Iowa 1978), indicate that cost increases of up to 58% do not constitute commercial impracticability. Furthermore, although Allegheny (D) would have lost money on the Louisiana Power & Light (P) contract, the plant producing the tubing remained profitable. Thus, Allegheny (D) could not defend the alleged breach of contract based upon commercial impracticability. Summary judgment granted to Louisiana Power and Light (P).

EDITOR'S ANALYSIS: U.C.C. § 2-615 allows impracticability as a defense upon "the occurrence of a contingency the non-occurrence of which was a basic assumption" of the parties at the time of the contract. It was intended to expand the common law defense of impossibility. However, many courts have treated § 2-615 as synonymous with common law impossibility.

QUICKNOTES

IMPRACTICABILITY - A doctrine relieving the parties to a contract from liability for nonperformance of their duties thereunder, if the subject matter of the contract ceases to exist.

NOTES:

CHAPTER 6
REMEDIES

QUICK REFERENCE RULES OF LAW

1. **Seller's Remedies.** The measure of damages for breach of contract by the buyer is the anticipated profit, including reasonable overhead, which the seller would have made but for the breach. (Teradyne, Inc. v. Teledyne Industries, Inc.)

2. **Buyer's Remedies.** (1) In calculating "cover" damages for the cost of substitute services, it is not error for a court to use the cost of what it determines are commercially reasonable substitutes instead of services that are identical to those involved in the contract. (2) In calculating "cover" damages for the cost of substitute services, it is not error for a court to project what actual performance would have been. (Hughes Communications Galaxy, Inc. v. United States)

3. **Buyer's Remedies.** When a seller breaches a sales contract, the proper measure of damages is the difference between the contract price and market price. (Tongish v. Thomas)

4. **The Statute of Limitations.** A cause of action for breach of a seller's agreement to repair any product defect that occurs during a warranty period and for a warranty claim arising from the same promise under the Magnusson-Moss Warranty Act does not accrue until the seller fails to perform the required repair within a reasonable time. (Poli v. DaimlerChrysler Corp.)

TERADYNE, INC. v. TELEDYNE INDUSTRIES, INC.
Buyer (P) v. Seller (D)
676 F.2d 865 (1st Cir. 1982).

NATURE OF CASE: Appeal from award of damages for breach of contract.

FACT SUMMARY: When Teledyne Industries (D) breached its contract with Teradyne (P) for the purchase of a transistor test system, Teradyne (P) filed suit to recover its lost profits.

CONCISE RULE OF LAW: The measure of damages for breach of contract by the buyer is the anticipated profit, including reasonable overhead, which the seller would have made but for the breach.

FACTS: After contracting to purchase a transistor test system from Teradyne (P), Teledyne Industries (D) breached the contract, offering to buy a less expensive machine instead. Teradyne (P) refused this offer. It then dismantled, tested, and reassembled the machine for sale to another purchaser, and filed suit for damages. Teradyne (P) would have made the sale to the second purchaser even if Teledyne Industries (D) had not broken its contract. It was not disputed that Teledyne Industries (D) broke the contract or that Teradyne's (P) right to damages was governed by U.C.C. § 2-708(2). What was disputed was the calculation of damages. The master concluded that the appropriate formula for calculating damages was "gross profit" including fixed costs but not costs saved as a result of the breach. The district court adopted the master's report, and this appeal followed.

ISSUE: Is the measure of damages for breach of contract by the buyer the anticipated profit, including reasonable overhead, which the seller would have made but for the breach?

HOLDING AND DECISION: (Wyzanski, J.) Yes. The measure of damages for breach of contract by the buyer is the anticipated profit, including reasonable overhead, which the seller would have made but for the breach. The master's formula made no deductions on account of the wages paid to testers, shippers, installers, and other Teradyne (P) employees who directly handled the machine in preparing it for sale to the subsequent purchaser, or on account of their fringe benefits amounting to 12% of wages. The work of those employees entered directly into producing and supplying the machine and should not be regarded as "reasonable overhead" within § 2-708(2). Thus, as a "direct cost," the wages of the testers, etc., should have been deducted from the contract price, and fringe benefits should also have been deducted as direct costs. Vacated and remanded with respect to the omitted direct labor costs specified.

EDITOR'S ANALYSIS: Section 2-708(2) applies only if the damages provided by § 2-708(1) are inadequate to put the seller in as good a position as he would have been had there been performance. Under § 2-708(1), the measure of damages is the difference between unpaid contract price and market price. Because the unpaid contract price here was $97,416, due to a discount, and the market price was $98,400, no damages would be recoverable under § 2-708(1). If Teledyne Industries (D) had performed, Teradyne (P) would have had the proceeds from two contracts, both Teledyne Industries' (D) and the subsequent purchaser's. Such losses by a "volume seller" are referred to as "lost volume profits."

QUICKNOTES

LOST PROFITS - The potential value of income earned or goods which are the subject of the contract; may be used in calculating damages where the contract has been breached.

NOTES:

HUGHES COMMUNICATIONS GALAXY, INC. v. UNITED STATES

Satellite manufacturer (P) v. Federal government (D)

271 F.3d 1060 (Fed. Cir. 2001).

NATURE OF CASE: Appeal of breach of contract damages calculation.

FACT SUMMARY: Hughes Communications Galaxy, Inc. (Hughes) (P) had a contract with NASA whereby NASA would use its best efforts to launch 10 Hughes satellites on space shuttles. As the result of the space shuttle Challenger explosion, NASA changed its program and informed Hughes (P) it would not use the space shuttles for launching any satellites. Hughes (P) then used expendable launch vehicles (ELVs) to launch its satellites at greater cost than it would have incurred by using the space shuttle. Hughes (P) sued the U.S. government (D) for breach of contract and was awarded $102,680,625 in contract damages.

CONCISE RULES OF LAW: (1) In calculating "cover" damages for the cost of substitute services, it is not error for a court to use the cost of what it determines are commercially reasonable substitutes instead of services that are identical to those involved in the contract. (2) In calculating "cover" damages for the cost of substitute services, it is not error for a court to project what actual performance would have been. (3) In calculating "cover" damages for the cost of substitute services, it is not error for a court to average actual costs to determine total damages. (4) In calculating "cover" damages for the cost of substitute services, it is not error for a court not to reduce damages by amounts passed through to customers.

FACTS: Huges (P) entered into a Launch Services Agreement (LSA) with NASA that required NASA to use its best efforts to launch 10 Hughes (P) HS-393 satellites on space shuttles before September 30, 1994. In January 1986, the space shuttle Challenger exploded. As a result, by August 1986, NASA decided not to launch commercial satellites on shuttles. After 1986, Hughes (P) launched three of its HS-393s on expendable launch vehicles (ELVs) and also launched similar satellites on ELVs, including six HS-601s. Hughes (P) incurred more costs by launching satellites on ELVs rather than on shuttles. Hughes (P) sued the U.S. government (D) for breach of contract. On remand, the Court of Federal Claims granted summary judgment for Hughes (P) for breach of contract, but before holding a trial on damages, that court ruled that the U.S. (D) could not produce evidence to reduce its damages by the amount Hughes (P) had passed on to its customers in increased prices. Hughes (P) presented two methods for calculating the increased costs. The first method, the Ten HS-393 Satellites Method, compared the costs of launching ten HS-393s on shuttles with the costs of launching ten HS-393s on ELVs. Because Hughes (P) had

actually launched only three HS-393s on ELVs, the method based the ELV launch costs on the actual costs of launching the three HS-393s. The second method, the Primary Method, compared Hughes' (P) actual costs of launching ten satellites on ELVs with the costs that Hughes (P) would have incurred by launching ten satellites on shuttles. The ten satellites included the three HS-393s, the six HS-601s, and one HS-376. The Court of Federal Claims used the Ten HS-393 Satellites Method to calculate Hughes' (P) cost of "cover." However, the court modified this method in several important ways: 1) the court found that even using its best efforts, NASA would have only launched five HS-393s under the LSA, so it only awarded Hughes (P) increased costs for five satellites; 2) the court averaged the costs of launching on shuttles the three HS-393s that were actually launched on ELVs and used that average for the fourth and fifth satellites, rather than individually calculating the cost of launching each satellite on a shuttle; 3) in calculating the ELV launch costs for the fourth and fifth satellites, the court escalated the costs using the midpoint between March 1989 and September 1994, rather than the midpoint between March 1989 and December 1995, as Hughes' (P) expert had done; 4) the court refused to award Hughes (P) prejudgment interest on its damages; 5) the court refused to award Hughes (P) reflight insurance costs and increased launch insurance costs for the five satellites. Based on these modifications, the court awarded Hughes (P) $102,680,625 in damages for its increased launch costs. Hughes (P) and the U.S. (D) both appealed.

ISSUES: (1) In calculating "cover" damages for the cost of substitute services, is it error for a court to use the cost of what it determines are commercially reasonable substitutes instead of services that are identical to those involved in the contract? (2) In calculating "cover" damages for the cost of substitute services, is it error for a court to project what actual performance would have been? (3) In calculating "cover" damages for the cost of substitute services, is it error for a court to average actual costs to determine total damages? (4) In calculating "cover" damages for the cost of substitute services, is it error for a court not to reduce damages by amounts passed through to customers?

HOLDING AND DECISION: (Rader, J.) No as to all issues. (1) The Court of Federal Claims awarded Hughes (P) "cover" damages—the difference between the cost of the substitute and the contract price plus other losses. Although the U.C.C. does not govern the LSA, it provides useful guidance. Under the U.C.C., substitute goods or services that are used for cover do not have

Continued on next page.

to be identical to those in the contract; they only have to be "commercially usable as reasonable substitutes under the circumstances." Whether cover provides a reasonable substitute is a question of fact. The U.S. (D) argues that Hughes (P) should be able to recover damages only for the three HS-393s that it actually launched. Although Hughes did not actually launch the fourth and fifth HS-393s that the trial court used to calculate damages, Hughes did incur costs in launching the HS-601s. However, based on the evidence presented, the trial court found that HS-601 launches were reasonable substitutes under the circumstances (the court believed that Hughes would not have developed the HS-601s but for the breach). This was an issue of credibility, a determination of which rarely is subject to reversal for clear error. As the victim of the breach, Hughes (P) was within its rights to obtain commercially reasonable substitute launch services even if the substitute services were not identical to those covered by the LSA. The trial court thus did not clearly err in holding that Hughes (P) successfully covered by launching HS-601s on ELVs. By using increased HS-393 launch costs (comparing the cost of ELV launches to shuttle launches) as a reasonable approximation for increased costs attributable to the substitute HS-601 launches, the trial court did not abuse its discretion. Moreover, these damages were direct because they represented increased launch costs only. In sum, there was no error for awarding damages for increased costs incurred by obtaining substitute launch services for two HS-601s in addition to the three HS-393s. (2) The Court of Federal Claims found that NASA could have launched five HS-393s during the LSA contract period using its best efforts. This finding was based on various sources of evidence, including NASA's manifests, expert testimony, and the circumstances surrounding NASA's revised shuttle program. Based on this evidence, the trial court did not clearly err in its finding of what actual performance would have been limited to. (3) Because Hughes (P) actually launched only three HS-393s, the trial court calculated the average costs of launching those three satellites on shuttles. Then, using the report of Hughes' (P) expert, it applied that average to project the shuttle launch costs of the fourth and fifth satellites. Hughes (P) asserted that the court should have used the shuttle launch costs for each individual satellite shown in the expert's report. However, the trial court's method was symmetrical with its calculation of the costs of ELV launches and was within the court's discretion. (4) The U.S. (D) wanted the court to reduce damages by the amount Hughes (P) recouped by increasing ("passing through") prices to its customers. As the trial court correctly noted, such mitigation is too remote, and allowing pass-through damages reduction in a breach of contract action would destroy symmetry between reduction and escalation of damages. Moreover, a standard for pass-through reductions would entail extremely

difficult burdens for the trial court. Thus, the trial court did not abuse its discretion by disallowing pass-through damages reductions. Affirmed.

EDITOR'S ANALYSIS: As this case repeatedly demonstrates, courts have discretion in determining what constitutes reasonable substitutes in determining "cover" damages. Because such a determination is heavily fact-driven, it is difficult to overturn on grounds of abuse of discretion or clear error.

NOTES:

TONGISH v. THOMAS
Sunflower seed grower (P) v. Buyers (D)
Kan. Ct. App., 16 Kan. App. 2d 809, 829 P.2d 916 (1992).

NATURE OF CASE: Appeal from judgment awarding damages for breach of contract.

FACT SUMMARY: Coop (D), the buyer, contended that damages awarded to it for Tongish's (P) breach of contract should be the market price differential, not lost profits.

CONCISE RULE OF LAW: When a seller breaches a sales contract, the proper measure of damages is the difference between the contract price and market price.

FACTS: The Decatur Coop Association (Coop) (D) contracted to buy sunflower seeds from Tongish (P). Coop (D) also contracted to sell the seeds to a third party at the same price, plus a set handling fee. Therefore, Coop (D) had no risk on fluctuating market prices in its contract with Tongish (P). By the time the seeds were ready to deliver, the market price of sunflower seeds had risen greatly. Tongish (P) refused to honor the contract and sold to another party, Thomas (D), at a higher price. After Tongish (P) successfully sued Thomas (D) for the sales price, Coop (D) intervened as a third party, alleging that Tongish (P) had breached its contract. The court awarded Coop (D) $455.51, the amount of his handling fee. Coop (D) appealed, contending that the appropriate measure of damages was the difference between the contract and market price.

ISSUE: When a seller breaches a sales contract, is the proper measure of damages the difference between the contract price and market price?

HOLDING AND DECISION: (Walton, J.) Yes. When a seller breaches a sales contract, the proper measure of damages is the difference between the contract price and market price. This is true even if this amount does not accurately reflect the buyer's anticipated profits. Commercial Code § 1-106 provides that the proper measure of damages for a breach of contract generally is the aggrieved party's lost profits. Section 2-713, however, prescribes that, when a seller breaches, the proper measure of damages is the difference between contract price and market price. Both sections could be applied here. However, § 1-106 is a general rule; § 2-713 is a specific statute. When a general rule and a specific statute conflict, the specific statute should prevail. Also, § 2-713, to a greater extent than § 1-106, tends to discourage breaches of contract and thus promotes commercial stability. Thus, the trial court should have applied § 2-713, not § 1-106. Reversed.

EDITOR'S ANALYSIS: Coop (D) received more than $5,000 under § 2-713, while its expected profit on the transaction would have only been $455.51. This seems unfair and, as between the parties here, may well have been. However, § 2-713 also serves a general deterrent purpose that was served here.

QUICKNOTES

LOST PROFITS - The potential value of income earned or goods which are the subject of the contract; may be used in calculating damages where the contract has been breached.

NOTES:

POLI v. DAIMLERCHRYSLER CORP.

Car buyer (P) v. Car manufacturer (D)

N.J. Super. Ct., 349 N.J. Super. 169, 793 A.2d 104 (2002).

NATURE OF CASE: Appeal from summary judgment dismissing action for breach of warranty as barred by the statute of limitations.

FACT SUMMARY: Poli (P) brought a new car along with a seven-year powertrain warranty from DaimlerChrysler Corp. (D). Over the next five years, the car's timing belt had to be repaired or replaced numerous times, and Poli (P) brought suit for, among other things, breach of warranty and claims under the Magnuson-Moss Warranty Act.

CONCISE RULE OF LAW: A cause of action for breach of a seller's agreement to repair any product defect that occurs during a warranty period and for a warranty claim arising from the same promise under the Magnusson-Moss Warranty Act does not accrue until the seller fails to perform the required repair within a reasonable time.

FACTS: In 1993, Poli (P) brought a new car along with a seven-year, 70,000 miles powertrain warranty from DaimlerChrysler Corp. (D). The warranty obligated Defendant to cover the cost of all parts and labor needed to repair or replace any covered part of the car. Over the next five years, the car's timing belt had to be repaired or replaced numerous times, and once, the failure of the belt caused other engine damage, which the dealer took six months to repair. In December 1998, Poli (P) brought suit for, among other things, breach of the powertrain warranty and claims under the Magnuson-Moss Warranty Act. Although Defendant acknowledged that the timing belt was covered by the powertrain warranty, Defendant moved for summary judgment on the ground that Poli's (P) claims were barred by a four-year statute of limitations. The trial court agreed with Defendant and dismissed.

ISSUE: Does a cause of action for breach of a seller's agreement to repair any product defect that occurs during a warranty period and for a warranty claim arising from the same promise under the Magnusson-Moss Warranty Act accrue until the seller fails to perform the required repair within a reasonable time?

HOLDING AND DECISION: (Skillman, P. J. A. D.) No. The U.C.C. establishes a four-year limitations period for breach of warranty claims. The limitations period under the U.C.C. for an action for breach of a sales contract is four years after the cause of action has accrued. The U.C.C. also provides that a cause of action accrues when the breach occurs, and that a breach of warranty occurs when delivery is made. However, an exception is where a warranty explicitly extends to future performance of the goods, and, where such a warranty is provided, the cause of action accrues when the breach is, or should have been, discovered. Defendant contends the warranty was an ordinary

sales warranty (action barred after four years from delivery—1997); Poli (P) contends it was a warranty of future performance (action barred after four years from discovery—2002). Here, the powertrain warranty was not a mere representation of the car's condition at the time of delivery but was a promise relating to its performance at a future time. Therefore, the claims for breach of this warranty did not accrue until Defendant allegedly breached its duty to repair the defect—the claim did not accrue at time of delivery. The correctness of this conclusion is made especially clear where the term of the warranty is longer than four years; if the warranty were an ordinary sales warranty, the express term in the warranty would be rendered meaningless. This conclusion is also supported by other decisions from other jurisdictions that have found that "a promise to repair defects that occur during a future period is the very definition of express warranty of future performance." Other jurisdictions find that although such a warranty is not an express warranty of future performance, the promise to repair is an independent obligation that is not breached until the seller fails to repair. In such instances, the cause of action also does not accrue at the time of delivery. Some commentators find that such a "warranty" is not a warranty at all, but, rather, is a remedial promise, with the action for the breach of which accrues when the remedial promise is not performed when due. Under any of these constructs, Poli's (P) complaint was timely filed in 1998. The Magnuson-Moss Warranty Act (the Act) does not establish a limitations period for actions brought under its provision. Where a federal statute does not establish a limitations period for a claim, the limitations period from the state statute of limitations that governs the state cause of action that is most closely analogous to the federal action is used. Here, the state cause of action most analogous to that under the Act is a breach of warranty claim under the U.C.C. It is also clear here that the powertrain warranty is a warranty of future performance under the Act's more expansive definition of warranty. Therefore, Poli's (P) claim under the Act did not accrue until Defendant allegedly breached its obligation to repair the defect. Reversed.

EDITOR'S ANALYSIS: Under the U.C.C., the parties to a sales agreement may reduce the Code's four-year period of limitations down to one year but may not extend it beyond four years. As this case indicates, however, it may not always be clear when that period accrues.

NOTES:

7

CHAPTER 7
NEGOTIABILITY

QUICK REFERENCE RULES OF LAW

1. **Implied Conditions.** Money orders that contain an unconditional promise to pay on demand are negotiable instruments. (Triffin v. Dillabough)

2. **Courier Without Luggage.** To be negotiable, a promissory note must not be cluttered by other promises, orders, obligations, or powers unless otherwise authorized. (Woodworth v. The Richmond Indiana Venture)

TRIFFIN v. DILLABOUGH
Money order holder (P) v. Order presenter (D)
Pa. Sup. Ct., 716 A.2d 605 (Pa. 1998)

NATURE OF CASE: Appeal from judgment in favor of defendant in an action demanding payment on a money order.

FACT SUMMARY: American Express (D) refused to pay on a stolen money order that it issued.

CONCISE RULE OF LAW: Money orders that contain an unconditional promise to pay on demand are negotiable instruments.

FACTS: American Express (D) issued many money orders that were stolen after they had been signed. Dillabough (D) presented two of these stolen money orders at a check cashing operation and received cash. The check cashing company presented the orders to American Express (D) who refused to pay on them because they had already been listed on a fraud log. The check cashing operation sold the money orders to Triffin (P) who filed suit against Dillabough (D) and American Express (D) to collect on the money orders. The trial court ruled that American Express (D) was not liable because the money orders were not negotiable instruments due to a statement on the back that the money order will not be paid if it has been stolen or forged. Triffin (P) appealed.

ISSUE: Are money orders containing unconditional promises to pay on demand negotiable instruments?

HOLDING AND DECISION: (Newman, J.) Yes. Money orders that contain an unconditional promise to pay on demand are negotiable instruments. The commercial code contains a four part test to determine whether a document qualifies as a negotiable instrument. It must 1) be signed by the maker; 2) contain an unconditional promise to pay; 3) be payable on demand; and 4) be payable to order or to bearer. The only contested issue in the present case is whether American Express' money orders contain an unconditional promise to pay. The legend on the back on the money order does not qualify as an unconditional promise for purposes of this test. Rather, it is more accurately viewed as a warning that American Express is reserving its statutory defenses. In the instant case, the statutory defenses are not applicable because Triffin (P) is a holder in due course as the assignee of the money order. Accordingly, American Express (D) is liable to Triffin (P) for the face value of the orders.

DISSENT: (Castille, J.) The express and explicit language on the American Express (D) money orders plainly contains a condition on payment. The majority is unjustified in construing it otherwise.

EDITOR'S ANALYSIS: The majority cited a Louisiana appellate court decision as persuasive. The dissent was unimpressed by this decision, especially since Louisiana hadn't adopted the U.C.C. at the time of the decision. U.C.C. § 3-106 contains the relevant provision to conditional orders.

QUICKNOTES
NEGOTIABLE INSTRUMENT - A signed writing promising to pay a specific sum of money either on demand or at a specified time.

NOTES:

WOODWORTH v. THE RICHMOND INDIANA VENTURE
Borrower (P) v. Lender (D)
Ohio Ct. Common Pleas, 13 U.C.C. Rep. Serv. 2d 1149 (1990).

NATURE OF CASE: Appeal from grant of plaintiff's partial motion for summary judgment in an action contesting negotiability of a promissory note.

FACT SUMMARY: When Woodworth (P) defaulted on the payments on his promissory note, he filed this action questioning the note's negotiability, since Richmond (D) had previously assigned the note to Signet Bank (D).

CONCISE RULE OF LAW: To be negotiable, a promissory note must not be cluttered by other promises, orders, obligations, or powers unless otherwise authorized.

FACTS: Woodworth (P) executed a promissory note in which he promised to pay Richmond (D), a limited partnership, $655,625. The note also contained a term providing for forfeiture of Woodworth's (P) partnership interest in Richmond (D) should he default on the payments. Woodworth (P) defaulted on the payments after the promissory note was assigned or negotiated to Signet Bank (D), and he filed this action contesting the note's negotiability on the ground that it was cluttered by an additional unnecessary term. Woodworth's (P) motion for partial summary judgment was granted, and Richmond (D) filed a motion for reconsideration.

ISSUE: To be negotiable, must a promissory note not be cluttered by other promises, orders, obligations, or powers unless otherwise authorized?

HOLDING AND DECISION: (Johnson, J.) Yes. To be negotiable, a promissory note must not be cluttered by other promises, orders, obligations, or powers unless otherwise authorized. In order to be negotiable, a promissory note must be a signed, unconditional promise to pay a sum certain in money which is payable on demand or at a definite, stated time. The additional term is clearly a forfeiture provision in addition to other remedies under the partnership agreement. Nothing in the U.C.C. authorizes this forfeiture term. Thus, the negotiability of the promissory note is doubtful. Where there is doubt, the decision should be against negotiability. Since the promissory note is not negotiable, Signet Bank (D) cannot claim the status of a holder in due course and is subject to ordinary contract defenses that Woodworth (P) may assert. As to the motion for reconsideration, it is persuasive that the forfeiture provision may be exercised at the option of the partnership, not the holder of the instrument. Including such provision in the instrument clutters the unconditional promise to pay and makes the commercial viability of this instrument less certain.

EDITOR'S ANALYSIS: The policy under pre-Code law was that instruments should be as concise as possible and free from collateral engagements. As seen in the rule above, the Code continues this policy. Since the forfeited interest here flowed to the partnership, that interest was not applied to the unpaid balance on the instrument. The court noted that any deleterious effects upon the flow of commercial instruments could be avoided by confining forfeiture provisions such as this one to the partnership agreement.

QUICKNOTES

PROMISSORY NOTE - A written promise to tender a stated amount of money at a designated time and to a designated person.

NOTES:

9

CHAPTER 9*
HOLDERS IN DUE COURSE

QUICK REFERENCE RULES OF LAW

1. **"Value".** A bank becomes a holder in due course and acquires a security interest in items deposited with it to the extent that the provisional credit given the customer in the item is withdrawn. (Falls Church Bank v. Wesley Heights Realty, Inc.)

2. **"Good Faith" and "Notice".** A holder in due course is one who takes the instrument for value, in good faith and without notice of any defense against it or claim to it on the part of any person. (General Investment Corp. v. Angelini)

3. **"Good Faith" and "Notice".** When an instrument is so incomplete as to call its validity into question, a purchaser of that instrument is on notice of the possibility of a claim against it and, thus, cannot be a holder in due course. (Winter & Hirsch, Inc. v. Passarelli)

4. **"Good Faith" and "Notice".** When an instrument is so incomplete as to call its validity into question, a purchaser of that instrument is on notice of the possibility of a claim against it and, thus, cannot be a holder in due course. (Jones v. Approved Bancredit Corp.)

5. **"Good Faith" and "Notice".** To be effective, notice to a purchaser of a negotiable instrument must be received at such time and in such manner as to give a reasonable opportunity to act on it. (Sullivan v. United Dealers Corp.)

6. **The Shelter Rule.** A holder in due course is entitled to enforce a negotiable instrument where there is no evidence presented that there is anything on the face of the instrument to indicate that the instrument has been forged or altered or is otherwise irregular. (Triffin v. Somerset Valley Bank)

7. **Defense Against a Holder in Due Course.** A holder in due course takes the instrument free from all defenses of any party to the instrument with whom the holder has not dealt except where misrepresentation has induced the party to sign the instrument with neither the knowledge nor reasonable opportunity to obtain knowledge of its character or its essential terms. (Federal Deposit Insurance Corp. v. Culver)

8. **Defense Against a Holder in Due Course.** Checks drawn for gambling purposes are void and unenforceable. (Sea Air Support, Inc. v. Herrmann)

9. **Defense Against a Holder in Due Course.** Unless the instrument arising from a contract is itself made void by statute, the illegality defense is not available to bar the claim of a holder in due course. (Kedzie & 103rd Currency Exchange, Inc. v. Hodge)

10. **Procedural Issues.** The party seeking recovery on an instrument is not required to prove that any signature is genuine until the defendant introduces evidence which would support a finding that the signature is forged. (Virginia National Bank v. Holt)

11. **Defenses Against a Non-Holder in Due Course.** One otherwise liable on an instrument may, as against a nonholder in due course, present evidence that the instrument was never intended to be binding. (Herzog Contracting Corp. v. McGowen Corp.)

* There are no cases in Chapter 8.

FALLS CHURCH BANK v. WESLEY HEIGHTS REALTY, INC.
Bank (P) v. Check casher (D)
256 A.2d 915 (D.C. 1969).

NATURE OF CASE: Appeal from judgment denying award of damages to a holder in due course.

FACT SUMMARY: When Wesley Heights (D) stopped payment on a check it issued to a Bank (P) customer after the Bank (P) approved the customer's withdrawal of a portion of the check's value, the Bank (P) sought to collect the withdrawal amount from Wesley Heights (D).

CONCISE RULE OF LAW: A bank becomes a holder in due course and acquires a security interest in items deposited with it to the extent that the provisional credit given the customer in the item is withdrawn.

FACTS: Wesley Heights (D) drew a check payable to the order of a customer of the Bank (P). After the customer deposited the check in his account, the Bank (P) allowed him to withdraw a small portion of the check prior to learning that Wesley Heights (D) had stopped payment on the check. The customer, who could not be found, left no credits in his account on which to recover the amount withdrawn. When Wesley Heights (D) refused the Bank's (P) demand to pay the amount of the withdrawal, the Bank (P) filed suit. At trial, Wesley Heights (D) moved for summary judgment on the grounds that the Bank (P) "was an agent for collection only, had no security interest, and was not a holder in due course for value." The trial court granted the motion, and the Bank (P) appealed.

ISSUE: Does a bank become a holder in due course and acquire a security interest in items deposited with it to the extent that the provisional credit given the customer in the item is withdrawn?

HOLDING AND DECISION: (Hood, J.) Yes. A bank becomes a holder in due course and acquires a security interest in items deposited with it to the extent that the provisional credit given the customer in the item is withdrawn. As a holder in due course as to the amount withdrawn, the Bank's (P) claim cannot be defeated except by those defenses set out in U.C.C. § 3-305(2), none of which were alleged herein. Reversed.

EDITOR'S ANALYSIS: Under the Code, a bank will be permitted to recover if it is out of pocket for anything and can prove that it paid value for the check. The crucial point in such instances is whether a bank permitted its customer to withdraw money before the subject check was cleared through the bank upon which it was drawn. A bank is deemed by the U.C.C. to be an agent of its customer and may be a holder in due course while acting as a collecting agent for its customer. Citizens Bank of Booneville v. National Bank of Commerce, 334 F.2d 257, 261 (10th Cir. 1964).

QUICKNOTES

HOLDER IN DUE COURSE - A party who takes an instrument in good faith and for consideration without notice of any claims therein.

SECURITY INTEREST - An interest in property that may be sold upon a default in payment of the debt.

NOTES:

GENERAL INVESTMENT CORP. v. ANGELINI
Corporation (P) v. Homeowners (D)
N.J. Sup. Ct., 58 N.J. 396, 278 A.2d 193 (1971).

NATURE OF CASE: Appeal from a money judgment in favor of the plaintiff.

FACT SUMMARY: When the contractor the Angelinis (D) hired to repair their home sold their installment payment note to General Investment (P) and then failed to complete the repairs for which they had contracted, the Angelinis (D) refused to make the periodic payments provided for in the note.

CONCISE RULE OF LAW: A holder in due course is one who takes the instrument for value, in good faith and without notice of any defense against it or claim to it on the part of any person.

FACTS: After contracting to repair the Angelinis' (D) home, Lustro sold the Angelinis' (D) note for monthly installment payments to General Investment Corp. (P). Due to General Investment's (P) past experience with Lustro, it knew that the homeowner's obligation to make payments did not come into being until 60 days after the home improvements were completed. The Angelinis (D) promptly returned a payment book received from General Investment (P), informing it that Lustro never completed the work and that its part performance neither conformed to the contract nor met reasonable workmanlike standards. General Investment (P) filed this action. The trial judge held that General Investment (P) was a holder in due course and was immune from any defenses asserted by the Angelinis (D). General Investment (P) was awarded damages. The appellate division affirmed, and this appeal followed.

ISSUE: Is a holder in due course one who takes the instrument for value, in good faith, and without notice of any defense against it or claim to it on the part of any person?

HOLDING AND DECISION: (Francis, J.) Yes. A holder in due course is one who takes the instrument for value, in good faith, and without notice of any defense against it or claim to it on the part of any person. Here, General Investment (P) neither demanded a certificate of completion from Lustro nor inquired of the Angelinis (D) as to completion. Instead it chose to accept the contractor's representation in the note endorsement form that he had fulfilled his contractual obligation. Such conduct justifies a strong inference that General Investment (P) willfully failed to seek actual knowledge on the subject of completion because of a belief or a fear that an inquiry would disclose a failure of consideration of the note. The evidence and the inferences drawn therefrom establish that General Investment (P) did not acquire the note in "good faith" and cannot claim the status of a holder in

due course. Consequently, it holds the instrument as an assigneee and is subject to the defense of failure of consideration. Reversed.

EDITOR'S ANALYSIS: The basic philosophy of the holder in due course status is to encourage free negotiability of commercial paper by removing certain anxieties of one who takes the paper as an innocent purchaser knowing no reason why the paper is not as sound as its face would indicate. Good faith is determined by looking to the mind of the particular holder. It would seem to follow, therefore, that the more the holder knows about the underlying transaction, the less he fits the role of a good-faith purchaser for value.

QUICKNOTES

GOOD FAITH - An honest intention to abstain from any unconscientious advantage of another.

GOOD FAITH PURCHASER FOR VALUE - A party who purchases property in good faith and for valuable consideration without notice of a defect in title.

HOLDER IN DUE COURSE - A party who takes an instrument in good faith and for consideration without notice of any claims therein.

NOTES:

WINTER & HIRSCH, INC. v. PASSARELLI
Lender (P) v. Borrower (D)
Ill. App. Ct., 122 Ill. App. 2d 372, 269 N.E.2d 312 (1970).

NATURE OF CASE: Appeal from denial of motion to vacate a judgment by confession.

FACT SUMMARY: Because Winter & Hirsch (P) issued a check to Equitable for purchase of a note before the note was formalized, Winter & Hirsch (P) was deemed to be a co-originator of the loan and on notice of its usurious rate and, thus, not to be a holder in due course.

CONCISE RULE OF LAW: When an instrument is so incomplete as to call its validity into question, a purchaser of that instrument is on notice of the possibility of a claim against it and, thus, cannot be a holder in due course.

FACTS: In return for a promissory note, Equitable loaned Passarelli (D) $10,000, with repayment totaling $16,260. Ten days prior to the time Passarelli (D) formally executed the note, Winter & Hirsch (P), by check, purchased it from Equitable for $11,000. Winter & Hirsch (P) claimed it made an effective purchase of the note from Equitable. Passarelli (D) defaulted on the note, and Winter & Hirsch (P) obtained a judgment by confession. It was uncontested that Equitable charged a usurious rate of interest on the note. Passarelli (D) moved to vacate the judgment, claiming that Winter & Hirsch (P) purchased the note with knowledge of the usurious interest and consequently could not have become a holder in due course. The trial court denied the motion, and this appeal followed.

ISSUE: When an instrument is so incomplete as to call its validity into question, is a purchaser of that instrument on notice of the possibility of a claim against it and is, thus, not a holder in due course?

HOLDING AND DECISION: (McCormick, J.) Yes. When an instrument is so incomplete as to call its validity into question, a purchaser of that instrument is on notice of the possibility of a claim against it and, thus, is not a holder in due course. Winter & Hirsch (P) was a cooriginator of the note since it advanced the funds for the usurious loan before the note was formalized, and it thus became charged with the knowledge of the terms of the loan, including the interest rate information. The difference between what Winter & Hirsch (P) paid Equitable and the amount due to be repaid on the note was so great that Winter & Hirsch (P) was on notice of a possible violation of the usury statute. Because the principal sum of the loan extended to Passarelli (D) did not appear on its face, the instrument was "so incomplete" as to call its validity into question after Winter & Hirsch (P) learned that it was able buy it for only $11,000. Winter & Hirsch (P) should have inquired how much money was loaned to Passarelli (D). Thus Winter & Hirsch (P) had "reason to know" there was a good defense against the note. Reversed and remanded.

EDITOR'S ANALYSIS: The court declared that parties cannot be permitted to intentionally keep themselves in ignorance of facts which, if known, would defeat their lawful purpose. Where it appears from the facts and circumstances of a particular transaction that a reasonably prudent businessman would have found the purchase suspicious, he should inquire as to the truth. The suspicion is even more compelling when the paper is bought from a broker in the business of selling such paper for profit.

QUICKNOTES
HOLDER IN DUE COURSE - A party who takes an instrument in good faith and for consideration without notice of any claims therein.

NOTES:

JONES v. APPROVED BANCREDIT CORP.
Homeowner (D) v. Bank (P)
Del. Sup. Ct., 256 A.2d 739 (Del. 1969).

NATURE OF CASE: Appeal from award of foreclosure of mortgage.

FACT SUMMARY: When Jones (D) refused to pay for construction of a home which was never finished and which had to be demolished at her expense, Bancredit (P), holder of the promissory note and mortgage, sought to foreclose on the mortgage and collect payments for the balance of the contract, as a holder in due course.

CONCISE RULE OF LAW: The more a holder knows about the underlying transaction which is the source of the paper or controls or participates in it, the less he fits the role of good faith purchaser for value which would accord him the protected status of holder in due course.

FACTS: Jones (D), after signing a purchase order contract and credit application, made a deposit to have a house built on her land by Albee Dell Homes, Inc. (hereafter, "Dell") Dell's representative presented a series of documents to sign; the representative immediately endorsed the paper and assigning it to Bancredit (P). When the builder's employee knocked the partially completed house off its foundations, the builder refused to go forward with the work, and Jones (D) eventually had to pay for demolition of the structure. Bancredit (P) subsequently sought to foreclose on the mortgage and collect the unpaid balance. The trial court entered judgment for Bancredit (P) as a holder in due course, even though Dell and Bancredit (P) were both wholly owned subsidiaries of a holding company, Albee Homes, with Albee Homes and Bancredit (P) having the same officers and directors. Jones (D) appealed.

ISSUE: Does the more a holder knows about the underlying transaction which is the source of the paper or controls or participates in it, make him less fit the role of good faith purchaser for value which would accord him the protected status of holder in due course?

HOLDING AND DECISION: (Hermann, J.) Yes. The more a holder knows about the underlying transaction which is the source of the paper or controls or participates in it, the less he fits the role of good-faith purchaser for value which would accord him the protected status of holder in due course. Under the circumstances, Bancredit (P) was so involved in the transaction that it may not be treated as a subsequent purchaser for value. By reason of its sister corporation relationship to Dell and the established course of dealing between them, Bancredit (P) was more nearly an original party to the transaction than a subsequent purchaser of the paper and should thus be denied the protected status of holder in due course. Reversed and remanded.

EDITOR'S ANALYSIS: The court pointed out that the problem arises in holder-in-due-course cases involving the financing of installment sales. There is a need to balance the interest of the commercial community in the unrestricted negotiability of commercial papers against the interest of installment buyers in the preservation of their normal remedy of withholding payment whenever there has been misrepresentation, failure of consideration, etc. While some jurisdictions protect finance companies from purchaser defenses on the ground that the free flow of credit is an overriding consideration in assuring easy negotiability of commercial paper, most courts follow a guideline whereby the closer the financial institution is to the underlying transaction, the less likely it will be protected as a holder in due course.

QUICKNOTES

GOOD FAITH PURCHASER FOR VALUE - A party who purchases property in good faith and for valuable consideration without notice of a defect in title.

HOLDER IN DUE COURSE - A party who takes an instrument in good faith and for consideration without notice of any claims therein.

MORTGAGE - An interest in land created by a written instrument providing security for the payment of a debt or the performance of a duty.

NOTES:

SULLIVAN v. UNITED DEALERS CORP.
Borrower (P) v. Lender (D)
Ky. App. Ct., 486 S.W.2d 699 (1972).

NATURE OF CASE: Appeal from award for breach of promissory note.

FACT SUMMARY: Sullivan (D), who had executed a promissory note that was subsequently purchased by United (P), defaulted on the payments, alleging that the house for which he got the construction loan was built in an unworkmanlike manner.

CONCISE RULE OF LAW: To be effective, notice to a purchaser of a negotiable instrument must be received at such time and in such manner as to give a reasonable opportunity to act on it.

FACTS: Sullivan (D), in contracting for construction of a prefabricated dwelling, executed and delivered a negotiable promissory note to the contractor, who then negotiated the note and assigned it to United Dealers (P). Sullivan (D) delivered written statements to United (P) that the foundation and framing members of the house had been properly installed in a workmanlike manner. Sullivan (D) then defaulted on the note, and United (P) filed suit. In defense, Sullivan (D) pleaded that United (P) was not a holder in due course because the contractor had constructed the house in an unworkmanlike manner. The trial court found that United (P) was a holder in due course; therefore, the defense was not assertable against it. Sullivan (D) appealed.

ISSUE: To be effective, must notice to a purchaser of a negotiable instrument be received at such time and in such manner as to give a reasonable opportunity to act on it?

HOLDING AND DECISION: (Reed, J.) Yes. To be effective, notice to a purchaser of a negotiable instrument must be received at such time and in such manner as to give a reasonable opportunity to act on it. "Notice" means notice at the time of the taking or at the time the instrument is negotiated and not subsequently. Here, the maker of the note, Sullivan (D), had represented that the contractor was one in compliance with the duties imposed by the contract. The evidence failed to demonstrate any bad faith on the part of United (P) at the time of the negotiation and transfer of the note to it. Indeed, all of the evidence demonstrated a complete lack of notice that would justify a finding that United (P) failed to acquire the status of a holder in due course. Affirmed.

EDITOR'S ANALYSIS: The court expressed the thought that the policy of the U.C.C. is to encourage the supplying of credit for the buying of goods by insulating the lender from lawsuits over the quality of the goods. The insulation provided, however, appears intended primarily for finance institutions that act independently to supply credit, rather than to protect a manufacturer who finances his own sales either in his own name or in the name of a subsidiary he controls. Although United (P) and the contractor had a frequent course of dealing between them, the instant case demonstrates the point that knowledge of the underlying transaction is not the same thing as notice of a claim or a defense to a claim arising out of that transaction.

QUICKNOTES

COURSE OF DEALING - Previous conduct between two parties to a contact which may be relied upon to interpret their actions.

NEGOTIABLE INSTRUMENT - A signed writing promising to pay a specific sum of money either on demand or at a specified time.

NOTES:

TRIFFIN v. SOMERSET VALLEY BANK

Purchaser of dishonored checks (P) v. Bank (D)

N.J. Super. App. Div., 343 N.J. Super. 73, 777 A.2d 993 (2001).

NATURE OF CASE: Appeal from summary judgment on liability for dishonored checks.

FACT SUMMARY: Triffin (P) purchased dishonored checks from check cashing companies and brought suit against the issuer, Hauser Contracting Co. (Hauser Co.) (D). No proof was presented that the checks on their face indicated forgery, alteration, or other irregularity, and summary judgment was granted for Triffin (P).

CONCISE RULE OF LAW: A holder in due course is entitled to enforce a negotiable instrument where there is no evidence presented that there is anything on the face of the instrument to indicate that the instrument has been forged or altered or is otherwise irregular.

FACTS: Triffin (P) is in the business of purchasing dishonored negotiable instruments, and he purchased 18 dishonored checks from check cashing companies, totaling $8,826.42. All the instruments on their face were issued by Hauser Co. (D), and Triffin (P) sued to enforce Hauser Co.'s (D) liability on the checks. Although none of the checks had been authorized, they were all signed with a facsimile stamp and otherwise manifested no signs of forgery, alteration, or other irregularities. The trial court, concluding that the checks at issue seemed genuine and that the check cashing companies took them in good faith, granted summary judgment to Triffin (P).

ISSUE: Is a holder in due course entitled to enforce a negotiable instrument where no evidence is presented that there is anything on the face of the instrument to indicate that the instrument has been forged or altered or is otherwise irregular?

HOLDING AND DECISION: (Cuff, J.) Yes. As a threshold matter, the checks at issue met the definition of a negotiable instrument. Although Hauser Co. claimed that the checks were not negotiable instruments because they had not been authorized, lack of authorization is a separate issue from whether an instrument is negotiable. The issue raised by lack of authorization is whether the checks are unenforceable by holders in due course as a result of the lack of authorization or forgery. Here, the check cashing companies were each holders in due course, a fact Hauser Co. (D) did not dispute. Also, Triffin (P) complied with the U.C.C.'s requirement for check transfers, and, again, Hauser Co. (D) did not dispute this fact. Hauser Co. (D) instead argued that the checks were per se invalid because they were fraudulent and unauthorized. Under the U.C.C., a person is not a holder in due course if the instrument bears "apparent evidence of forgery or alteration" or is otherwise "so irregular…" Here, however, Hauser Co. (D) did not present any evidence, other than conclusory assertions, that it was apparent on the face of the checks that they were forged, altered, or irregular. Thus, the U.C.C.'s presumption that the signature on a check is valid remains unless it is rebutted by a defendant. Here, Hauser Co. (D) did not meet its burden of proof, and, therefore, did not raise any genuine issues of material fact. Affirmed.

EDITOR'S ANALYSIS: This case is a clear illustration of the U.C.C.'s shelter rule, codified in § 3-203(b), which gives the transferee of a holder in due course the holder's rights, even though the transferee would otherwise not be entitled to those rights. The business of purchasing dishonored checks and pursuing their issuer's liability would not be possible without this rule.

NOTES:

FEDERAL DEPOSIT INSURANCE CORP. v. CULVER
Bank (P) v. Borrower (D)
640 F. Supp. 725 (D. Kan. 1986).

NATURE OF CASE: Motion for summary judgment in action for breach of promissory note.

FACT SUMMARY: After Culver (D), who had received a loan from the now-insolvent bank and later signed a promissory note which he was told was a receipt and which contained no essential terms, he attempted to assert a defense of fraud in the factum against the FDIC (P), which took over as receiver.

CONCISE RULE OF LAW: A holder in due course takes the instrument free from all defenses of any party to the instrument with whom the holder has not dealt except where misrepresentation has induced the party to sign the instrument with neither the knowledge nor reasonable opportunity to obtain knowledge of its character or its essential terms.

FACTS: After Culver (D) received $30,000 in a wire transfer from the Rexford State Bank, he was approached by an individual who asked him to sign a document which Culver (D) was told was merely a receipt for the money. However, the document was a preprinted promissory note form containing no execution date, no maturity date, no principal amount, and no interest rate. Those were filled in later, with the principal amount shown as $50,000. When the bank became insolvent, the FDIC (P) was appointed as its receiver. Culver (D) defaulted on the note, and the FDIC (P) filed this action for payment. Because the FDIC (P) was a holder in due course, Culver (D) sought to assert the "real" defense of fraud in the factum against it. The FDIC (P) moved for summary judgment.

ISSUE: Does a holder in due course take the instrument free from all defenses of any party to the instrument with whom the holder has not dealt except where misrepresentation has induced the party to sign the instrument with neither knowledge nor reasonable opportunity to obtain knowledge of its character or its essential terms?

HOLDING AND DECISION: (O'Connor, J.) Yes. A holder in due course takes the instrument free from all defenses of any party to the instrument with whom the holder has not dealt except where misrepresentation has induced the party to sign the instrument with neither knowledge nor reasonable opportunity to obtain knowledge of its character or its essential terms. The test for the defense of fraud in the factum is that of excusable ignorance of the contents of the writing signed. Being literate in English language, Culver (D) was negligent in relying on another's assurance that the note was only a receipt. He has also failed to show the "excusable ignorance" needed to establish fraud in the factum, since he had a "reasonable opportunity to obtain

knowledge of the document's character" before he signed it. As a holder in due course, the FDIC (P) is thus entitled to enforce this note as completed. Motion for summary judgment granted.

EDITOR'S ANALYSIS: A prior Kansas Supreme Court ruling held that if a party is in possession of his faculties and able to read, he can know the character of every instrument to which he put his signature. Further, he owes a duty to any party who may be subsequently affected by his act to know what it is he signs. Ort v. Fowler, 2 P.580 (Kan. 1884). Moreover, K.S.A. § 84-3-407 provides, in part, that a subsequent holder in due course may in all cases enforce the instrument according to its original tenor, and when an incomplete instrument has been completed, he may enforce it as completed.

QUICKNOTES

FRAUD IN THE FACTUM - Occurs when a testator is induced to execute a testamentary instrument as a result of a misrepresentation as to the nature of the document or its provisions.

MISREPRESENTATION - A statement or conduct by one party to another that constitutes a false representation of fact.

NOTES:

SEA AIR SUPPORT, INC. v. HERRMANN
Debt holder (P) v. Gambler (D)
Nev. Sup. Ct., 613 P.2d 413 (1980).

NATURE OF CASE: Appeal from dismissal of action to recover on a gaming debt.

FACT SUMMARY: Sea Air Support, Inc. (P) attempted to collect on a dishonored check made payable to a casino by Herrmann (D).

CONCISE RULE OF LAW: Checks drawn for gambling purposes are void and unenforceable.

FACTS: Herrmann (D) wrote a check for $10,000 payable to a casino to cover the cost of gaming chips he had purchased earlier. After discovering that Herrmann (D) did not have sufficient funds in his account, the casino assigned the debt to Sea Air Support, Inc. (P), which sued Herrmann (D) to recover the $10,000. The trial court dismissed the action as barred by the Statute of Anne, which provides that all notes drawn for gambling purposes are void. Sea Air (P) appealed, arguing that the court should either enforce the gambling debt or consider Sea Air (P) a holder in due course and, therefore, immune to Statute of Anne defense.

ISSUE: Are checks drawn for gambling purposes void and unenforceable?

HOLDING AND DECISION: (Per curiam) Yes. Checks drawn for gambling purposes are void and unenforceable. Nevada law incorporates the common law of gambling as modified by the Statute of Anne. The Statute of Anne provides that notes drawn for the purpose of reimbursing or repaying any money knowingly advanced for gaming are void and unenforceable. Here, Herrmann's (D) check was clearly drawn for the purpose of repaying money knowingly advanced for gaming. Therefore, it was void and unenforceable. Furthermore, Sea Air (P) was not a holder in due course, defined as one who takes a negotiable instrument (1) for value; (2) in good faith; and (3) without notice of having been dishonored or of any defense against it. A promise to enforce collection in the future—as was made by Sea Air (P) to the casino in exchange for assignment of the debt—is not taking for value. Also, Sea Air (P) had constructive notice of the Statute of Anne defense and actual notice that the check had been dishonored. Affirmed.

EDITOR'S ANALYSIS: Although the court concluded that Sea Air (P) was not a holder in due course, a contrary conclusion would have resulted in the same outcome. Although holders in due course are, indeed, immune to most personal defenses, U.C.C. § 3-305(2) expressly subjects them to so-called "real" defenses—including the defense of illegality raised by Herrmann (D) in this case. Therefore, even if Sea Air (D) had successfully claim HDC status, it still would not have been able to enforce the check. Three years after Sea Air Support was decided, the Nevada legislature modified state law to permit casinos to sue on checks issued to pay gambling debts. Nev. Rev. Stat. § 463.368 (1983).

QUICKNOTES

HOLDER IN DUE COURSE - A party who takes an instrument in good faith and for consideration without notice of any claims therein.

NOTES:

KEDZIE AND 103RD CURRENCY EXCHANGE, INC. v. HODGE

Bank (P) v. Putative checkwriter (D)

Ill. Sup. Ct., 156 Ill.2d 112, 691 N.E.2d 732 (1993).

NATURE OF CASE: Appeal from order dismissing action seeking to collect on a negotiable instrument.

FACT SUMMARY: Hodge (D), drawer of a check, contended that she was not liable to the Currency Exchange (P), the holder in due course, because she had drawn the check to pay a plumber who was not licensed as required by state law.

CONCISE RULE OF LAW: Unless the instrument arising from a contract is itself made void by statute, the illegality defense is not available to bar the claim of a holder in due course.

FACTS: Hodge (D) hired Fentress (D) to perform plumbing services. Fentress (D) was not licensed to perform these services as required by Illinois law. Hodge (D) drew a check for $500, payable to Fentress (D). When Fentress (D) failed to perform, Hodge (D) stopped payment. In the meantime, Fentress (D) negotiated the check to Kedzie and 103rd Currency Exchange, Inc. (P). When Currency Exchange (P) presented the check to the drawee bank, the bank refused to pay. Currency Exchange (P) sued Hodge (D) and Fentress (D). Hodge (D) moved to dismiss, claiming the defense of illegality based on Fentress' (D) unlicensed status. The trial court dismissed, and Currency Exchange (P) appealed.

ISSUE: Is the illegality defense available to bar the claim of a holder in due course if the instrument arises from an obligation that has not been expressly declared void by the legislature?

HOLDING AND DECISION: (Freeman, J.) No. Unless the instrument arising from a contract is itself made void by statute, the illegality defense is not available to bar the claim of a holder in due course. When local law renders an obligation null and void, as opposed to merely voidable, illegality exists as a defense to a claim by one of the contracting parties. But unless the instrument memorializing the obligation is also declared void by the legislature, an innocent third party — i.e., a holder in due course — will be protected and will be permitted to make a claim for payment. For example, an instrument associated with a debt incurred by illegal gambling is void by law no matter who possesses it, and illegality could be raised as a defense in that case. In contrast, an obligation to an unlicensed contractor is merely voidable at the option of the obligor. In this case, the transaction between Hodge (D) and Fentress (D) was voidable by Hodge (D), but the instrument itself was not void under Illinois law. Therefore, the illegality defense is unavailable to Hodge (D). Reversed.

DISSENT: (Bilandic, J.) U.C.C. § 3-305 makes it clear that where a transaction's illegality renders the maker's obligation a nullity, the illegality defense is available. The legislature need not declare the instrument void too, as the majority contends. Since the contract at issue here was illegal and void, the action against Hodge (D) should be dismissed.

EDITOR'S ANALYSIS: The holder in due course concept represents an exercise in choosing the lesser of evils. Commercial practice requires that negotiable instruments be exchangeable with a high degree of certainty. Therefore, a holder can be reasonably sure he can negotiate such instruments, and the occasional injustice to a maker, such as Hodge (D) here, will not change this. However, as the dissent noted, free negotiability is not absolute. Certain transactions such as those involving duress, illegality, or misrepresentation are disfavored on public policy grounds.

QUICKNOTES

HOLDER IN DUE COURSE - A party who takes an instrument in good faith and for consideration without notice of any claims therein.

NOTES:

VIRGINIA NATIONAL BANK v. HOLT
Bank (P) v. Putative note signer (D)
Va. Sup. Ct., 216 Va. 500, 219 S.E.2d 881 (1975).

NATURE OF CASE: Appeal from denial of award of damages in action to recover on a promissory note.

FACT SUMMARY: Virginia National Bank (P) sued Holt (D) on a promissory note that Holt (D) claimed she had not signed.

CONCISE RULE OF LAW: The party seeking recovery on an instrument is not required to prove that any signature is genuine until the defendant introduces evidence which would support a finding that the signature is forged.

FACTS: Virginia National Bank (P) filed suit against Holt (D), seeking recovery on a promissory note allegedly bearing her signature. In her pleadings, Holt (D) denied that she had signed the note. Holt (D) did not testify at trial, but her denial was admitted in the form of a statement from her discovery deposition. The only other evidence offered in her behalf were admissions from the Bank's (P) witnesses that they did not see Holt (D) sign the note. The Bank (P) moved for summary judgment, contending that Holt (D) had failed to overcome the presumption that her signature was genuine. After the judge denied the motion, the case was submitted to the jury, which returned a verdict in Holt's (D) favor. The Bank (P) appealed.

ISSUE: Is the party seeking recovery on an instrument required to prove that the instrument's signature is genuine if the defendant has not introduced evidence which would support a finding that the signature is forged?

HOLDING AND DECISION: (Compton, J.) No. The party seeking recovery on an instrument is not required to prove that the signature on the instrument is genuine until the defendant introduces evidence which would support a finding that the signature is forged. Motivated by the rarity of forged or unauthorized signatures, U.C.C. § 3-307 established a presumption that a signature on an instrument is genuine or authorized. Under § 3-307, each signature on an instrument is admitted, unless the party denying the validating of the signature is able to introduce sufficient evidence to establish grounds for her denial. If she can, then the burden of establishing the genuineness of the signature shifts to the party who is claiming under the signature. In this case, Holt (D) initially put the genuineness of the signature on the promissory note in issue by denying that she signed the note. Pursuant to § 3-307, the signature was presumed to be genuine. But, merely presenting one statement from a deposition is not sufficient to make a showing supporting a finding that she did not in fact write her name on the note. Therefore, the § 3-307 presumption required the trial judge to make a finding that the signature on the instrument was genuine and effective, rather than submit the case

to the jury. The Bank (P) was entitled to recover on the note. Reversed.

EDITOR'S ANALYSIS: If, at the very least, Holt (D) had testified on her own behalf that the signature on the note was not hers, she may have been able to overcome the § 3-307 presumption that her signature was genuine. Even an equivocal denial of genuineness by a purported signer has been held sufficient to overcome the presumption and to raise a factual issue for the jury to decide. The burden of establishing the effectiveness of Holt's (D) signature by a preponderance of the evidence would then have been on the Bank (P). See, e.g., Metropolitan Mortgage Fund v. Basiliko, 407 A.2d 773 (1979).

QUICKNOTES
PRESUMPTION - A rule of law requiring the court to presume certain facts to be true based on the existence of other facts, thereby shifting the burden of proof to the party against whom the presumption is asserted to rebut.

NOTES:

HERZOG CONTRACTING CORP. v. McGOWEN CORP.
Corporation (P) v. Corporation (D)
976 F.2d 1062 (7th Cir. 1992).

NATURE OF CASE: Appeal from summary judgment in a diversity suit to enforce two promissory notes.

FACT SUMMARY: McGowen Corp.'s (D) evidence offered to prove that promissory notes it had given Herzog Contracting Corp. (P) had in fact been a sham to disguise a sales installment payment in order to minimize tax liability was ruled inadmissible.

CONCISE RULE OF LAW: One otherwise liable on an instrument may, as against a nonholder in due course, present evidence that the instrument was never intended to be binding.

FACTS: Herzog (P) purchased certain assets from McGowen (D) for five annual installments of $500,000. That same year, McGowen (D) gave Herzog (P) two notes totaling $400,000 in exchange for that amount from Herzog (P). When the notes became due, Herzog (P), whose relations with McGowen (D) had soured, sued for payment. McGowen (D) admitted receiving the $400,000 but contended that the "loan" had actually been a disguised prepayment by Herzog (P) for the second installment and that the notes had only been designed to make the transaction look like a loan in order to lessen tax liability. The district court held evidence of the purported purpose to be inadmissible and entered summary judgment against McGowen (D), which appealed.

ISSUE: May one otherwise liable on an instrument, as against a nonholder in due course, present evidence that the instrument was never intended to be binding?

HOLDING AND DECISION: (Posner, J.) Yes. One otherwise liable on an instrument, as against a nonholder in due course, may present evidence that the instrument was never intended to be binding. Per U.C.C. § 3-305(b), one other than a holder in due course takes an instrument subject to all defenses thereto. It is well settled that a document or contract that was never meant to be binding will not be so held. At common law, courts were reluctant to allow parol evidence in actions based on negotiable instruments (as opposed to contracts in general) for any reason other than showing mistake or fraud in formation. However, the trend for well over a century has been to allow parol evidence to show any "special purpose" behind an instrument that may not be apparent on its face. The parol evidence rule now applies to instruments as much as it does to contracts: it may not be used as evidence of additional or different terms, but may be used to explain the terms themselves. Here, McGowen (D) was not trying to change the terms in the promissory notes but was only trying to show that they were intended to fool the IRS, rather than to create

a legally enforceable obligation. It should have been allowed to do so. Reversed and remanded.

EDITOR'S ANALYSIS: This case illustrates the wide protections that a holder in due course enjoys that a party to an instrument does not. Of course, like Herzog (P), one may sue on an instrument whether or not one is a holder in due course. In fact, under some circumstances, one need not even be a holder in order to enforce the instrument — the true owner of a lost instrument, for example, enjoys this right. A holder's due course status only becomes significant once a defense to an instrument is raised.

QUICKNOTES

HOLDER IN DUE COURSE - A party who takes an instrument in good faith and for consideration without notice of any claims therein.

PAROL EVIDENCE RULE - Doctrine precluding parties to an agreement from introducing evidence of prior or contemporaneous agreements in order to repudiate or alter the terms of a written contract.

NOTES:

CHAPTER 10
THE NATURE OF LIABILITY

QUICK REFERENCE RULES OF LAW

1. **The Underlying Obligation.** Until a check is presented and honored, no one is directly liable on the check itself, and the underlying obligation represented by the check is suspended. (Ward v. Federal Kemper Insurance Co.)

2. **The Accommodation Party.** A guarantee as against "loss" is a guarantee of collection rather than payment. (Floor v. Melvin)

3. **Section 3-605.** Where the collateral is in the possession of the debtor, inaction by the creditor, negligent or otherwise, does not release a guarantor who has waived the creditor's obligation to protect and preserve the collateral. (Chemical Bank v. PIC Motors Corp.)

4. **Section 3-605.** Consent to alter a suretyship contract need not be express but may be implied from the surety's conduct. (London Leasing Corp. v. Interfina, Inc.)

5. **Presentment and Dishonor.** A thumbprint signature is a form of reasonable identification that may be requested by a bank of a non-account holder wishing to cash a check drawn on a bank's customer account. (Messing v. Bank of America, N.A.)

6. **Excuse.** Formal notice of presentment and dishonor may be excused if defendant's rights will not be injured or prejudiced in any way. (Makel Textiles, Inc. v. Dolly Originals, Inc.)

7. **The Non-Bank Acceptor.** If a bill is presented to a drawee for his acceptance, he will be considered an acceptor if he does anything to it or with it which does not clearly indicate that he will not accept it. (Norton v. Knapp)

8. **Checks.** A check is not an assignment of the drawer's funds in the hands of the drawee and creates no lien on the money which the holder can enforce against the bank. (Galyen Petroleum Co. v. Hixson)

9. **Signature by an Agent.** Under New Hampshire law, a representative may be held personally liable on a promissory note, which does not unambiguously show that the representative's signature is made on behalf of a represented person identified in the instrument, to a holder in due course who takes the instrument without notice that the defendant did not intend to be personally liable and to any other party unless the defendants prove the original parties did not intend them to be personally liable. (Mundaca Investment Corp. v. Febba)

10. **Signature by an Agent.** When a corporation is named on a note by use of its assumed name, extrinsic evidence is allowed to show that the signer was not personally obligated. (Nichols v. Seale)

WARD v. FEDERAL KEMPER INS. CO.

Insured (P) v. Insurance company (D)

Md. Ct. App., 62 Md. App. 351, 489 A.2d 91 (1985).

NATURE OF CASE: Appeal from denial of declaratory judgment in insurance claim.

FACT SUMMARY: After Federal Kemper Ins. Co. (D) overpaid Ward (P) with a refund check that Ward (P) never negotiated, it canceled his insurance policy when he failed to return the difference.

CONCISE RULE OF LAW: Until a check is presented and honored, no one is directly liable on the check itself, and the underlying obligation represented by the check is suspended.

FACTS: Federal Kemper (D) sent Ward (P) a $12 check representing a refund of an overpaid premium, only to discover that the proper refund should have been $4.50. Ward (P) received the check but never negotiated it. Federal Kemper (D) billed Ward (P) for the $7.50 difference. When Ward (P) failed to pay, Federal Kemper (D) canceled his insurance policy. Ward (P) subsequently had a car accident, but Federal Kemper (D) refused to provide coverage, contending that its cancellation was a proper response to Ward's (P) failure to pay the premium due balance included in the unnegotiated $12 check. The trial court agreed and ruled in Federal Kemper's (D) favor. Ward (P) appealed.

ISSUE: Is direct liability on a check suspended, along with the underlying obligation represented by the check, until a check is presented and honored?

HOLDING AND DECISION: (Adkins, J.) Yes. Until a check is presented and honored, no one is directly liable on the check itself, and the underlying obligation represented by the check is suspended. The drawer does not own the funds it has on deposit with the drawee. The drawee owns them. When the drawer draws a check on the drawee and delivers the check to the payee, the check is regarded as only a conditional payment on the underlying obligation, the conditions being presentment and dishonor. Until those conditions are met, the check does not itself operate as an assignment of any funds in the hands of the drawee. In this case, Ward (P) received the check, but the funds it represented were never transferred to Ward (P) because he never presented the check to the bank (the drawee). Thus, Federal Kemper (D) never became liable directly on the check, and its underlying obligation (to refund $4.50 to Ward) (P) was never actually discharged. Since Ward (P) did not owe any premium to Federal Kemper (D), Federal Kemper (D) could not lawfully cancel Ward's (P) policy for nonpayment of a premium. Reversed.

EDITOR'S ANALYSIS: Ward is an exception to the typical check case where the suspension of the underlying obligation has little practical significance because the parties expect the check to be presented promptly. Compare the situation in which a party gives the other a note due in 90 days. Now the suspension of the underlying obligation is more meaningful since the payee gives up a valuable right to insist on immediate payment and the maker acquires valuable time to get more money together. At the other end of the spectrum, transferring a cashier's check extinguishes the underlying obligation completely since the bank is both the drawer and the drawee, and there is no recourse on the instrument against the transferor.

QUICKNOTES

DECLARATORY JUDGMENT - A judgment of the rights between opposing parties that is binding, but does not grant coercive relief (*i.e.* damages.)

NOTES:

FLOOR v. MELVIN

Holder of note (P) v. Decedent's estate (D)
Ill. App. Ct., 5 Ill. App. 3d 463, 283 N.E.2d 303 (1972).

NATURE OF CASE: Appeal from dismissal of action to recover on a promissory note.

FACT SUMMARY: Melvin's estate (D) argued that, as a guarantor against "loss" rather that nonpayment, its decedent was only secondarily liable on a promissory note issued to Floor (P).

CONCISE RULE OF LAW: A guarantee as against "loss" is a guarantee of collection rather than payment.

FACTS: Melcro, Inc. issued a $12,000 promissory note payable to the order of Floor (P). The back of the note contained the statement: "[W]e irrevocably guarantee Floor (P) against loss by reason of nonpayment of this note." It also contained the signature of Melvin's (D) decedent. Melcro, Inc. failed to pay when the note became due, and Floor (P) sued Melvin's estate (D) to recover the $12,000. Melvin's estate (D) moved to dismiss for failure to state a cause of action, arguing that its decedent was not liable because Floor (P) had not yet prosecuted her claim against the maker of the note. The trial court agreed and dismissed the case. Floor (P) appealed.

ISSUE: Is a guarantee against "loss" a guarantee of collection rather than payment?

HOLDING AND DECISION: (Alloy, J.) Yes. A guarantee against "loss" is a guarantee of collection rather than payment. U.C.C. § 3-416 declares that contracts of guaranty of negotiable instruments are of two kinds: (1) contracts guaranteeing the collection of the notes and (2) contracts guaranteeing the payment of the notes. A contract guaranteeing the collection of a note is conditional, in that the guarantor agrees to pay the debt if the owner of the note first attempts to collect payment from the maker but is unable to do so. On the other hand, a contract guaranteeing the payment of a note is an absolute contract; if the note is not paid upon maturity, the guarantor may be sued immediately. In this case, the terms of the guarantee were made conditional upon collection of the note. Although Melvin's decedent (D) did not actually use the word "collection," the guarantee against "loss" was, in effect, a guarantee of collection and not of payment. Since Floor (P) neither alleged that she prosecuted an unsatisfied claim against Melco, Inc., the maker of the note, nor that Melco became insolvent, she failed to comply with U.C.C. § 3-416(2), and dismissal of her action was proper. Affirmed.

EDITOR'S ANALYSIS: Under U.C.C. § 3-416(5), the liability of an endorser who adds "payment guaranteed" to his signature is virtually indistinguishable from that of a comaker. One who adds "collection guaranteed," on the other hand, forestalls liability until the holder has a judgment and unsatisfied execution against the principal debtor. Note, however, that under § 416(2), the holder may fulfill this requirement by showing that proceeding to judgment and execution would be a useless act.

NOTES:

CHEMICAL BANK v. PIC MOTORS CORP.

Bank (P) v. Car dealership (D)

N.Y. App. Div., 87 A.D.2d 447, 452 N.Y.S.2d 41 (1982).

NATURE OF CASE: Appeal from summary judgment awarding recovery on a loan.

FACT SUMMARY: Siegel (D) claimed that Chemical Bank's (P) failure to keep track of Pic Motors Corp.'s (D) inventory of cars discharged his obligations as a guarantor.

CONCISE RULE OF LAW: Where the collateral is in the possession of the debtor, inaction by the creditor, negligent or otherwise, does not release a guarantor who has waived the creditor's obligation to protect and preserve the collateral.

FACTS: Chemical Bank (P) agreed to periodically loan funds to Pic (D), using Pic's (D) inventory of automobiles as collateral . Chemical Bank (P) verified Pic's (D) sales by periodic inspections. Siegel (D), Pic's (D) director, personally guaranteed the loans "absolutely and unconditionally." When Pic (D) was unable to account for 50% of its inventory, Chemical Bank (P) demanded repayment of its loan and instituted suit against Pic (D) and Siegel (D). Siegel (D) denied liability, arguing that Chemical Bank (P) had impaired the collateral by failing to regularly inspect the inventory and, furthermore, that its employees had submitted false inventory reports and approved loans on nonexistent cars. Concluding that Siegel (D) was an unconditional guarantor, the lower court granted Chemical Bank's (P) motion for summary judgment. Siegel (D) appealed.

ISSUE: Where the collateral is in the possession of the debtor, does inaction by the creditor release a guarantor who has waived the creditor's obligation to protect and preserve the collateral?

HOLDING AND DECISION: (Fein, J.) No. Where the collateral is in the possession of the debtor, inaction by the creditor, negligent or otherwise, does not release a guarantor who has waived the creditor's obligation to protect and preserve the collateral. A surety may waive any obligation of a creditor, including an obligation not to impair the security. Here, Chemical Bank (P) was not obligated by either its agreement with Pic (D) or by the guaranty to conduct inspections or to preserve or protect the collateral. Also, the terms of the guaranty allowed Chemical Bank (P) to release or surrender the collateral or extend further credit without notifying or discharging Siegel (D). Therefore, the alleged actions by Chemical Bank's (P) employees did not serve to discharge Siegel (D). Affirmed.

DISSENT: (Milonas, J.) A waiver of a creditor's obligation to protect the collateral should not be enforced to bind a guarantor on the underlying obligation where the creditor has engaged in negligent, fraudulent, or tortious conduct. Enabling a creditor to shield itself by inserting a waiver clause is contrary to the spirit of the U.C.C. and to public policy.

EDITOR'S ANALYSIS: Sureties like Siegel (D) have an interest in how the creditor handles the collateral because, once the principal debtor defaults and the surety pays off the creditor, thereby acquiring the debt, the surety is entitled to the collateral. The creditor's conduct regarding the collateral (in the absence of a waiver) is measured by a "reasonable care" standard. See Comment 5 to U.C.C. § 3-606.

QUICKNOTES

COLLATERAL - Property that secures the payment of a debt.

GUARANTOR - A party who agrees to be liable for the debt or default of another.

NEGLIGENCE - Conduct falling below the standard of care that a reasonable person would demonstrate under similar conditions.

NOTES:

LONDON LEASING CORP. v. INTERFINA, INC.
Corporation (P) v. Corporation (D)
N.Y. App. Div., 53 Misc. 2d 657, 279 N.Y.S.2d 209 (1967).

NATURE OF CASE: Motion for summary judgment in action to recover on promissory note.

FACT SUMMARY: Evans (D) argued that he should not be personally liable on a note that he executed in his corporate capacity as well as endorsed in his personal capacity since he did not personally consent to an agreement extending the time for payment of the note.

CONCISE RULE OF LAW: Consent to alter a suretyship contract need not be express but may be implied from the surety's conduct.

FACTS: Interfina, Inc. (D) made and delivered to London Leasing Corp. (P) a promissory note in the amount of $52,000, signed by Evans (D), as president of Interfina (D), and also personally endorsed by him. Then, acting solely in his corporate capacity, he sought, negotiated, and signed an agreement with London Leasing (P), extending the time for payment of the note. When Interfina (D) defaulted on the note, London Leasing (P) sued Interfina (D) and Evans (D). Evans (D) contended that the extension agreement discharged him from personal liability on the note because he had not consented personally to the extension. London Leasing (P) moved for summary judgment.

ISSUE: May consent to alter a suretyship contract be implied from the surety's conduct?

HOLDING AND DECISION: (Crawford, J.) Yes. Consent to alter a suretyship contract need not be express but may be implied from the surrounding circumstance or from the surety's conduct. Parties to a contract may always alter the contract by mutual agreement. However, under U.C.C. § 3-606, the holder discharges any party to the instrument to the extent that the holder agrees to suspend the right to enforce the instrument without such party's consent. However, if the surety does consent to a modification of the contract between the principal creditor and the debtor, he will not be discharged from liability. Although the U.C.C. does not define consent, Stearns Law of Suretyship (5th ed., § 6.13) states that consent by a surety need not be expressly given but may be implied from the surrounding circumstances or from his conduct. In this case, Evans (D) applied for, negotiated, and received the agreements extending the time for payment and then signed them in his corporate capacity. Evans' (D) conduct exceeded mere knowledge or acquiescence in the extension agreements and, under the circumstances, constituted consent. Motion for summary judgment granted.

EDITOR'S ANALYSIS: Under U.C.C. § 3-606(2), if a creditor wants to grant a debtor an extension of time to make payments,

but the surety refuses to consent, the creditor may still prevent a surety's claim to discharge by "expressly reserving" his rights against the surety. Theoretically, the surety is not harmed by the creditor's express reservation of rights because the surety can immediately pay the instrument and then exercise his right of recourse against the principal debtor. Note, however, that § 3-606 does not require the creditor to notify the surety when he expressly reserves his rights against him, and the surety can hardly exercise his option to pay and sue if he has no knowledge of the creditor's actions.

QUICKNOTES

SURETYSHIP - A situation in which one party guarantees payment of the debt of another party to a creditor.

NOTES:

MESSING v. BANK OF AMERICA, N.A.
Non-account check holder (P) v. Bank (D)
Md. Spec. App. Ct., 143 Md. App. 1, 792 A.2d 312 (2002).

NATURE OF CASE: Appeal from summary judgment dismissing action against a bank's thumbprint signature requirement for non-account holders.

FACT SUMMARY: Messing (P) attempted to cash a check drawn on a Bank of America (Bank) (D) customer account at a Bank of America branch. The Bank required a thumbprint signature from all non-account holders before cashing a check drawn on one of its customer's accounts. When Messing (P) refused to provide his thumbprint, the Bank (D) refused to cash the check. Messing (P) sued, claiming the thumbprint requirement was unlawful.

CONCISE RULE OF LAW: A thumbprint signature is a form of reasonable identification that may be requested by a bank of a non-account holder wishing to cash a check drawn on a bank's customer account.

FACTS: Messing (P) attempted to cash a $976 check at a Bank of America branch. The check was made out to Messing (P) and was drawn on a Bank of America customer's checking account. The teller asked for identification, and Messing (P) presented his driver's license and a major credit card. The teller then asked Messing (P) if he was a Bank of America customer. When Messing replied he was not, the teller asked him to place his thumbprint signature on the check by applying his thumb to an inkless fingerprinting device that is neither messy nor time consuming. This was in accordance with the Bank's (D) policy relating to non-account holders, which was posted at every teller station. When Messing (P) refused, the teller put away the cash she had counted out. The branch manager confirmed that the Bank's policy did not permit cashing the check without Messing's (P) thumbprint signature, and that this policy was pursuant to an agreement with the Bank's customers. Messing (P) sued, claiming the Bank's (D) policy was unlawful. He also claimed that the Bank unlawfully dishonored his check. The trial court granted the Bank's motion for summary judgment and dismissed with prejudice.

ISSUE: Is a thumbprint signature a form of reasonable identification that may be requested by a bank of a non-account holder wishing to cash a check drawn on a bank's customer account?

HOLDING AND DECISION: (Krauser, J.) Yes. The Bank's thumbprint requirement is a form of "reasonable identification" under the U.C.C. for several reasons. First, this form of identification has been accepted by drafters of the Maryland U.C.C. as an effective, reliable, and accurate way to authenticate a writing on a negotiable instrument, i.e., a signature may be a thumbprint. Second, the process that a non-account holder goes through to provide a thumbprint signature is unobtrusive and is not unreasonably inconvenient. Third, this procedure is a reasonable and necessary response to the growing incidence of check fraud, and has been endorsed by numerous bank groups for that purpose. Finally, although a thumbprint cannot confirm the true identity of a non-account holder at the time of presentment, it nevertheless serves the purpose of reasonable identification. Messing (P) also claimed that the trial court had erred in holding that the Bank (D) had not dishonored the check. His argument rested on the assumption that the Bank (D) had accepted the check, but in fact, the bank had not accepted the check. In that situation, there is no dishonor if presentment fails to comply with an agreement of the parties. The Bank (D) had the authority to refuse payment in accordance with the deposit agreement it had with each account holder, which gave it authority to refuse payment unless "reasonable identification" was presented. Messing's (P) failure to provide his thumbprint rendered the presentment ineffective. Remanded.

EDITOR'S ANALYSIS: Although the court in the instant case concludes that a thumbprint signature is a form of "reasonable identification," it does not expressly address the question that the plaintiff seemed to be raising, which is why his proffer of his driver's license and/or a major credit card, which are also recognized as forms of "reasonable identification," was not enough to satisfy the reasonable identification requirement. The decision seems to imply that those non-physical forms of identification are not as sound as the thumbprint in combating fraud, but the court never comes out and explicitly says so.

NOTES:

MAKEL TEXTILES, INC. v. DOLLY ORIGINALS, INC.

Corporation (P) v. Corporation (D)

N.Y. App. Div., 4 U.C.C. Rep. Serv. 95 (1967).

NATURE OF CASE: Action to recover on promissory notes.

FACT SUMMARY: Having made, endorsed, and defaulted on two promissory notes, Goldberg (D) claimed he was relieved of liability because the notes had never been presented for payment.

CONCISE RULE OF LAW: Formal notice of presentment and dishonor may be excused if defendant's rights will not be injured or prejudiced in any way.

FACTS: Goldberg (D), president and principal officer of Dolly Originals, Inc. (D), executed two promissory notes and, together with Kushner (D), endorsed them on the back. These notes were given to Makel Textiles, Inc. (P) as repayment on a loan. When Dolly Originals (D) defaulted on the notes, Makel (P) sued Goldberg (D) and Kushner (D) in addition to Dolly Originals (D). Goldberg (D) and Kushner (D) moved for a dismissal, contending that the promissory notes had never been presented for payment and thus their obligation was discharged. [No lower court decisions were included in the casebook excerpt, but as Makel (P) was the appellant, it apparently received an adverse judgment].

ISSUE: May formal notice of presentment and dishonor be excused if defendant's rights will not be injured or prejudiced in any way?

HOLDING AND DECISION: (Spiegel, J.) Yes. Formal notice of presentment and dishonor may be excused if defendant's rights will not be injured or prejudiced in any way. Here, the usual obligation of presentment and notice of dishonor was unnecessary because Goldberg (D) was an active participant in Dolly Original's (D) affairs and knew that the notes he had executed and endorsed could not be paid from corporate funds. On the other hand, there was no evidence of any corporate activity or participation by Kushner (D); presentment and notice of dishonor were required to hold him liable. Judgment for Makel (P) dismissed as to Kushner (D).

EDITOR'S ANALYSIS: U.C.C. § 3-511(2) specifies when the formality of presentment and notice of dishonor will be excused. For example, an endorser may expressly waive his right to have the instrument presented by including a waiver either in the body or on the back of the instrument. Presentment and notice of dishonor will also be excused when an endorser has played an active role in causing an instrument to be dishonored. An endorser's mere knowledge of the maker's insolvency, however, is not sufficient to excuse the technical requirements.

NOTES:

NORTON v. KNAPP
Seller (P) v. Buyer (D)
Sup. Ct. of Iowa, 64 Iowa 112, 19 N.W. 867 (1884).

NATURE OF CASE: Action for payment on a sight draft.

FACT SUMMARY: When Knapp (D) received a sight draft for the price of a mill delivered to him by Norton (P), he wrote "Kiss my foot" on the back of the draft and signed it.

CONCISE RULE OF LAW: If a bill is presented to a drawee for his acceptance, he will be considered an acceptor if he does anything to it or with it which does not clearly indicate that he will not accept it.

FACTS: Norton (P) delivered a mill, priced at $80, to Knapp (D). When Knapp (D) did not pay the $80, Norton (P) drew a draft on Knapp (D) payable on sight. When Knapp (D) received the sight draft, he wrote "Kiss my foot" on the back and signed his name. Claiming that Knapp's (D) writing and signature constituted a valid acceptance, Norton (P) sued for the unpaid draft.

ISSUE: If a bill is presented to a drawee for his acceptance, will he be considered an acceptor if he does anything to it or with it which does not clearly indicate that he will not accept it?

HOLDING AND DECISION: (Seevers, J.) Yes. If a bill is presented to a drawee for his acceptance, he will be considered an acceptor if he does anything to it or with it which does not clearly indicate that he will not accept it. If the drawee writes anything on the bill which does not clearly negative an intention to accept, he can be charged as an acceptor. The term "kiss my foot" may be vulgar, but, when used in reply to a request, it is understood to signify one thing only: refusal. In this case, drawee Knapp's (D) use of the term "kiss my foot" was clearly meant to emphasize his intention not to accept the sight draft or, for that matter, to have anything to do with it or with Norton (P). Therefore, Knapp's (D) signature accompanied by the words "kiss my foot" was not a legal or valid acceptance.

EDITOR'S ANALYSIS: When a drawee "accepts" a draft other than a check, he becomes primarily liable upon the instrument. Comment 4 to U.C.C. § 3-410 specifies the formalities required for accepting an instrument. Customarily the signature is written vertically across the face of the instrument, but a drawee's signature anywhere on the instrument is sufficient to manifest acceptance. Comment 4 states that nothing in § 3-410 is intended to change such decisions as Knapp. Thus, although a signature need not be accompanied by such words as "accepted," an instrument must not bear any words indicating an intent to refuse to honor the bill.

NOTES:

76

GALYEN PETROLEUM CO. v. HIXSON
Corporation (P) v. Account holder (D)
Neb. Sup. Ct., 213 Neb. 683, 331 N.W.2d 1 (1983).

NATURE OF CASE: Appeal from summary judgment in suit to recover on three checks.

FACT SUMMARY: Drawee Commercial Bank (D) refused payment on three checks drawn by Hixson (D) presented by Galyen (P) despite sufficient funds in the account to pay some of the checks.

CONCISE RULE OF LAW: A check is not an assignment of the drawer's funds in the hands of the drawee and creates no lien on the money which the holder can enforce against the bank.

FACTS: On November 12, Galyen (P) personally presented three checks totaling $6,883, drawn by Hixson (D) to drawee Commercial Bank (D). Commercial Bank (D) unconditionally refused payment of all three checks, although Hixson's (D) account had a credit balance of approximately half that amount. Later that same day, Commercial Bank (D) set off Hixson's (D) account against payment of two notes made payable to it, virtually depleting the account, although the credited notes were not due at that time. Galyen (P) filed suit against Commercial Bank (D) for unlawfully refusing payment of the checks on presentment. Summary judgment was granted in favor of Commercial Bank (D), and Galyen (P) appealed.

ISSUE: Is a check an assignment of the drawer's funds in the hands of the drawee (the bank), creating a lien on the money which the holder can enforce against the bank?

HOLDING AND DECISION: (Colwell, J.) No. A check is not an assignment of the drawer's funds in the hands of the drawee and creates no lien on the money which the holder can enforce against the drawee bank. Absent special circumstances, a check gives the holder of the check no right of action against the drawee and no valid claim to the fund of the drawer in its hands, even though the drawer has on deposit sufficient funds to pay the check. There were no special circumstances in this case that would warrant a different result. Galyen (P) had no standing or cause of action against Commercial Bank (D), based on its refusal to honor the three checks. Affirmed.

EDITOR'S ANALYSIS: Although, in general, the drawer's writing of a check does not create any immediate rights in the checking account funds, there are special circumstances when a drawee bank may become liable to the holder prior to acceptance. Liability may arise apart from the instrument itself. U.C.C. § 3-409(2) states: "Nothing in this section shall affect any liability in contract, tort or otherwise arising from any letter of credit or other obligation or representation which is not an acceptance." This provision preserves the common law rule that allows the drawer, by special agreement, to immediately assign bank-held funds in order to give the holder of the check a claim against the drawee bank prior to acceptance.

QUICKNOTES
ASSIGNMENT - A transaction in which a party conveys his or her entire interest in property to another.

LIEN - A claim against the property of another in order to secure the payment of a debt.

NOTES:

MUNDACA INVESTMENT CORP. v. FEBBA

Receiver (P) v. Trustees (D)

N.H. Sup. Ct., 727 A.2d 990 (1999).

NATURE OF CASE: Appeal from summary judgment holding defendants liable on two promissory notes.

FACT SUMMARY: Mundaca (P) brought suit against the trustees (D) of L.T.D. Trust, seeking to hold them personally liable for amounts due on two promissory notes executed by the trustees (P) for the purchase of two condominium units.

CONCISE RULE OF LAW: Under New Hampshire law, a representative may be held personally liable on a promissory note, which does not unambiguously show that the representative's signature is made on behalf of a represented person identified in the instrument, to a holder in due course who takes the instrument without notice that the defendant did not intend to be personally liable and to any other party unless the defendants prove the original parties did not intend them to be personally liable.

FACTS: Trustees (D) of L.T.D. Trust purchased two condominium units for trust. To finance the purchase, they executed two promissory notes secured by two mortgages, payable to Dartmouth Savings Bank. The notes identified trustees (D) as the "borrowers," but the trust was not identified. Mundaca (P) acquired the notes as receiver for the bank and notified the trustees (P) they were in default. Mundaca (P) foreclosed on the condominiums and filed suit against the trustees (D) individually for the remaining amount due. Both parties moved for summary judgment and the trial court ruled in favor of Mundaca (P) on the basis that the trustees' (P) signatures did not clearly show that they were acting in a representative capacity. Trustees (D) appealed, arguing that reading the mortgages and notes together unambiguously shoed that they were acting in a representative capacity and that there was a genuine issue if material fact as to whether the original parties intended the trustees (D) to be personally liable.

ISSUE: Under New Hampshire law, may a representative may held personally liable on a promissory note, which does not unambiguously show that the representative's signature is made on behalf of a represented person identified in the instrument, to a holder in due course who takes the instrument without notice that the defendant did not intend to be personally liable and to any other party unless the defendants prove the original parties did not intend them to be personally liable?

HOLDING AND DECISION: (Brock, C.J.) Yes. Under New Hampshire law, a representative may be held personally liable on a promissory note, which does not unambiguously show that the representative's signature is made on behalf of a represented person identified in the instrument, to a holder in due course who takes the instrument without notice that the defendant did not intend to be personally liable and to any other party unless the defendants prove the original parties did not intend them to be personally liable. Because here the represented person, the trust, was not identified in the instrument as required by state law, the case falls under RSA 382-A:3-402(b)(2) which states that the trustees (D) could be personally liable in two situations: 1) to a holder in due course who takes the instrument without notice that the defendants did not intend to be held personally liable; and 2) to any other party unless the defendants prove the original parties did not intend to hold them personally liable. The trustees (D) argued that summary judgment was inappropriate because there was a genuine issue of material fact as to the intent of the original parties. This court agrees. The record contains conflicting evidence regarding the intent of the original parties. Since the court did not address the issue of whether Mundaca (P) was a holder in due course without notice that the defendants did not intend to be held personally liable, this issue is to be resolved by the trial court on remand. Reversed and remanded.

EDITOR'S ANALYSIS: The trustees (D) also argued that the mortgages served as a defense to their personal liability on the promissory notes. This argument was erroneous. They only provided a defense to the extent the mortgages modified, supplemented or nullified the trustees' (D) liability on the notes, which they did not do here. While the mortgages were issued as collateral for the notes, both instruments failed to clearly identify the borrower.

NOTES:

NICHOLS v. SEALE
Business owner (D) v. Check holder (P)
Tx. Civ. App., 493 S.W.2d 589 (1973).

NATURE OF CASE: Appeal from summary judgment awarding recovery on a promissory note.

FACT SUMMARY: Nichols (D) argued that a note that contained his corporation's assumed name and his signature was sufficiently ambiguous to allow parol evidence to show that he signed in his corporate capacity only.

CONCISE RULE OF LAW: When a corporation is named on a note by use of its assumed name, extrinsic evidence is allowed to show that the signer was not personally obligated.

FACTS: Nichols (D) signed a note on behalf of his corporation, Mr. Carls Fashion, Inc., doing business as (dba) The Fashion Beauty Salon. Only the dba name appeared on the note. Seale (P), the payee, sued on the note, and the trial court upheld its motion for summary judgment against Nichols (D), concluding that Nichols (D) was personally liable on the note because the note neither named the corporation nor showed that Nichols (D) signed in his individual capacity. Nichols (D) appealed.

ISSUE: When a corporation is named on a note by use of its assumed name, is extrinsic evidence allowed to show that the signer was not personally obligated?

HOLDING AND DECISION: (Guittard, J.) Yes. When a corporation is named on a note by use of its assumed name, extrinsic evidence is allowed to show that the signer was not personally obligated. Under U.C.C. § 3-403, a representative who signs his own name to an instrument is personally obligated if the instrument neither names the person represented (here, the corporation) nor shows that he signed in a representative capacity. In this case, Nichols' (D) use of an assumed name did "name the person represented" within the meaning of the Code, which expressly authorizes use of an assumed name in a negotiable instrument under § 3-401(2). Furthermore, corporations are expressly permitted to use assumed names under state law. When a corporation is "named" by use of its assumed name, § 3-403(2) does not forbid extrinsic evidence to show that, as between the original parties, the signer was not personally obligated. Such proof is admissible to explain an ambiguity with respect to the capacity of the signer. Therefore, summary judgment in this case was not appropriate. Reversed and remanded.

EDITOR'S ANALYSIS: The Texas Supreme Court reversed on appeal. Apparently Nichols' (D) affidavit stated that he signed the note as president of the corporation, indicating his subjective intent to sign as an agent, but he did not state that he had ever disclosed his intent to Seale (P). Texas law provides that in order for an agent to avoid liability for his signature on a contract, he must communicate his intent to sign as a representative to the other contracting party. Consequently, Nichols (D) did not raise an issue of fact, and Seale's (P) motion was properly granted by the trial court. Seale v. Nichols, 505 S.W.2d 251 (Tex. 1974).

NOTES:

CHAPTER 11
BANKS AND THEIR CUSTOMERS

QUICK REFERENCE RULES OF LAW

1. **Wrongful Dishonor.** Damages resulting from mental anguish are recoverable, even though they cannot be determined with exactness. (Twin City Bank v. Isaacs)

2. **Bank's Right of Setoff.** Absent insolvency, a bank does not have a priority of right in equity where it seeks to set off an unmatured indebtedness. (Walter v. National City Bank of Cleveland)

3. **Customer's Right to Stop Payment.** A single digit error in the amount of a check in a stop payment order does not deprive a bank of a reasonable opportunity to act on the stop payment order. (Parr v. Security National Bank)

4. **Customer's Right to Stop Payment.** Where a bank has improperly paid on checks redeposited a second time, but the payment was to the IRS, a rebuttable presumption will be raised in favor of the bank that no harm has come to the depositor. (Canty v. Vermont National Bank)

5. **Final Payment.** A payor bank which holds a check past the dishonoring deadline is liable when a party is damaged thereby. (Rock Island Auction Sales, Inc. v. Empire Packing Co.)

6. **Final Payment.** The U.C.C.'s "midnight deadline" does not apply with respect to checks returned in order to avoid a check-kiting scheme. (First National Bank of Chicago v. Standard Bank & Trust)

7. **Charge Back.** Punitive damages are permissible under Article 4 of the U.C.C. where the defendant acts willfully and maliciously. (Gordon v. Planters & Merchants Bancshares, Inc.)

TWIN CITY BANK v. ISAACS
Bank (D) v. Account holders (P)
Ark. Sup. Ct., 263 Ark. 127, 672 S.W.2d 651 (1984).

NATURE OF CASE: Appeal from denial of defense motion for new trial upon award of damages for wrongful dishonor.

FACT SUMMARY: After the Isaacs (P) were awarded damages for mental anguish they suffered when Twin City (D) wrongfully dishonored their checks and wrongfully withheld their funds, Twin City (D) appealed the denial of its motion for a new trial on the basis that damages were speculative.

CONCISE RULE OF LAW: Damages resulting from mental anguish are recoverable, even though they cannot be determined with exactness.

FACTS: After discovering their checkbook missing, the Isaacs (P) reported the loss to Twin City Bank (Twin City) (D). They later learned that two forged checks totalling $2,050 had been written on their account and honored by Twin City (D) before they realized the checkbook was missing. Nevertheless, Twin City (D), believing the Isaacs (P) were somehow involved with the forged checks, issued a hold order on the account, leaving the balance at approximately $2,000. As a result, the Isaacs (P) sued for wrongful dishonor of their checks and wrongful withholding of their funds, and the jury, finding substantial evidence of mental anxiety, awarded them compensatory and punitive damages. Twin City (D) moved for a new trial, contending that damages awarded on the basis of mental anguish were speculative. The district court denied its motion, and Twin City (D) appealed.

ISSUE: Although they cannot be determined with exactness, are damages resulting from mental anguish recoverable?

HOLDING AND DECISION: (Hays, J.) Yes. Damages resulting from mental anguish are recoverable, even though they cannot be determined with exactness. This rule is based in U.C.C. § 4-402. Although this section appears to circumscribe the old common law rule that damages may not be had where they are speculative, a majority of courts addressing this issue have allowed recovery. (See esp. Wasp Oil v. Arkansas Oil & Gas, 280 Ark. 420, 658 S.W.2d 397 (1983).) In the instant case, there was substantial evidence establishing mental anxiety on the part of the Isaacs (P) occasioned by their financial strain. The district court did not err in denying Twin City's (D) motion for a new trial after the jury found it liable to the Isaacs (P) for compensatory and punitive damages awarded on the basis of their mental anguish. Affirmed.

EDITOR'S ANALYSIS: The court above awarded punitive damages, stating that they were not excessive since Twin City (D) was in a favorable financial condition. Interestingly enough, however, these damages are usually awarded in the case of mental anguish where the defendant intended to engage in wrongful activity that naturally brings about such anguish on the part of the plaintiff. Punitive damages can also be awarded where the defendant's conduct is not intentional, but unreasonable under the circumstances. The degree of unreasonableness of the defendant's conduct will naturally influence the amount of punitive damages awarded.

NOTES:

WALTER v. NATIONAL CITY BANK OF CLEVELAND
Creditor (P) v. Bank (D)
Ohio Sup. Ct., 42 Ohio St. 2d 524, 330 N.E.2d 425 (1975).

NATURE OF CASE: Appeal from grant of summary judgment awarding recovery for conversion.

FACT SUMMARY: Walter (P) successfully sued National (D) for conversion, thereby receiving a priority of right to funds owed him by Ritzer, whose account at National (D) he had garnished after National (D) withheld the sum Ritzer owed it before paying Walter (P).

CONCISE RULE OF LAW: Absent insolvency, a bank does not have a priority of right in equity where it seeks to set off an unmatured indebtedness.

FACTS: After Ritzer opened a commercial account with National City Bank of Cleveland (D), National (D) made a loan to Ritzer, against collateral of an unmatured 90-day promissory note for $3,600, despite knowing that Ritzer was insolvent. Subsequently, when Walter (P) recovered a judgment against Ritzer for $6,831.95, he served National (D) by mail as garnishee with an order in aid of execution. At the time of service, Ritzer had on deposit with National (D) the sum of $3,651.75 and the unmatured debt on National's (D) promissory note, which then totaled $3,626.25, interest included. After National (D) set off the amount of its loan, leaving a balance of $25.50, it mailed this amount to Walter (P) to satisfy his judgment. Consequently, Walter (P) sued National (D) for conversion, claiming a priority of right to the funds in Ritzer's account. At trial, both sides moved for summary judgment, and the district court granted Walter's (P) motion, which was affirmed on appeal. National (D) appealed.

ISSUE: Absent insolvency, does a bank have a priority of right in equity where it seeks to set off an unmatured indebtedness?

HOLDING AND DECISION: (Stern, J.) No. Absent insolvency, a bank does not have a priority of right in equity where it seeks to set off an unmatured indebtedness. This rule represents the general principle courts have applied to unmatured indebtedness, which is in stark contrast to the principle followed when the indebtedness is matured. An unmatured debt is not presently due or collectible and is not available for setoff since setoff would alter the contract made by the parties. In the case of insolvency, however, a bank may set off an unmatured indebtedness where equitable principles dictate. In the instant case, since National (D) voluntarily granted Ritzer a loan on a 90-day promissory note, which had not matured, despite knowing that Ritzer was insolvent, the later, specific terms of this note controlled over the general language of National's (D) rules and regulations that would allow it to apply the balance of the commercial account to the note. Under these circumstances, the lower courts did not err in granting and upholding summary judgment in Walter's (P) favor. Affirmed.

EDITOR'S ANALYSIS: According to § 362(a)(7) of the Bankruptcy Code, the filing of a petition in bankruptcy creates an automatic stay against creditor collection activity, specifically including the exercise of the right of setoff. Individuals injured by a violation of the automatic stay may sue under Bankruptcy Code § 362(h) and recover "actual damages, including costs and attorney fees, and, in appropriate circumstances, may recover punitive damages."

NOTES:

PARR v. SECURITY NATIONAL BANK
Checking account holder (P) v. Bank (D)
Okla. Ct. App., 680 P.2d 648 (1984).

NATURE OF CASE: Appeal from denial of recovery of stop payment amount.

FACT SUMMARY: Parr (P) appealed from a decision denying her the right to recover the amount of a check paid by Security National Bank (Bank) (D), upon which she had requested a stop payment, contending a single digit error in the amount made in the stop payment order did not deprive the Bank (D) of a reasonable opportunity to stop payment.

CONCISE RULE OF LAW: A single digit error in the amount of a check in a stop payment order does not deprive a bank of a reasonable opportunity to act on the stop payment order.

FACTS: Parr (P) wrote a check to Champlin, mailing it on September 14, 1981. During the next two days, Parr (P), both by phone and in person, ordered payment stopped on the check. Both orders were accurate in their descriptions of the check except that a $0.50 error was made in identifying the amount of the check. The Bank's (D) computer keyed on the amount of the check, and, as a result, the Bank (D) paid the check on September 17, 1981. Parr (P) sued to recover the amount of the check, plus interest and attorney fees. The Bank (D) argued that Parr's (P) error as to the amount of the check relieved it from liability, as its computer was programmed to stop payment only if the amount of the check as reported was correct. The Bank (D) prevailed, and Parr (P) appealed, contending the error in the check amount did not deprive the Bank (D) of a reasonable opportunity to stop payment.

ISSUE: Will a single digit error in the amount of a check in a stop payment order deprive a bank of a reasonable opportunity to act on the stop payment order?

HOLDING AND DECISION: (Reynolds, J.) No. A single digit error in the amount of a check in a stop payment order does not deprive a bank of a reasonable opportunity to act on the stop payment order. Parr's (P) stop payment order was accurate in all respects except as to the reported check amount. The U.C.C. contains the applicable law as to stop payment orders and makes clear the policy that losses through failure to stop payment should be borne by the banks. Most cases have held that a single digit error in the reported check amount still provides the banks with notice of sufficient accuracy so as to allow the bank to stop payment. In those cases where a different result is reached, the bank has informed the customer of the importance of an accurate check amount. It is not contended that the Bank (D) informed Parr (P) that any discrepancy in check amount would prevent compliance with the stop payment order. With the check described with sufficient accuracy in other respects, and U.C.C. policy being clear, the Bank (D) should bear the responsibility for failing to have effected the stop payment order. Reversed and remanded.

EDITOR'S ANALYSIS: Many states have amended the U.C.C. language so as to require more specificity in a stop payment order, somewhat relieving the bank of liability for failure to stop payment. These amendments are in part a response to the failure of the U.C.C. to keep pace with the advances associated with modern computerized banking techniques.

NOTES:

CANTY v. VERMONT NATIONAL BANK
Account holder (P) v. Bank (D)
Vt. Sup. Ct., 25 U.C.C. Rep. Serv. 2d 1184 (1994).

NATURE OF CASE: Motion for summary judgment in a suit to recover improperly paid funds.

FACT SUMMARY: The IRS redeposited checks which had already been paid and received payment a second time.

CONCISE RULE OF LAW: Where a bank has improperly paid on checks redeposited a second time, but the payment was to the IRS, a rebuttable presumption will be raised in favor of the bank that no harm has come to the depositor.

FACTS: Canty (P) had a checking account with Vermont National Bank (D). The IRS asked Canty (P) for cancelled checks to verify that he had paid obligations owing to the IRS. The IRS then redeposited the cancelled checks, which Vermont National Bank (D) paid a second time. Canty (P) sued to recover the funds improperly paid twice.

ISSUE: If a bank improperly paid on checks redeposited a second time, but the payment was to the IRS, will it be presumed that no harm has accrued to the depositor?

HOLDING AND DECISION: (Katz, J.) Yes. Where a bank has improperly paid on checks redeposited a second time, but the payment was to the IRS, a rebuttable presumption will be raised in favor of the bank that no harm has come to the depositor. A depositor with a bank has a valid expectation that drafts drawn on his account will be paid out only once. However, a problem arises when a draft is paid on twice. If the twice-paid check satisfies some obligation, a recrediting of the account by the bank will unjustly enrich the depositor. The depositor will have both paid on an obligation and received a recredit. In this case, the problem is particularly clear. By recrediting Canty's (P) account, he would have both paid a future tax bill and received the funds back. Such an unjust enrichment cannot be proper. Since the IRS was the entity paid twice, it is presumed, as a matter of law, that Vermont National Bank (D) has raised a presumption that no actual loss has occurred. Canty's (P) motion for summary judgment is denied; unless he can show actual loss, his claims will be dismissed.

EDITOR'S ANALYSIS: This particular rule of law favors the bank at the expense of the depositor. Unjust enrichment could also be avoided if the bank was forced to recredit, but was given a right to recover, the funds improperly paid. The court's reasoning in this case is flawed. A depositor is harmed whenever funds are paid out in an unplanned fashion. Interest on the money is lost, but the harm may merely be the outrage at paying on an obligation sooner than was planned.

QUICKNOTES

REBUTTABLE PRESUMPTION - A rule of law, inferred from the existence of a particular set of facts, that is conclusive in the absence of contrary evidence.

UNJUST ENRICHMENT - The unlawful acquisition of money or property of another for which both law and equity require restitution to be made.

OBLIGATION - A debt; a duty that a person is legally or morally bound to perform; an action or forbearance that a party promises to do or refrain from doing.

NOTES:

ROCK ISLAND AUCTION SALES, INC. v. EMPIRE PACKING CO.

Seller (P) v. Buyer (D)

Ill. Sup. Ct., 32 Ill. 2d 269, 204 N.E.2d 721 (1965).

NATURE OF CASE: Appeal from award of damages for breach of the "midnight deadline."

FACT SUMMARY: Illinois National Bank (D), the payor bank of a check, held it past the statutory deadline for dishonoring a check.

CONCISE RULE OF LAW: A payor bank which holds a check past the dishonoring deadline is liable when a party is damaged thereby.

FACTS: Rock Island Auction Sales (P) sold certain cattle to Empire Packing Co. (D). Empire (D) paid with a check drawn from Illinois National Bank (D). Rock Island (P) deposited the check, and it was sent by the depositary bank to Illinois National (D) on September 27, 1962. Illinois held it until October 2 before dishonoring it due to insufficient funds and returning it. Empire (D) later declared bankruptcy. Rock Island (P) brought an action against Illinois National (D) for damages it suffered as a result of the delay in dishonoring the check. The trial court awarded Rock Island (P) the amount of the check, and Illinois National (D) appealed.

ISSUE: Is a payor bank which holds a check past the dishonoring deadline liable when a party is damaged thereby?

HOLDING AND DECISION: (Schaffer, J.) Yes. A payor bank which holds a check past the dishonoring deadline is liable when a party is damaged thereby. U.C.C. § 4-302 provides that a payor bank is accountable for the amount of a check if it does not honor or dishonor the check by midnight of the banking day it is received. In the context of this statute, "accountable" is synonymous with "liable," Illinois National's (D) protestations to the contrary notwithstanding. The disparate treatment between depository and payor banks does not violate equal protection because the legislature could rationally conclude that they are in materially different positions in the check-processing chain. Here, since Illinois National (D) held the check for well past the statutory deadline, it is liable therefor. Affirmed.

EDITOR'S ANALYSIS: Federal legislation has, since this case was decided, marginally affected § 4-302. The Expedited Funds Availability Act allows a bank to miss the midnight deadline, so long as the check gets back to the presenting bank the next day. In practice, the difference is minimal, and the effect is the same.

NOTES:

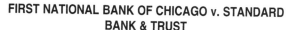

**FIRST NATIONAL BANK OF CHICAGO v. STANDARD
BANK & TRUST**
Bank (P) v. Bank (D)
172 F.3d 472 (7th Cir. 1999).

NATURE OF CASE: Action for declaratory judgment.

FACT SUMMARY: First National Bank of Chicago (NBD at the time of the suit) (P) brought suit seeking declaratory judgment alleging that Standard (D) failed to return some $4 million in checks to NBD (P) in a time fashion as required by federal law.

CONCISE RULE OF LAW: The U.C.C.'s "midnight deadline" does not apply with respect to checks returned in order to avoid a check-kiting scheme.

FACTS: An individual presented checks to both NBD (P) and Standard (D) for approximately $4 million. NBD (P) opted not to honor the checks and Standard (D) also attempted to dishonor the checks. NBD (P) brought suit alleging that Standard (D) failed to return the checks in as timely fashion under the Expedited Funds Availability Act. The district court granted summary judgment to Standard (D) and awarded Standard (D) prejudgment interest on the returned checks. Standard (D) claimed it was entitled to the prime rate, but the court used the three-month Treasury Bill rate compounded quarterly. Both parties appealed.

ISSUE: Does the UCC's "midnight deadline" apply with respect to checks returned in order to avoid a check-kiting scheme?

HOLDING AND DECISION: (Flaum, J.) No. The U.C.C.'s "midnight deadline" does not apply with respect to checks returned in order to avoid a check-kiting scheme. The issue here is whether Standard's (D) return of the checks complies with Federal Reserve Board Regulation CC sec. 229.30(c)(1), which extends the U.C.C.'s Amidnight deadline. NBD (P) argued the extension did not apply here since the legislative history of the regulation indicates the extension was intended to be limited to banks regularly using courier services to return checks. Firth the plain language of the regulation must be considered before resorting to legislative history. The regulation's plain language extends the U.C.C. deadline when a paying bank expedites delivery of a returned check. Moreover, the use of the singular "check" indicates that the regulation was intended to apply to one-time singular check transactions. This reading is further substantiated by the second clause of the regulation, which allows a bank to extend the deadline when it "uses a means of delivery that would ordinarily result in the returned check being received by the bank to which it is sent on or before the receiving bank's next business day following the otherwise applicable deadline." Furthermore, the board issued a clarifying amendment to remove any doubt as to whether the midnight deadline applies

to checks retuned to avoid a kiting scheme. The district court's finding that NBD (P) should have honored the checks was correct. Judgment on pleadings in favor of Standard (D) affirmed. Grant of prejudgment interest vacated and remanded to enter an award consistent with the average prime rate for the applicable period.

EDITOR'S ANALYSIS: The U.C.C.'s "midnight deadline" permits a paying bank to dishonor or revoke payment on a check before midnight in the following business day after receiving the check. The purpose of the U.C.C. provision is to expeditiously deal with dishonored checks; however, the regulation in issue here extends the requirement that the return process be commenced by midnight on the basis that it might have the indirect effect of slowing the process since many banks would elect to return the checks by mail rather than wait till the following day to dispatch a courier service.

NOTES:

GORDON v. PLANTERS & MERCHANTS BANCSHARES, INC.
Farmer (P) v. Bank (D)
Ark. Sup. Ct., 326 Ark. 1046, 935 S.W.2d 544 (1996).

NATURE OF CASE: Suit for wrongful charge back of a check.

FACT SUMMARY: Gordon (P) brought suit against Planters Bank (D) claiming the bank wrongfully charged back a check to his account after final settlement and seeking punitive damages plus interest and attorney's fees.

CONCISE RULE OF LAW: Punitive damages are permissible under Article 4 of the U.C.C. where the defendant acts willfully and maliciously.

FACTS: Gordon (P) and Wallace were partners in a farming business which ended when Wallace decided to take a job with Planters (D). Gordon (P) paid Wallace $67,000 for what he believed to be the right to all assets formerly belonging to the partnership. Gordon (P) then received a $2,494.21 check issued by Stuttgart Cooperative Buyers' Association (Co-op) made payable to Gordon Wallace Farms. He endorsed the check "Gordon Wallace Farms" and deposited it in his personal account at Planters (D). Two days after the check was deposited, Wallace called the Gordon (P) home inquiring whether he received a check from the Co-op. Without speaking to Gordon (P) personally, he called a friend at First National to tell him that the check had been improperly endorsed. Planters (D) received the check from First National marked "Return to Maker." Wallace instructed the bookkeeper to charge back the check against Gordon's (P) account. Gordon (P) spoke with the bank president who told Gordon (P) that this was a personal matter between him and Wallace. Gordon (P) then brought suit against Planters (D) claiming the bank was strictly liable when it charged back the check after final settlement, seeking the amount of the check plus interest and punitive damages. The trial court dismissed for failure to state a claim and this court reversed. On remand the trial court entered a directed verdict to Planters (D) on the issue of punitive damages and awarded Gordon (P) the amount of the check plus interest and attorney's fees of $335. Gordon (P) appeals contending the trial court erred in granting the directed verdict as to punitive damages and the amount of attorney's fees awarded.

ISSUE: Are punitive damages permissible under Article 4 of the UCC where the defendant acts willfully and maliciously?

HOLDING AND DECISION: (Roaf, J.) Yes. Punitive damages are permissible under Article 4 of the U.C.C. where the defendant acts willfully and maliciously. Planters (D) admitted that it wrongfully charged-back Gordon's (P) account; thus, the only issue addressed here is whether Gordon (P) sufficiently pled and submitted evidence to support a punitive damages award. This requires the court to find that: (1) punitive damages are permissible under the wrongful charge back provision of Ark. Code Ann. § 4-4-4215(d); (2) there was sufficient evidence to allow the issue to be submitted to the jury; and (3) Planters (D) may be held vicariously liable for Wallace's wrongful conduct. Other courts have held that punitive damages are permitted under the U.C.C. where a wrongdoer acts willfully or maliciously. Moreover Article 4 of the U.C.C. provides for other damages when a bank acts in bad faith in dealing with its customers. This court has authorized the award of punitive damages in wrongful dishonor cases, which are also governed by Article 4 of the U.C.C., although the wrongful dishonor provision did not expressly provide for them. Furthermore § 4-1-203 provides that every contract imposes an obligation of good faith. Planters' (D) argument that punitive damages are not recoverable since Gordon's (P) case is based in contract and not in tort, does not defeat the right to punitive damages pursuant to the duty of good faith under § 4-1-203. In order to avoid a directed verdict as to the issue of punitive damages, Gordon (P) was required to present substantial evidence that Planters (D) acted wantonly in causing the injury or with such conscious indifference that malice may be inferred. Gordon (P) met his burden and the issue should have gone to the jury. Last, the court must determine whether an agency relationship existed between Wallace and Planters (D) when Wallace caused the check to be charged back to Gordon's (P) account. Under the doctrine of respondeat superior, an employer may be held liable for punitive damages for the acts of its employees acting within the scope of his employment at the time of the conduct. This depends upon whether the person is carrying out the "object and purpose of the enterprise" rather than acting in his own interest. While it is true that Wallace was motivated by his own personal, pecuniary interests, he used his position with the bank to do so. Moreover, the bank president when approached by Gordon (P) told him to take up the matter with Wallace and refused to assist him, thereby demonstrating "conscious indifference" and ratification of Wallace's conduct. Reversed and remanded.

DISSENT: (Corbin, J.) There was no substantial evidence presented at trial to support an award of punitive damages to Gordon (P).

EDITOR'S ANALYSIS: The statutory right of charge back provided in the U.C.C. § 4-214 provides the depositary bank with a remedy against the depositor when a payor bank dishonors a check.

12

CHAPTER 12
WRONGDOING AND ERROR

QUICK REFERENCE RULES OF LAW

1. **Conversion Liability.** (1) Where a payee's agent wrongfully alters an instrument so that it is payable to the agent, a depository bank is strictly liable for conversion of the altered instrument. (2) Where a payee's agent wrongfully alters an instrument so that it is payable to the agent, a drawer/drawee/payor bank is not strictly liable for conversion of the altered instrument. (Leeds v. Chase Manhattan Bank, N.A.)

2. **Forgery of the Drawer's Name.** A party accepting a draft has no recourse against a good-faith endorser if the draft had originally been forged. (Price v. Neal)

3. **Forgery of the Drawer's Name.** Presentment and transfer warranties are not made to a drawee bank when a presenting bank submits for payment to the drawee bank a check that has on it a forged drawer's name. (Decibel Credit Union v. Pueblo Bank & Trust Co.)

4. **Common Law Validation.** A party whose attorney forges an endorsement on a settlement check may not recover her converted funds from the tortfeasor. (Hutzler v. Hertz Corp.)

5. **The Negligence Rule.** The failure of a drawer of an instrument to exercise ordinary care that contributes to forgery of the instrument results in the drawer being comparatively liable for any resulting loss. (The Bank/First Citizens Bank v. Citizens and Associates)

6. **The Bank Statement Rule.** Section 4-406(f) of the U.C.C. does not bar suits brought beyond the time limitation set forth in that section where plaintiff-customer alleges that the bank acted in bad faith in paying items that are the subject of suit. (Falk v. Northern Trust Co.)

LEEDS v. CHASE MANHATTAN BANK, N.A.
Payee on check (P) v. Bank (D)
N.J. Sup. App. Div., 752 A.2d 332 (2000).

NATURE OF CASE: Appeal from summary judgment dismissing strict liability for conversion for payment on an altered check by the depository bank and the drawer/drawee/payor bank.

FACT SUMMARY: A Summit Bank teller's check made payable to Leeds (P) was altered by his attorney to be made payable to the attorney. The attorney deposited the altered check in an account with Chase Manhattan Bank, N.A. (Chase) (D) and Summit Bank (Summit) (D) honored the check. The attorney paid moneys owing to Leeds (P) out of an account the attorney held at Trust Company of New Jersey (Trustco) by using moneys that rightfully belonged to Shrewbury State Bank (Shrewsbury). Trustco sought repayment of the monies traceable to the attorney's fraud from the attorney, as well as from Leeds. Leeds then brought suit alleging strict liability for conversion for payment on the altered check against both Chase (D) and Summit (D).

CONCISE RULES OF LAW: (1) Where a payee's agent wrongfully alters an instrument so that it is payable to the agent, a depository bank is strictly liable for conversion of the altered instrument. (2) Where a payee's agent wrongfully alters an instrument so that it is payable to the agent, a drawer/drawee/payor bank is not strictly liable for conversion of the altered instrument.

FACTS: Leeds (P) hired Egnasko, an attorney, for his representation in a real estate transaction. Egnasko accepted a settlement check for $87,293.56 on Leeds' (P) behalf. The check was made payable to Leeds (P) and was a Summit Bank (D) teller's check. Unbeknownst to Leeds (P), Egnasko altered the check by making it payable to himself as attorney for Leeds. Egnasko then deposited the check into his attorney trust account with Chase Manahattan Bank (D). Summit (D) honored its own check upon presentment. Then Egnasko drew a check for $92,050 payable to Leeds from another attorney trust account he had at Trust Company of New Jersey (Trustco). However, the funds in that account came from Egansko's alteration of a check payable to Shrewsbury State Bank (Shrewsbury). Facing a claim of conversion from Shrewsbury, Trustco filed suit against Egnasko and Leeds (P) in New York, seeking repayment of the monies traceable to Egnasko's fraud. Leeds (P) contested liability in that action and then filed an action alleging strict liability for conversion against Chase (D), as the depository bank, including damages related to the cost of defending the New York action, and Summit (D), as the drawer/drawee/payor bank. The defendants moved for summary judgment, which the trial court granted. Leeds (P) appealed.

ISSUES: (1) Where a payee's agent wrongfully alters an instrument so that it is payable to the agent, is a depository bank strictly liable for conversion of the altered instrument? (2) Where a payee's agent wrongfully alters an instrument so that it is payable to the agent, is a drawer/drawee/payor bank strictly liable for conversion of the altered instrument?

HOLDING AND DECISION: (Wecker, J.A.D.) Yes as to issue #1. No as to issue #2. (1) The check was not delivered to Leeds (P); it was delivered to Egnasko as Leeds' (P) attorney. Therefore, Leeds (P) is entitled to bring the action for conversion against Chase (D) as one who received delivery of the instrument through delivery to an agent. Section 3-420a of the U.C.C. makes it clear that Egnasko was a person, who by virtue of his altering the check, was not entitled to enforce the check or receive payment on it—his actions constituted forgery. By crediting Egnasko's account, Chase (D) paid a person not entitled to receive payment. Under the U.C.C., a depository bank is strictly liable for conversion on a forged instrument. Therefore, Chase (D) is strictly liable on Leeds' (P) claim for conversion. Chase (D) had argued in favor of its summary judgment motion that Leeds (P) had been paid and therefore suffered no damages. This defense of payment is not persuasive in light of Leeds' continuing exposure to the New York action, and Chase (D) is not entitled to summary judgment. (2) A drawee bank, like Summit (D), is strictly liable for conversion when it pays on a forged endorsement. However, U.C.C. §3-420a limits damages for conversion where the actions by such a party have been made in good faith. Here, there were no allegations that Summit (D) acted in bad faith, and, therefore, it cannot be liable to Leeds for conversion. Summary judgment is, therefore, affirmed in favor of Summit (D).

EDITOR'S ANALYSIS: Although Leeds' (P) strict liability action against Summit (D) failed, Leeds (P) could have brought an action against Summit (D) for negligence. Because Summit (D) was the drawer of the check, Leeds (P) would likely have had a strong case that Summit (D) was negligent in failing to detect the alteration on its own teller's check.

NOTES:

PRICE v. NEAL
Lender (P) v. Borrower (D)
3 Burr. 1354, 97 Eng. Rep. 871 (1762).

NATURE OF CASE: Action seeking recovery on a draft.

FACT SUMMARY: Price (P) accepted as payment of a debt a pair of drafts endorsed by Neal (D) which had been forged prior to Neal's (D) possession of them.

CONCISE RULE OF LAW: A party accepting a draft has no recourse against a good-faith endorser if the draft had originally been forged.

FACTS: Neal (D) owed £80 to Price (P). Neal (D) endorsed a pair of £40 drafts that had come into his possession, supposedly having been drawn on one Sutton. In fact, they had been forged and were worthless. Price (P) accepted the drafts as payment for the debt. When they were found to be forgeries, Price (P) sued Neal (D) for the debt.

ISSUE: Does a party accepting a draft have any recourse against a good-faith endorser if the draft had originally been forged?

HOLDING AND DECISION: (Lord Mansfield) [In a rather brief summary of the judge's opinion, the reporter noted that the judge was of the opinion that since both parties were equally blameless, it would not be appropriate for the law to shift the loss from one party to the other. Rather, the parties would be left as they were, with Price (P) bearing the loss.]

EDITOR'S ANALYSIS: The rule stated here still has much vitality. Essentially, a drawee accepting a negotiable instrument cannot pass off the risk of forgery. U.C.C. § 3-418 to some extent codifies this rule.

NOTES:

DECIBEL CREDIT UNION v. PUEBLO BANK & TRUST CO.
Drawee bank (P) v. Presenting bank (D)
Co. Ct. App., 996 P.2d 784 (2000).

NATURE OF CASE: Appeal from summary judgment on breach of warranty of presentment and transfer claims.

FACT SUMMARY: Checks belonging to a customer of Decibel Credit Union (Decibel) (P) were stolen, the drawer's name was forged, and the checks were cashed at Pueblo Bank & Trust Co. (Pueblo Bank) (D) during a 40-day period. As soon as the forgeries were discovered, Decibel notified Pueblo Bank (D) and demanded reimbursement from it. Pueblo Bank (D) declined, and Decibel (D) sued.

CONCISE RULE OF LAW: Presentment and transfer warranties are not made to a drawee bank when a presenting bank submits for payment to the drawee bank a check that has on it a forged drawer's name.

FACTS: A thief stole blank checks furnished by Decibel (P) to one of its customers. The thief forged the customer's signature on 14 checks totaling $2,350 and during a 40-day period cashed the forged checks at Pueblo Bank (D) where the thief had an account. Pueblo Bank (D) processed all the forged checks through the Federal Reserve System to Decibel (P), and Decibel (P) paid the checks. When the customer discovered the forgeries upon receipt of his bank statement, the customer immediately notified Decibel (P), which in turn immediately notified Pueblo Bank (D). Decibel (P) made demand on Pueblo Bank (D) for reimbursement, and, when Pueblo Bank (D) declined, Decibel (P) sued. The trial court granted summary judgment for Decibel (P) on the ground that Pueblo Bank (D) had triggered its presentment and transfer warranties when it submitted the checks to Decibel (P) for payment. Pueblo Bank (D) appealed.

ISSUE: Are presentment and transfer warranties made to a drawee bank when a presenting bank submits for payment to the drawee bank a check that has on it a forged drawer's name?

HOLDING AND DECISION: (Ruland, J.) No. For purposes of the U.C.C., Decibel (P) was the drawee bank and Pueblo Bank (D) was the presenting bank. With regard to the presentment warranty in § 4-208(a), subsection (a)(1) provides only a warranty that there are no unauthorized or missing endorsements on the check. Other subsections do not apply because the checks were not altered and because Pueblo Bank (D) had no knowledge of the forged signatures. If a bank in the position of Pueblo Bank (D) had to warrant that all signatures were genuine, the Code's final payment doctrine, which creates certainty as to which bank must bear a loss, would be rendered meaningless. Therefore, Pueblo Bank (D) did not extend any presentment warranties to Decibel (P) when it presented the checks for payment. As to the transfer warranty, assuming there was a transfer here, it is well settled that a transfer warranty as to the genuineness of the drawer's signature does not apply for the benefit of the drawer bank. Therefore, Pueblo Bank (D) did not extend any transfer warranties to Decibel (D). Reversed and remanded.

EDITOR'S ANALYSIS: The result in this case rests on the distinction between forgeries of the drawer's name and forgeries of endorsements. The reviewing court had the straightforward task of applying well established principles under the Code that the presentment and transfer warranties apply to forgeries of endorsements (unless there is knowledge on the part of the presenting bank of the forged drawer's name).

NOTES:

92

HUTZLER v. HERTZ CORP.
Claimant (P) v. Corporation (D)
N.Y. Ct. App., 39 N.Y.2d 209, 347 N.E.2d 627, 383 N.Y.S. 2d 266 (1976).

NATURE OF CASE: Appeal from award of damages for negligence.

FACT SUMMARY: After her attorney converted the proceeds of a settlement from Hertz (D) by forging her signature in the endorsement area on the back of a check, Hutzler (P) sued Hertz (D) for negligence.

CONCISE RULE OF LAW: A party whose attorney forges an endorsement on a settlement check may not recover her converted funds from the tortfeasor.

FACTS: Hertz Corp. (D), as settlement of a tort claim against it by Hutzler (P), executed a check in the amount of $10,929, payable to her and Yudow, her attorney. To make it appear that Hutzler (P) endorsed the check, Yudow forged her signature, took the funds, and disappeared from the scene. Hutzler (P), upon learning of this, sued Hertz (D) for negligence and the drawee bank for conversion. The trial court granted summary judgment in favor of Hutzler (P), which the appellate division modified slightly. Hertz (D) appealed.

ISSUE: May a party whose attorney forges an endorsement on a settlement check recover her converted funds from the tortfeasor?

HOLDING AND DECISION: (Jasen, J.) No. A party whose attorney forges an endorsement on a settlement check may not recover her converted funds from the tortfeasor. An attorney retained to collect a debt is an agent and has at least apparent authority to receive payment from a settlor or judgment-debtor. From this relationship it has long been the rule that a debtor's liability is discharged when a check payable to the creditor is wrongfully endorsed by the creditor's agent and paid by the drawee bank. This is true in the attorney-client relationship. To hold otherwise would inject unhealthy uncertainty into legal transactions. It is true that U.C.C. § 3-401 (1) states that an unauthorized signature is inoperative against the person whose name is signed. However, under the aforementioned agency principles, a client in a situation such as Hutzler (P) is estopped from denying as unauthorized the signature of her agent. Reversed.

EDITOR'S ANALYSIS: The rule stated here would appear to comport with the majority of jurisdictions in this country. It is embodied in the Restatement (Second) of Agency, at § 178. The view is that, between a blameless client and blameless tortfeasor, the client, who made the unwise attorney selection, should bear the loss.

THE BANK/FIRST CITIZENS BANK v. CITIZENS AND ASSOCIATES

Depository bank (P) v. Drawer (D)

Tenn. Ct. App., 44 U.C.C. Rep. Serv. 2d 1072 (2001).

NATURE OF CASE: Appeal from comparative fault determination in an action to determine who bears the loss of a bank's acceptance of forged instruments.

FACT SUMMARY: Citizens and Associates (Citizens) (D) gave three checks totaling $50,000 to Gray, a branch manager for Allied Mortgage Capital Corp. (Allied), for the purpose of purchasing an Allied franchise. Instead of forwarding the checks, which were payable to Allied, Gray deposited the checks in her personal account in Bank/First Citizens Bank (the Bank) (P). The Bank (P) delivered them to the First Tennessee Bank, which paid the checks.

CONCISE RULE OF LAW: The failure of a drawer of an instrument to exercise ordinary care that contributes to forgery of the instrument results in the drawer being comparatively liable for any resulting loss.

FACTS: Gray was the branch manager of Allied Mortgage Capital Corp. (Allied), and convinced Citizens (D) to invest in Allied through a franchise. Citizens (D) did not independently verify the transaction with Allied. Over the next thirty days, Citizens (D) issued three checks to Allied Mortgage, in the total amount of $50,000, and it gave these checks to Ms. Gray for delivery to Allied's main office in Texas. However, Ms. Gray did not forward the checks to the main office. Instead, she endorsed each in the name of the corporation and deposited the instruments in her personal account at the Bank (P). The Bank (P), as the depository bank, presented these checks to First Tennessee Bank, the drawee bank, which paid the checks and deducted the amounts paid from Citizens' (D) account. In an action to determine liability for the loss, the trial court determined under U.C.C. § 3-406 that both Citizens (D) and the Bank (P) had failed to exercise ordinary care in the transactions and allocated the loss at 80 percent to Citizens (D) and 20 percent to the Bank (P). Citizens (D) appealed.

ISSUE: Does the failure of a drawer of an instrument to exercise ordinary care that contributes to forgery of the instrument result in the drawer being comparatively liable for any resulting loss?

HOLDING AND DECISION: (Franks, J.) Yes. The U.C.C. in § 3-406 requires the Bank (P) to prove that Citizens (D) failed to exercise ordinary care. Here, Citizens' (D) principals were experienced businessmen and, as the trial court found, failed to exercise ordinary care by delivering the checks to Gray without having any written documentation and without independently verifying the transaction, or Gray's authority, with Allied itself. Accordingly, Citizens was negligent and careless in its business practices. Citizens (D) argues that even if it was negligent, its negligence did not "substantially contribute" to the forged endorsements as required by § 3-406. However, it was Citizens' (D) negligence that put the checks at her disposal and, thus, contributed to her ability to forge the endorsement, and was a substantial factor in bringing it about. Under § 3-406, where a drawer negligently issues an instrument so as to contribute to its alteration or forgery, he must be judged by a comparative fault test. Therefore, the evidence did not preponderate against the trial court's findings and holding. Affirmed.

CONCURRENCE IN PART AND DISSENT IN PART: (Susano, Jr., J.) The Bank (P) should be responsible 100 percent for the loss. Because Gray was without question an employee of Allied and was authorized to receive documents and checks for her employer, Citizens (D) did not fail to exercise the ordinary care contemplated by § 3-406. Moreover, the cases cited by the majority all involved transactions where checks were negligently entrusted to third parties for delivery to the payee, whereas here the checks were entrusted to the payee's agent. Accordingly, Citizens (D) acted reasonably under the circumstances and did not contribute to the forgery.

EDITOR'S ANALYSIS: On appeal, the Tennessee Supreme Court reversed, holding that the bank could not assert that the drawer was precluded from asserting the forgery against it under § 3-406 because it did not show that any failure by the drawer to exercise ordinary care substantially contributed to the making of the forged endorsements.

NOTES:

FALK v. NORTHERN TRUST CO.
Account holder (P) v. Bank (D)
Ill. App. Ct., 763 N.E.2d 380 (2001).

NATURE OF CASE: Appeal from dismissal of damages and accounting action as time-barred.

FACT SUMMARY: Falk's (P) personal assistant and bookkeeper misappropriated over $2 million from his accounts at The Northern Trust Co. (the Bank) (D) over the course of four years. He sued the Bank (D) for damages and an accounting. His suit was dismissed as time-barred by § 4-406(f) of the U.C.C.

CONCISE RULE OF LAW: Section 4-406(f) of the U.C.C. does not bar suits brought beyond the time limitation set forth in that section where plaintiff-customer alleges that the bank acted in bad faith in paying items that are the subject of suit.

FACTS: Falk (P) employed Podmokly as his personal assistant and bookkeeper for over 13 years. In 1984, she was made a signatory on his accounts at the Bank (D) and held a position of a fiduciary with respect to Falk (P), a fact known to the Bank (D). In 1993, Podmokly began misappropriating funds from Falk's (P) accounts at the Bank (D) for her own benefit. Over the next four years, she misappropriated over $2 million from Falk (P). Podmokly maintained her own account at the Bank (D). Falk (P) sued the Bank (D) for damages and an accounting, claiming that the Bank (D) had been placed on notice of Podmokly's misappropriations because of the number of changes and irregularities in Falk's (P) accounts and by virtue of knowing her personal information—the Bank (D) was aware that her income was insufficient to support the account and loan activity she was generating. The Bank (D) moved to dismiss under U.C.C. § 4-406(f), which requires that a bank's customer notify the bank of any irregularities within one year after receiving bank his bank statements. The trial court granted the motion and dismissed. Falk (P) appealed.

ISSUE: Does § 4-406(f) of the U.C.C. bar suits brought beyond the time limitation set forth in that section where plaintiff-customer alleges that the bank acted in bad faith in paying items that are the subject of suit?

HOLDING AND DECISION: (Hall, J.) No. An amendment to § 4-406 eliminated the requirement that the bank pay items in "good faith" in order for the customer to have to report unauthorized signatures or alterations to the bank within one year of receiving the items and a bank statement relating to those items. Prior to the amendment, the Seventh Circuit in Appley v. West, 832 F.2d 1021 (7th Cir. 1987) held that the time limitation did not apply where the plaintiff alleged that the bank acted in bad faith in allowing the plaintiff's fiduciary to misappropriate funds from plaintiff's accounts. The Bank (D) maintains that Appley is no longer controlling, given that the requirement the bank pay items in good faith was eliminated. However, Appley is persuasive precedent, unlike the cases the Bank (D) relies on, because it encompasses a scenario in which the bank acted in bad faith in paying an item. The issue, then, is whether the amendment to § 4-406 requires a result different from that in Appley. As a matter of statutory construction, § 4-406(f) does not bar suits brought beyond the one-year time limitation where bad faith on the part of the bank is alleged. That is because the other subsections of § 4-406 now require the bank and the customer to share the loss where the bank did not use ordinary care in paying an item and because new § 4-406 now allows customers to avoid preclusion altogether if they can prove the bank did not pay an item in good faith. Moreover, the U.C.C. requires good faith in the performance of every duty or obligation. Therefore, the Bank (D) was required to pay the items in good faith in order to claim the protection of the one-year notice requirement in § 4-406(f)—the public policy behind that protection is not served where "the bank is a party, either actively or passively, to a scheme to defraud the customer." However, the customer must allege sufficient facts to establish "bad faith." Here, Falk (P) alleged sufficient facts to show that the Bank (D) was on notice that Podmokly was acting in breach of her fiduciary duties to Falk (P). Given the number of years and the number of transactions involved, the Bank's (D) failure to investigate was more than a lack of care. Thus, Falk (P) alleged sufficient facts to establish that the Bank (D) acted in bad faith. Reversed and remanded.

DISSENT: (Cerda, J.) Because the legislature did not insert a "good faith" requirement into § 4-406(f), the Bank (D) should not be required to have paid the items in dispute in good faith for the statute's one-year period to apply.

EDITOR'S ANALYSIS: The definition of "bad faith" in the instant case does not have to do with dishonesty, but rather with whether it is commercially unjustifiable for the payee to disregard and refuse to learn facts that are readily available. It is remaining passive in the light of obvious circumstances that constitutes "bad faith."

NOTES:

CHAPTER 13
ELECTRONIC BANKING

QUICK REFERENCE RULES OF LAW

1. **Wire Transfers**. In the funds transfer context, the originator of the funds transfer is the party who bears the risk of loss. (Grain Trader, Inc. v. Citibank, N.A.)

2. **Transmission Errors.** Under Florida law, acceptance of a wire transfer by the recipient bank is precluded where the name, bank account or other identifying information of the beneficiary is nonexistent or unidentifiable. (Corfan Banco Asuncion Paraguay v. Ocean Bank)

3. **Transmission Errors.** A bank is entitled to restitution from the beneficiaries for the amount of an unauthorized transfer despite its own negligence, unless the beneficiaries have, in good faith, applied the overpayment to a pre-existing debt owed by the originator. (Bank of America N.T.S.A. v. Sanati)

GRAIN TRADERS, INC. v. CITIBANK, N.A.
Bank (P) v. Bank (D)
960 F. Supp. 784 (S.D.N.Y. 1997).

NATURE OF CASE: Diversity action seeking recovery of funds lost in an electronic funds transfer.

FACT SUMMARY: Grain Traders (P) brought suit against Citibank (D) seeking the refund of money it allegedly lost in the process of an electronic funds transfer.

CONCISE RULE OF LAW: In the funds transfer context, the originator of the funds transfer is the party who bears the risk of loss.

FACTS: Grain Traders (P) initiated a funds transfer designed to move $310,000 from Grain Traders (P) to Kraemer in one day. The transfer was to proceed as follows: (1) Grain Traders' (P) account at BCN was to be debited $310,000; (2) the funds would be transferred to BCI at Citibank by means of a debit to BCI's Citibank (D) account and a corresponding credit to BCN's Citibank (D) account; (3) the funds were in turn to be transferred from BCI to Banco Extrader, S.A.; and (4) the funds finally transferred to Kraemer's account at Extrader. Just before BCI's account at Citibank (D) was credited it was placed on a "hold for funds" status. Since BCI's account with Citibank (D) was overdrawn by more than $12 million, BCI was prevented form making further withdrawals from the account. Kraemer never received a credit to his account for the $310,000. Grain Traders (P) brought suit against Citibank (D) seeking a refund under UCC § 4-A-402, for a refund as well as reasonable expenses and attorney's fees under UCC §§ 4-A-209, 4-A-301, and 4-A-305, for breach of the obligation to deal in good faith under § 1-203 and for conversion under the common law.

ISSUE: In the funds transfer context, is the originator of the funds transfer the party who bears the risk of loss?

HOLDING AND DECISION: (Chin, J.) Yes. In the funds transfer context, the originator of the funds transfer is the party who bears the risk of loss. In the first cause of action, Grain Traders (P) claims it is entitled to a refund under the "money back guarantee" of § 4-A-402. Citibank (D) argued that under that provision a party to a funds transfer may only recover against the next party or bank in line; thus Grain Traders (P) may only seek a refund from BCN. This court agrees. First the plain language of § 4-A-402 and other provisions of Article 4-A clearly state that a party to a fund transfer may only recover a refund from the specific party to whom it made payment. Moreover, § 4-A-402(5) makes clear that there is no right to a refund between the originator and an intermediary bank. The official comments to the section also states that when the originator chooses an intermediary bank that is financially unable to complete its part of the funds transfer, the originator bears the risk of loss. In addition, § 4-A-305(2) provides that a receiving

bank is liable to the originator for interest and expenses under certain circumstances. This section shows that when the drafters or Article 4-A wanted to give the originator the right to bring a cause of action against any bank in the funds transfer chain, they knew how to make that clear. They failed to do so with respect to an intermediary bank. Thus summary judgment is granted for Citibank (D) as to the first claim for relief. Grain Traders (P) also alleged that since Citibank (D) intended to use the funds as a set-off to the debt owed by BCI, it did not intend to carry out the payment order received by BCN and thus did not constitute "execution" or "acceptance" under §§ 4-A-209 and 4-A-301. The record, however, shows that Citibank (D) properly executed the payment order it received, thereby satisfying its obligation to issue a payment order intended to carry out the payment order received by the sender. Thus the second claim for relief is dismissed. Grain Traders (P) also asserted Citibank's (D) conduct violated § 1-203, which imposes an obligation of good faith and fair dealing on a party's performance of or enforcement of any contract or duty within the scope of the U.C.C., seeking damages. Section 1-203 only imposes an obligation of good faith and fair dealing on the performance of a contract or duty. Here no contract is alleged to have existed between Citibank (D) and Grain Traders (P). There is also no statutory duty since Grain Traders failed to state a claim under Article 4-A. Since there is no contractual or statutory duty this claim is dismissed as well. Last, Grain Traders (P) asserted a claim for relief based on the common law torts of "conversion" and "money had and received." These claims must be dismissed as well since Grain Traders (P) failed to present evidence in support of either of these claims.

EDITOR'S ANALYSIS: A funds (or wire) transfer is a method of payment by which the originator (the person making the payment) transmits an instruction to a bank to make payment to a beneficiary or to instruct another bank to make the payment to the beneficiary. It consists of several such orders and is accomplished via a series of debits and credits to bank accounts.

NOTES:

CORFAN BANCO ASUNCION PARAGUAY v. OCEAN BANK

Transnational bank (P) v. Florida bank (D)

Fla. Dist. Ct. App., 715 So. 2d 967 (1998).

NATURE OF CASE: Appeal from summary judgment for defendant on causes of action for violation of the U.C.C. and common law negligence.

FACT SUMMARY: Corfan (P) erroneously sent two wire transfers to the same person and brought suit against Ocean Bank (D) for repayment of one.

CONCISE RULE OF LAW: Under Florida law, acceptance of a wire transfer by the recipient bank is precluded where the name, bank account or other identifying information of the beneficiary is nonexistent or unidentifiable.

FACTS: Corfan (P) originated a wire transfer of $72,972 via its intermediary Swiss Bank to the account of Silva in Ocean Bank (D). Ocean Bank (D) noticed a discrepancy in the account numbers and did not inform Corfan (P) or Swiss of the error. Once the correct account number was confirmed by Silva, Ocean (D) accepted the wire transfer and credited his account. Corfan (P) became aware of the discrepancy and issued a second wire transfer of $72,972 to Silva's correct account number at Ocean (D). The second transfer did not indicate that it was a correction or replacement of the first transfer. The transfer was automatically credited to Silva's account. Several days later Corfan (P) inquired regarding the transfers indicating that only one was intended. Silva had already withdrawn both transfers from the account. When Ocean (D) refused to repay $72,972 to Corfan (P), Corfan (P) brought suit under the U.C.C. and for common law negligence. The trial court granted Ocean's (D) motion for summary judgment as to the U.C.C. count and dismissed the negligence count.

ISSUE: Under Florida law, is acceptance of a wire transfer by the recipient bank is precluded where the name, bank account or other identifying information of the beneficiary is nonexistent or unidentifiable?

HOLDING AND DECISION: (Sorondo, J.) Yes. Under Florida law, acceptance of a wire transfer by the recipient bank is precluded where the name, bank account or other identifying information of the beneficiary is nonexistent or unidentifiable. The plain language of Florida Statutes § 670.207(1) states that "if, in a payment order received by the beneficiary's bank, the name, bank account number, or other identification of the beneficiary refers to a nonexistent or unidentifiable person or account, no person has rights as a beneficiary of the order and acceptance cannot occur." Here the payment order referred to a nonexistent bank account number. Thus, under the clear and unambiguous terms of the statute, acceptance of the order could not have occurred. The trial court dismissed the negligence count on the basis that the statutory scheme preempted any common law negligence claim. Since the duty claimed to have been breached by Ocean (D) in the negligence claim (the duty of care to follow the accepted banking practice of the community and to return the funds from the first transfer upon receipt due to a nonexistent account number) is exactly the same duty now governed by statute, the statutory scheme preempts the negligence claim and the dismissal of the claim is affirmed. Reversed in part and affirmed in part.

DISSENT: (Nesbitt, J.) Corfan (P) was negligent in handling the wire transaction by incorrectly listing Silva's account number on the first wire transfer and then by compounding that error by sending the second wire transfer with no indication that it constituted a correction of the first, resulting in Corfan's (P) loss. Moreover, Ocean's (D) actions here were not precluded by the statute since reading the statutory scheme in its entirety shows that the receiving bank is permitted to look to other identification in accepting the wire transfer.

EDITOR'S ANALYSIS: It is common practice with respect to wire transfers for the recipient bank to ignore the name of the beneficiary and look only to the account number specified. U.C.C. § 4A-207 deals with this issue and allows the recipient bank to ignore the name identified as the beneficiary and to only look to the account number.

NOTES:

BANK OF AMERICA N.T.S.A. v. SANATI
Bank (P) v. Account holder (D)
Cal. Ct. App., 14 Cal. Rptr. 2d 615 (1992).

NATURE OF CASE: Appeal from judgment granting plaintiff's motion for summary judgment in an action for unjust enrichment.

FACT SUMMARY: After Mr. Sanati (D) left the United States, having arranged for monthly interest payments from an account held solely in his name to be made to his wife (D) and two children in California, the Bank of America (P) erroneously transferred the principal of the account as well as the interest to his wife (D).

CONCISE RULE OF LAW: A bank is entitled to restitution from the beneficiaries for the amount of an unauthorized transfer despite its own negligence, unless the beneficiaries have, in good faith, applied the overpayment to a pre-existing debt owed by the originator.

FACTS: When Mr. Sanati (D) permanently left the United States, he arranged for monthly interest payments to be made to Mrs. Sanati (D) and their two children in California from a London account held in Mr. Sanati's (D) name only. The Bank of America (P) later erroneously transferred the principal as well as the interest — a total of $203,750 — to the California account. Mrs. Sanati (D) withdrew the principal, depositing it into bank accounts she and her children controlled, and refused the Bank's (P) request for restitution. The Bank (P) then filed an action for unjust enrichment. Mrs. Sanati (D) argued that the U.C.C. controlled and that she had a quasi-community property interest in the London account. Applying the common law, the trial court granted the Bank's (P) motion for summary judgment. Sanati (D) appealed.

ISSUE: Is a bank entitled to restitution from the beneficiaries for the amount of an unauthorized transfer despite its own negligence?

HOLDING AND DECISION: (Johnson, J.) Yes. A bank is entitled to restitution from the beneficiaries for the amount of an unauthorized transfer despite its own negligence, unless the beneficiaries have, in good faith, applied the overpayment to a pre-existing debt owed by the originator. The general common law and equitable principles applied at the time of the fund transfer in this case. However, even if the U.C.C. did apply, the Bank (P) would be entitled to restitution, unless Mrs. Sanati (D) had detrimentally relied on the payment without notice of the mistake or unless she had, in good faith, applied the erroneous payment to a pre-existing debt or lien owed to her by Mr. Sanati (D). While Mrs. Sanati (D) raises a reasonable inference of a potential quasi community property interest in the funds, this does constitute a pre-existing debt or lien at the time of the transfer. Moreover, she and her children do not contend that they changed

their position to their detriment in reliance on the erroneously transmitted funds. The Bank (P) is entitled to restitution. Affirmed.

EDITOR'S ANALYSIS: In recognizing a reasonable inference of a pre-existing debt or lien, courts have applied the "discharge for value" rule. The Restatement of Restitution describes the rule as applying to debts that are liquidated, concrete, and pre-existing, not merely probable and undetermined. This case would raise entirely different issues if there had been a pre-existing judgment dividing the couple's assets, but Mrs. Sanati (D) did not file for dissolution until several months after the erroneous fund transfer.

QUICKNOTES

RESTITUTION - The return or restoration of what the defendant has gained in a transaction to prevent the unjust enrichment of the defendant.

UNJUST ENRICHMENT - The unlawful acquisition of money or property of another for which both law and equity require restitution to be made.

NOTES:

CHAPTER 14
INVESTMENT SECURITIES

QUICK REFERENCE RULES OF LAW

1. **The Issuer and the Holder.** When duplicate bonds are issued due to the malfeasance of an agent of the issuer, the issuer is obligated to pay on the duplicate bonds. (First American National Bank v. Christian Foundation Life Insurance Co.)

2. **Registration.** When an agent of an issuer of registered bonds accepts forged documents and reregisters them, the holder of the bonds is still entitled to his interest therein. (Jennie Clarkson Home for Children v. Missouri, Kansas & Texas Railway)

3. **Security Entitlements.** Where an investment agreement requires more than one entitlement holder signature to authorize a transfer, an entitlement order made by only one entitlement holder is ineffective. (Powers v. American Express Financial Advisors, Inc.)

FIRST AMERICAN NATIONAL BANK v. CHRISTIAN FOUNDATION LIFE INSURANCE CO.
Bank (P) v. Church (D)
Ark. Sup. Ct., 242 Ark. 678, 420 S.W.2d 912 (1967).

NATURE OF CASE: Appeal from declaratory judgment holding denying validity to duplicate.

FACT SUMMARY: An employee of a bond issuer's agent fraudulently sold bonds which were duplicates of bonds previously used as collateral for a loan.

CONCISE RULE OF LAW: When duplicate bonds are issued due to the malfeasance of an agent of the issuer, the issuer is obligated to pay on the duplicate bonds.

FACTS: First Methodist Church of Mena (D) authorized a $90,000 bond issue. The fiscal agent for the issue was Institutional Finance Co. (D). Unbeknownst to anyone, Hayes, the president of Institutional (D), had an extra $25,000 worth of bonds printed, which he used as collateral to obtain a loan. The other bonds were sold to investors. The situation came to Mena's (D) attention when duplicate bond holders presented interest coupons for payment. Mena (D) refused to pay until the validity of the bonds was established. First American National Bank (P), which had made the loan to the now-deceased Hayes, brought an action for a declaratory judgment that its bonds (the bonds it held as collateral for the loan it made to Hayes) were valid. The trial court held they were invalid, and First American (P) appealed.

ISSUE: When duplicate bonds are issued due to the malfeasance of an agent of the issuer, is the issuer obligated to pay on the duplicate bonds?

HOLDING AND DECISION: (Smith, J.) Yes. When duplicate bonds are issued due to the malfeasance of an agent of the issuer, the issuer is obligated to pay on the duplicate bonds. U.C.C. § 8-205 provides that an unauthorized security is valid if held by a bona fide purchaser for value and was signed or otherwise authenticated by an authenticating agent. This is precisely what occurred here. Hayes, employee of issuer agent Institutional Finance (D), authorized the duplicate bonds. They therefore were effective against the issuer. Reversed.

DISSENT: (Jones, J.) Section 8-202(3) provides that lack of genuineness of a security is a complete defense for the issuer. A forged security is not genuine. Therefore, the bonds should not be effective.

EDITOR'S ANALYSIS: A theme running through the U.C.C. is that a loss should fall on the party who is in the best position to prevent such a loss. Section 8-205 is an example of this. An issuer is in a better position to guarantee the fidelity of its agent than is the investor. Thus, a loss occurring because of the agent's dishonesty should fall on the issuer.

JENNIE CLARKSON HOME FOR CHILDREN v. MISSOURI, KANSAS & TEXAS RAILWAY
Bond holder (P) v. Bond issuer (D)
N.Y. Ct. App., 182 N.Y. 47, 74 N.E. 571 (1905).

NATURE OF CASE: Appeal from award of interest on fraudulently registered bonds.

FACT SUMMARY: An agent of the Railway (D) registered bonds it had previously issued when he accepted forged documents presented by the treasurer of Jennie (P), the bondholder, and reregistered them in the forger's name.

CONCISE RULE OF LAW: When an agent of an issuer of registered bonds accepts forged documents and reregisters them, the holder of the bonds is still entitled to his interest therein.

FACTS: Jennie Clarkson Home for Children (P) held certain long-term bonds issued by Missouri, Kansas & Texas Railway (D). At one point Jennie's (P) treasurer converted them to his own use. To do this, he had to forge a resolution by Jennie's (P) board of directors authorizing the transfer because the bonds were registered to Jennie (P). The treasurer had been told of this necessity by Gibson, an employee of the brokerage firm employed by the Railway (D) to handle its securities. Jennie (P) sued Railway (D) for interest due on the bonds. The trial court granted such relief, and the appellate division affirmed. The court of appeals granted review.

ISSUE: When an agent of an issuer of registered bonds accepts forged documents and reregisters them, is the holder of the bonds still entitled to his interest therein?

HOLDING AND DECISION: (Haight, J.) Yes. When an agent of an issuer of registered bonds accepts forged documents and reregisters them, the holder of the bonds is still entitled to his interest therein. When an agent of an issuer of bonds is instrumental in the false transfer thereof, the defrauded former holder retains the right to assert his interest in the bonds. In addition, New York Stock Exchange rules provide that an endorsement by a member of the exchange on a security is considered a guaranty of its correctness. Here, Gibson, an agent of the Railway (D) and an Exchange member, so endorsed the transfer. He also was instrumental in the fraudulent transfer in that he (inadvertently) advised the defrauder on how to effect his theft. Gibson had the opportunity to check on the treasurer's good faith but failed to do so. Therefore, the Railway (D), as Gibson's principal, must bear the loss. Affirmed.

EDITOR'S ANALYSIS: The present case predates the U.C.C. by many years. However, its rule remains vital under the Code. Section 8-311 provides that an unauthorized endorsement is ineffective against the issuer. This would appear to apply to the facts of this case.

POWERS v. AMERICAN EXPRESS FINANCIAL ADVISORS, INC.

Entitlement holder (P) v. Securities intermediary (D)

238 F.3d 414, 43 U.C.C. Rep. Serv. 2d 425 (4th Cir. 2000).

NATURE OF CASE: Appeal from summary judgment awarding damages to an entitlement holder

FACT SUMMARY: Powers (P) and D'Ambrosia had a joint investment account with American Express Financial Advisors, Inc. (American Express) (D). The signature of both owners was required for transfers of $50,000 or more. On the instructions of D'Ambrosia alone, American Express (D) transferred all the funds (over $86,000) to a joint account that D'Ambrosia then liquidated. Powers (P) sued to recover the money.

CONCISE RULE OF LAW: Where an investment agreement requires more than one entitlement holder signature to authorize a transfer, an entitlement order made by only one entitlement holder is ineffective.

FACTS: Powers (P) and D'Ambrosia had a joint investment account with American Express Financial Advisors, Inc. (American Express) (D). Section C of the investment application required the signature of both owners for redemption requests of $50,000 or more. In a memo signed only by D'Ambrosia that he faxed to American Express (D), D'Ambrosia instructed American Express (D) to close the couple's account and transfer all the funds (over $86,000) to a joint bank account held by Powers (P) and D'Ambrosia, which American Express (D) did. D'Ambrosia then absconded with the money. Powers (P) sued to recover the money and moved for summary judgment, claiming that American Express' (D) transfer had been ineffective. The district court granted summary judgment in favor of Powers (P), and American Express (D) appealed.

ISSUE: Where an investment agreement requires more than one entitlement holder signature to authorize a transfer, is an entitlement order made by only one entitlement holder ineffective?

HOLDING AND DECISION: (Per Curiam.) Yes. The reasoning of the district court was correct and was as follows. Under U.C.C. § 8-507(b), a securities intermediary, like American Express (D), which transfers funds pursuant to an "ineffective entitlement order," is liable to an entitlement holder for any damages caused by the improper transfer. Although D'Ambrosia was an "appropriate person" to give an entitlement order to American Express (D), when an intermediary has agreed (as American Express (D) did in the investment application) that the "appropriate person" to make an order is both owners of a joint account, both owners must make the order for it to be effective. Because Powers (P) did not ratify the transfer of the funds

ordered by D'Ambrosia, the transfer was ineffective. The district court was also correct in rejecting American Express' (D) contention that the $50,000 threshold only applied to transfers from a single mutual fund account (the couple had four), because the plain language of the investment application applied to redemption requests generally, not to redemption requests out of individual funds. The district court was also correct that Powers (P) was not barred under § 8-115 from seeking damages. Under that section, a securities intermediary is not liable to an individual who has an adverse claim to an asset that the intermediary transfers at the direction of a customer—Powers (P) was not an adverse claimant because she was one of two entitlement holders on the account. Finally, the district court was correct that American Express (D) did not have standing to seek a constructive trust on behalf of D'Ambrosia's former employer, from whom D'Ambrosia had been embezzling money.

EDITOR'S ANALYSIS: Under § 8-507(a)(2), when an "appropriate person" gives an entitlement order to a securities intermediary, the intermediary has a duty to execute the order. Although the district court acknowledged that D'Ambrosia was an "appropriate person," it was able to restrict the literal meaning of that subsection by looking to § 1-103 of the Code, which states that principles of law and equity shall supplement the Code. Thus, the outcome in this case was the result, ultimately, of the application of general principles and not a strict adherence to the Code itself.

NOTES:

CHAPTER 15
DOCUMENTS OF TITLE

QUICK REFERENCE RULES OF LAW

1. **Basic Bailment Law.** When bailed goods disappear without explanation, the bailee is liable. (Procter & Gamble Distribution Co. v. Lawrence American Field Warehouse Corp.)

2. **Basic Bailment Law.** A provision in a contract of bailment limiting liability to a certain amount per pound per article is valid. (Dunfee v. Blue Rock Van & Storage, Inc.)

3. **Bills of Lading: The Basic Idea.** (1) A bill of lading may be treated as negotiable where it is consigned "To Order" and is not marked as nonnegotiable and where the holder has purchased the bill of lading for value and considers it to be negotiable. (2) Where a shipper has assigned a bill of lading, a carrier who misdelivers goods upon instructions of the shipper, by failing to require surrender of the original bill of lading, is liable to the holder of the original negotiable bill of lading. (3) Acceptance of partial payment for a claim on a bill of lading does not constitute accord and satisfaction where there is evidence that acceptance of the partial payment is an effort at mitigation of damages. (BII Finance Co. v. U-States Forwarding Services Corp.)

4. **Bills of Lading: Misdescription.** A creditor who loans money secured by a straight bill of lading has no recourse against the carrier for inaccuracies in the bill. (GAC Commercial Corp v. Wilson)

5. **Due Negotiation: The Basic Concept.** A purchaser of crops who does not inquire as to the existence of a landlord's lien thereon is subject to the lien. (Cleveland v. McNabb)

6. **Due Negotiation: The Section 7-503 (I) Owner.** (1) Where there are genuine issues of fact as to whether a document of title has been duly negotiated and as to whether a secured party has acquiesced in the procurement of that document, those questions are for a trier of fact. (2) A secured party may not entrust goods that it does not own. (Agricredit Acceptance, LLC v. Hendrix)

7. **Liability of the Collecting Bank.** A collecting bank in an international transaction may be liable to the vendor for failing to notify it of the vendee's failure to pay an invoice. (Rheinberg Kellerei GmbH v. Brooksfield National Bank of Commerce)

PROCTER & GAMBLE DISTRIBUTING CO. v. LAWRENCE AMERICAN FIELD WAREHOUSE CORP.
Bailor (P) v. Bailee (D)
N.Y. Ct. App., 16 N.Y.2d 344, 213 N.E.2d 8973 (1965).

NATURE OF CASE: Appeal from award of damages for breach of a bailment.

FACT SUMMARY: Certain merchandise bailed by Proctor & Gamble (P) to Lawrence American (D) for storage disappeared without explanation.

CONCISE RULE OF LAW: When bailed goods disappear without explanation, the bailee is liable.

FACTS: Proctor & Gamble (P), bailor, placed in the custody of Lawrence American Field Warehouse Corp. (D), bailee, a large amount of soybean oil. It was converted by unknown persons and never traced. P & G (P) sued for the value of the merchandise. The trial court awarded damages in the amount of the value of the oil upon Lawrence's (D) failure to explain the loss. The appellate division affirmed, and Lawrence (D) appealed.

ISSUE: When bailed goods disappear without explanation, is the bailee liable therefor?

HOLDING AND DECISION: (Van Voorhis, J.) Yes. When bailed goods disappear without explanation, the bailee is liable therefor. Section 7-403 of the U.C.C., along with other provisions of New York's General Business Law, provides that a bailee is liable for the loss of bailed goods absent the exercise of due care. As the bailee is in a much better position than the bailor to account for a loss of bailed goods, it is incumbent upon the bailee to prove due care, not the bailor to prove otherwise. When goods mysteriously disappear, the bailee cannot escape liability by placing the burden on the bailor to demonstrate why possessions in the control of the bailee are missing. The bailee, having taken possession of the goods, must account for them or compensate the bailor. Such is the case here. [The court affirmed with the modification that the value of the oil was to be determined by reference to the highest value between time of delivery and time of P & G's (P) notification of the loss.]

EDITOR'S ANALYSIS: Normally, in a bailment loss, the value of the lost goods is measured by reference to market value at the time of loss. Here, the time of loss was unknown. To have measured the value as of the time of P & G's (P) notification would have allowed Lawrence (D) to have control over the measure of damages, a result the court considered unfair.

QUICKNOTES
DUE CARE - the degree of care that can be expected from a reasonably prudent person under similar circumstances; synonymous with ordinary care.

DUNFEE v. BLUE ROCK VAN & STORAGE, INC.
Bailor (P) v. Bailee (D)
Del. Sup. Ct., 266 A.2d 187 (1970).

NATURE OF CASE: Motion for judgment n.o.v. upon award of damages for breach of a bailment.

FACT SUMMARY: A bailment contract between Dunfee (P) and Blue Rock (D) called for a limitation of liability of $1,000 or $.60 per pound per article.

CONCISE RULE OF LAW: A provision in a contract of bailment limiting liability to a certain amount per pound per article is valid.

FACTS: Dunfee (P) stored certain goods with Blue Rock Van & Storage, Inc. (D). The contract between them limited liability to $1,000 or $.60 per pound per article, whichever was less. Dunfee's (P) goods weighed 4,340 pounds. After a fire destroyed the goods, Dunfee (P) sued Blue Rock (D) for the value of the bailed goods, and the jury awarded him $5,500. Blue Rock (D) moved for judgment n.o.v., based on the contract.

ISSUE: Is a provision in a contract of bailment limiting liability to a certain amount per pound per article valid?

HOLDING AND DECISION: (Per curiam) Yes. A provision in a contract of bailment limiting liability to a certain amount per pound per article is valid. U.C.C. § 7-204 allows a warehouseman to limit liability "per article or item, or value per unit of weight." Technically, this section does not permit a limitation per pound per article. However, the section stands for the general proposition that a bailee may limit his liability. It is unlikely that the section's drafters intended the two types of limitations cited to be pigeonholes into which all bailment situations had to be put. Here, Blue Rock (D) and Dunfee (P) contracted for such a limitation, and it should be enforced. Motion granted.

EDITOR'S ANALYSIS: Prior to adoption of the U.C.C., warehouseman liability was governed partly by the Uniform Warehouse Receipts Act and partly by common law. The circumstances under which liability could be limited varied greatly from state to state. Section 7-204 (2) was intended to add greater uniformity and clarity to the law in this area.

QUICKNOTES
BAILMENT - The delivery of property to be held in trust and which is designated for a particular purpose, following the satisfaction of which the property is either to be returned or disposed of as specified.

JUDGMENT N.O.V. - A judgment entered by the trial judge reversing a jury verdict if the jury's determination has no basis in law or fact.

BII FINANCE CO. v. U-STATES FORWARDING SERVICES CORP.

Holder of bills of lading (P) v. Shipping carrier (D)
Cal. Ct. App., 115 Cal. Rptr. 2d 312, 46 U.C.C. Rep. Serv. 2d 827 (2002).

NATURE OF CASE: Appeal from judgment in action for breach of contract and conversion.

FACT SUMMARY: BII Finance Co. (BII) (P) was the holder of original bills of lading consigned "To Order." U-States Forwarding Services Corp. (U-States) (D) delivered goods covered by the bills of lading without requiring surrender of the original bills of lading. BII (P) had not received full payment for the goods and sued U-States (D) for the balance.

CONCISE RULES OF LAW: (1) A bill of lading may be treated as negotiable where it is consigned "To Order" and is not marked as nonnegotiable and where the holder has purchased the bill of lading for value and considers it to be negotiable. (2) Where a shipper has assigned a bill of lading, a carrier who misdelivers goods upon instructions of the shipper, by failing to require surrender of the original bill of lading, is liable to the holder of the original negotiable bill of lading. (3) Acceptance of partial payment for a claim on a bill of lading does not constitute accord and satisfaction where there is evidence that acceptance of the partial payment is an effort at mitigation of damages.

FACTS: Primaline, Inc. (Primaline), an agent for the shipping carrier U-States Forwarding Services Corp. (U-States) (D), issued four bills of lading in favor of Shineworld Industrial Ltd. (Shineworld), a Hong Kong manufacturer. Although the goods covered by the bills of lading were to be shipped to the buyer, Jacobs & Turner, Ltd. (Jacobs & Turner) in Scotland, they were consigned "TO ORDER." Jacobs & Turner issued a letter of credit for the stated value of the goods, $200,000, and Shineworld assigned the bills of lading to BII Finance Co. (BII) (P), a commercial bank, for a loan of $200,000. While the goods were in transit, BII (P) sent the shipping documents to Jacobs & Turner's bank, requesting payment under the letter of credit. That bank refused to release the funds to BII (P) because it had found discrepancies between the letter of credit and the bills of lading and was awaiting waiver of the discrepancies from Jacobs & Turner. BII (P) notified Shineworld about this problem. Shineworld's (inexplicable) response was to send a letter to Primaline requesting that it release the goods to Jacobs & Turner without requiring the original bills of lading, which is what Primaline, as agent for U-States (D), did, presumably because U-States (D) did not know that Shineworld had assigned the bills of lading to BII (P). Jacobs & Turner had not, however, waived the discrepancies, nor paid for the goods. BII (P) sued Jacobs & Turner, which claimed the goods were defective but which settled with BII (P) for 65% of the goods' value. BII (P) then sued U-States (D) for the balance in breach of contract and conversion. The trial

court found that U-States (D) misdelivered the goods, that BII (P) made efforts to mitigate, and that the unpaid balance was owing, along with costs and attorneys' fees. U-States (D) appealed.

ISSUES: (1) May a bill of lading be treated as negotiable where it is consigned "To Order" and is not marked as nonnegotiable and where the holder has purchased the bill of lading for value and considers it to be negotiable? (2) Where a shipper has assigned a bill of lading, is a carrier who misdelivers goods upon instructions of the shipper, by failing to require surrender of the original bill of lading, liable to the holder of the original negotiable bill of lading? (3) Does acceptance of partial payment for a claim on a bill of lading constitute accord and satisfaction where there is evidence that acceptance of the partial payment is an effort at mitigation of damages?

HOLDING AND DECISION: (Mosk, J.) Yes as to issue #1. Yes as to issue #2. No as to issue #3. (1) The applicable law is U.C.C. which Section 7104 governs whether a bill of lading is negotiable or nonnegotiable. For a bill of lading to be negotiable, the first subdivision of § 7104 requires that by its terms it be delivered to the bearer or to the order of a named person, or, if it runs, to a named person or assigns. Subdivision 2 provides that any other document is nonnegotiable. Subdivision 3 (a California add-on) provides that a nonnegotiable bill must be conspicuously marked as nonnegotiable, and that if it is not so marked, a holder who purchased it for value may treat such a document as negotiable. Because the bills of lading were consigned "TO ORDER," they are not negotiable under subdivision 1. BII (P) argues that § 3109 of the Code converts "To Order" to "To Bearer," but that section, applying to commercial paper, is inapplicable to bills of lading, a form of document of title. Therefore, under subdivision 2, the bills of lading are nonnegotiable. Nonetheless, under subdivision 3, the evidence shows that BII (P) purchased the bills of lading for value, that the parties considered the bills of lading to be negotiable, and that BII (P) elected to treat them as negotiable. Accordingly, under that subdivision, U-States' (D) liabilities under the bills of lading are the same as if they had been negotiable. (2) The absence of an express term requiring surrender of the original bill of lading does not absolve U-States (D) for misdelivery. Where a bill of lading is negotiable, the law requires its surrender in exchange for the goods covered by it. U-States (D) argues that a provision in the bill of lading gave it the option of requiring or not requiring surrender of the bill of lading. That provision started with the phrase "if required by the carrier..." However, that provision simply made clear that U-States (D) may

Continued on next page.

require surrender of the original bill of lading, which requirement allows U-States (D) to protect itself from liability by ensuring that the party to whom it delivers the goods is entitled to them; it does not eliminate U-States' (D) duty to ensure delivery of the goods to the proper party. Delivery to a person who is not the holder, or is not authorized by the holder, is conversion and a breach of contract. Although a shipper may choose to follow a shipper's instructions to deliver goods without requiring surrender of the original bill of lading, as U-States (D) did here, the carrier does so at its own peril because the shipper may have negotiated the bill of lading before giving the instruction. Accordingly, U-States (D) is liable to BII (P) for misdelivery to Jacobs & Turner. (3) BII's (P) acceptance of partial payment from Jacobs & Turner did not constitute an accord and satisfaction, but, rather, constituted mitigation. Whether an agreement is an accord and satisfaction is a question of the parties intent, and, therefore, is a question of fact. Here, U-States (D) failed to present evidence of the terms of the agreement between BII (P) and Jacobs & Turner, and therefore did not establish the parties' intent that Jacobs & Turner's payment was in full satisfaction of BII's (P) claim under the bills of lading. There was evidence, however, that BII (P) intended its acceptance of payment from Jacobs & Turner to be a mitigation of its damages, as it did not surrender the bills of lading to Jacobs & Turner, but retained them and sued U-States (D). Therefore, there was sufficient evidence to support a determination that the partial payment did not extinguish BII's (P) claims against U-States (D). Affirmed.

EDITOR'S ANALYSIS: It is important to keep in mind that, given the international context of this case (Hong Kong shipper, Hong Kong commercial bank (BII), buyer in Scotland, California carrier (U-States)) the results of this case could have been different under the laws of other jurisdictions. The court in the instant case determined that choice of law considerations required application of California law. Even in the U.S., authorities have suggested that there should be a broad interpretation of negotiability and that documents of title, such as bills of lading, need not contain the exact words specified in the U.C.C. for negotiability. However, the California court in the instant case distinguished those authorities.

NOTES:

G.A.C. COMMERCIAL CORP. v. WILSON
Lender (P) v. Defendant (D)
271 F. Supp. 242 (S.D.N.Y. 1967).

NATURE OF CASE: Motion to dismiss action for damages for fraud.

FACT SUMMARY: G.A.C. (P) sued Norwood Railroad (D), a carrier, after it loaned money to St. Lawrence Pulp, secured by straight bills of lading which turned out to be fraudulent.

CONCISE RULE OF LAW: A creditor who loans money secured by a straight bill of lading has no recourse against the carrier for inaccuracies in the bill.

FACTS: G.A.C. Commercial Corp. (P) loaned money to St. Lawrence Pulp & Paper Corp. and took as collateral straight bills of lading, both interstate and intrastate. The carrier was Norwood Railroad (D). After St. Lawrence went bankrupt, the freight cars covered by the bills turned out to be empty. The "loading" had been effected by St. Lawrence, which had also filled out the bills. G.A.C. (P) sued Norwood (D) for $254,173.42, the amount it had loaned. Norwood (D) moved to dismiss, arguing that it was not liable to G.A.C. (P) under the Federal Bills of Lading Act.

ISSUE: Does a creditor who loans money secured by a straight bill of lading have recourse against the carrier for inaccuracies in the bill?

HOLDING AND DECISION: (Bryan, J.) No. A creditor who loans money secured by a straight bill of lading has no recourse against the carrier for inaccuracies in the bill. As to interstate shipments, the Federal Bills of Lading Act, 48 U.S.C. § 81 et seq., controls. This section allows recovery under a straight bill of lading against a carrier only by an owner of goods described in the bill. In a situation where the goods described in the bill don't exist, there can be no owner thereof; therefore, no recovery is possible. As to the intrastate goods, U.C.C. § 7-301 gives a remedy only to a "con-signee," i.e., the party to whom the goods were destined. A bank which loans money secured by such goods is rarely the consignee. Therefore, except in that unusual situation, a lender will have no recourse. Motion granted.

EDITOR'S ANALYSIS: Bills of lading come in two basic types: order and straight. An order of bill is considered a negotiable instrument; a straight bill is not. The former variety contains certain requirements not shared by straight bills and is treated differently under both the Bills of Lading Act and the U.C.C.

QUICKNOTES
BILL OF LADING - A receipt or other documentation given to a shipper by a carrier evidencing the contract to transport such goods and that the shipper possessed title to the goods shipped.

CLEVELAND v. McNABB
Landlord (P) v. Tenant (D)
312 F. Supp. 155 (W.D. Tenn. 1970).

NATURE OF CASE: Action to enforce lien on chattel.

FACT SUMMARY: Cleveland (P), landlord of farmer McNabb (D), sought to assert a lien on crops grown by McNabb (D) when he fell in arrears on the rent.

CONCISE RULE OF LAW: A purchaser of crops who does not inquire as to the existence of a landlord's lien thereon is subject to the lien.

FACTS: Cleveland (P) leased certain lands to McNabb (D), who grew cotton thereon. He sold it to, among others, the federal Government (D), through the Commodity Credit Corporation (D). No inquiry was made as to the source of the cotton or whether it was free of any liens. When McNabb (D) fell in rental arrears, Cleveland (P) filed an action to foreclose on a lien which state law gave to a landlord upon a tenant's crops. The Government (D) contended that it acquired title, as a bona fide purchaser, free of the lien.

ISSUE: Is a purchaser of crops who does not inquire as to the existence of a landlord's lien thereon subject to the lien?

HOLDING AND DECISION: (Brown, C.J.) Yes. A purchaser of crops who does not inquire as to the existence of a landlord's lien is subject to the lien. U.C.C. § 7-502 provides that the holder of a duly negotiated document of title who takes such document without knowledge of prior interests thereon takes the document, and the chattel it embodies, free of that interest. The Government (D) claimed such status. However, U.C.C. § 1-201 provides that a person has notice of a fact when he has reason to know it exists. Here, the evidence shows that the Government's (D) standard practice is to make an injury regarding the existence of liens. Sensible business practice would also demand such inquiry. As the Government (D) did not make such inquiry, it is not entitled to the protections of § 7-502. Judgment for Cleveland (P).

EDITOR'S ANALYSIS: A standard axiom in the law is that a transferor can give a transferee no greater rights that he himself possessed. This is, in fact, not always true. By U.C.C. § 7-502, which codified prior law, a transferee can take an instrument free of defenses thereto which would have been valid against the transferor.

QUICKNOTES
LIEN - A claim against the property of another in order to secure the payment of a debt.

AGRICREDIT ACCEPTANCE, LLC v. HENDRIX

Lender (P) v. Borrower (D)

82 F. Supp. 2d 1379 (S.D. Ga. 2000).

NATURE OF CASE: Motion for summary judgment on priority of security interest.

FACT SUMMARY: Agricredit Acceptance Corp. (AAC) (P) financed Hendrix's (D) cotton crop with a loan properly perfected and secured by the crop. Sea Island Cotton Trading (Sea Island), the selling agent, sold large quantities of cotton, including the Hendrix (D) cotton, to many cotton merchants (D), who paid Sea Island and received electronic warehouse receipts (EWRs) in their names. Sea Island never paid either AAC (P) or Hendrix (D) as it was obligated to do, and AAC (P) filed suit against the merchants (D) and others to foreclose on its security interest in the Hendrix (D) cotton.

CONCISE RULES OF LAW: (1) Where there are genuine issues of fact as to whether a document of title has been duly negotiated and as to whether a secured party has acquiesced in the procurement of that document, those questions are for a trier of fact. (2) A secured party may not entrust goods that it does not own.

FACTS: Agricredit Acceptance Corp. (AAC) (P) financed Hendrix's (D) 1997 cotton crop with a loan properly perfected and secured by the crop. Sea Island Cotton Trading (Sea Island) was designated as the selling agent through which the crop would be sold. Hendrix's (D) crop was stored in various warehouses, which issued electronic warehouse receipts (EWRs) for the cotton in a central filing system. In 1997 and 1998, various cotton merchants (D) bought large quantitites of cotton from Sea Island, including many bales from Hendrix's (D) crop. The merchants paid Sea Island for these bales, and the EWRs representing the bales were transferred into the names of the merchants (D). However, Sea Island never paid either AAC (P) or Hendrix (D) as it was obligated to do. Consequently, AAC (P) filed suit against the merchants (D) and others to foreclose on its security interest in the Hendrix (D) cotton. The merchants (D) argued that because the EWRs were duly negotiated to them by Sea Island and because AAC (P) entrusted the cotton to Hendrix (D) with apparent authority to sell it, the cotton was no longer subject to AAC's (P) security interest. The merchants (D) moved for summary judgment.

ISSUES: (1) Where there are genuine issues of fact as to whether a document of title has been duly negotiated and as to whether a secured party has acquiesced in the procurement of that document, are those questions for a trier of fact? (2) May a secured party entrust goods that it does not own?

HOLDING AND DECISION: (Nangle, J.) Yes as to issue #1. No as to issue #2. (1) Under the U.C.C., in §9-309, the rights of a holder to whom a negotiable document of title has been duly negotiated take priority over an earlier, perfected, security interest. A warehouse receipt, such as the EWRs involved here, is a negotiable document of title. To be duly negotiated, a document of title must be negotiated to a holder who 1) purchases in good faith 2) without any notice of any defense against it or claim to it and 3) for value. One of defendants' theories on which they base summary judgment is that the EWRs were duly negotiated to the merchants (D), and, therefore, the merchants' (D) interest in the cotton has priority over AAC's (P) interest. Here, it is undisputed that they purchased the EWRs for value. Here, too, the merchants (D) purchased in good faith—with honesty in fact. AAC (P) is incorrect that good faith requires the merchants (D) to perform a lien check on the cotton prior to purchase. The last hurdle for the merchants (D) to prove the EWRs were duly negotiated is for them to prove that they were purchasers without notice of defenses or claims. AAC (P) argues that their experience with the cotton industry and its willful ignorance as to the existence of liens on the cotton constitutes "reason to know" of AAC's (P) defense to the EWRs. Here, there is a genuine issue of fact whether the merchants (D) had notice of AAC's (P) claims to the cotton. On the one hand, they do not perform lien searches on cotton brought from merchants or gins. On the other hand, when buying directly from the producer, or in a state with a central lien filing system, they do perform lien searches. This shows that they knew of the possibility of liens. However, whether failure to search for liens resulted from deliberate indifference or ignorance to their existence is an issue for a jury. Even if the court were to find that the merchants (D) had no notice of AAC's (P) claims, and that the EWRs had been duly negotiated, that determination alone would not automatically provide priority to the merchants' (D) rights over AAC's (P) secured interest. The Code in § 7-503 provides priority to the holder of a duly negotiated document of title as against a holder of a perfected security interest in the goods underlying that document of title only where the holder of the security interest has neither entrusted the goods to the bailor nor acquiesced in the procurement by the bailor of the document of title. Here, the merchants (D) argue that AAC (P) waived the priority of its security interest by entrusting the cotton to Hendrix (D). The Code does not define "acquiesce." Here, AAC (P) may have acquiesced in the procurement of the EWRs. When a bank knows that a farmer is trying to sell his collateral, and it acquiesces in his procurement of documents of title to that collateral, the bank has waived its security interest in that collateral. Here, the evidence is insufficient for the court to rule on this issue as a matter of law, and the question of AAC's (P) acquiescence is best left for a jury. (2) With regard to whether AAC (P) entrusted the cotton to Hendrix (D), "entrusted" is only

Continued on next page.

defined in Article 2 (not in Article 1 or 7) of the Code. The courts of this state have interpreted that definition to apply only to owners of goods, because one cannot entrust goods one does not own. As a matter of statutory construction, the court must use that definition here. Therefore, because AAC (P) was not the owner of the cotton, it could not, as a matter of law, have entrusted it to Hendrix (D).

EDITOR'S ANALYSIS: As the court observes, § 9-309 (which is now § 9-331), applies when the negotiable document holder and the secured party are both claiming an interest in the document of title (the EWR), whereas § 7-503 covers disputes between competing interests in the underlying goods. Here, the court read those two provisions together to arrive at its decision.

NOTES:

RHEINBERG KELLEREI GMBH v. BROOKSFIELD NATIONAL BANK OF COMMERCE
Winemaker (P) v. Bank (D)
901 F.2d 481 (5th Cir. 1990).

NATURE OF CASE: Appeal from denial of award of damages for negligence.

FACT SUMMARY: Brooksfield Bank (D), the collecting bank in an international transaction, failed to inform Rheinberg (P), vendor, of vendee J & J Wine's (D) failure to pay an invoice.

CONCISE RULE OF LAW: A collecting bank in an international transaction may be liable to the vendor for failing to notify it of the vendee's failure to pay an invoice.

FACTS: J & J Wine (D), an American wine importer, placed an order for wine from winemaker Rheinberg Kellerei GmbH (P), a German corporation. Payment was to be made through a letter of collection to be sent from a German bank to Brooksfield National Bank (D). Payment was to be due upon arrival of the wine in Houston. On March 27, 1986, the collection letter was forwarded to J & J (D). J & J (D) did not pay but asked for an extension. The wine arrived in port on March 31, and the Bank (D) was never informed of the arrival. J & J (D) never paid and eventually went out of business. The Bank (D) never informed Rheinberg (P) of J & J's (D) failure to pay. Meanwhile, the wine deteriorated to an undrinkable condition. Rheinberg (P) sued the Bank (D) for negligence. The district court entered judgment for the Bank (D) because it never had been informed of the event triggering the payment obligation, the wine's arrival. Rheinberg (P) appealed.

ISSUE: May a collecting bank in an international transaction be liable to the vendor for failing to notify it of the vendee's failure to pay an invoice?

HOLDING AND DECISION: (Garza, J.) Yes. A collecting bank in an international transaction may be liable to the vendor for failing to notify it of the vendee's failure to pay an invoice. Article 20 (iii)(cc) of the International Rules for collection provides that a collecting bank must send without delay advice on nonpayment or advice of nonacceptance to the bank from which a collecting order was received. The question to be answered in this case is "what constitutes nonpayment," a term not defined in the Rules. However, the U.C.C. contains analogous concepts. Under § 4-502, a collecting bank need not present collection documents prior to payment being due, but if it elects to do so, it must notify the sender of the documents. This court believes this to be a sensible rule, which it finds applicable to the situation in this case. Here, had the Bank (D) informed Rheinberg (P) or its agent of J & J's (D) nonpayment, the loss of the merchandise could have been avoided. It was the Bank (D) that caused the loss. Reversed.

EDITOR'S ANALYSIS: Section 4-502 gives collecting banks a good deal of discretion. When collecting documents require presentment "on arrival," and the arrival date is uncertain, the bank can assume arrival in a reasonable time frame, based on its knowledge and experience. In the present case, the Bank (D) did not exercise any such discretion.

NOTES:

CHAPTER 16
LETTER OF CREDIT

QUICK REFERENCE RULES OF LAW

1. **The Issuer's Duties and Rights.** (1) A notice of refusal of a letter of credit is deficient where by its own terms it does not plainly state that the issuer is actually rejecting the beneficiary's documents or refusing to honor the letter of credit. (2) Discrepancies between a letter of credit and presentation documents that are technical or typographical in nature do not warrant the rejection of the documents where the whole of the documents obviously relate to the transaction on their face. (Voest-Alpine Trading Co. v. Bank of China)

2. **The Issuer's Duties and Rights.** A court can enjoin payment of drafts under a letter of credit where the caller's fraud has been called to the issuing bank's attention before the drafts and documents have been presented for payment. (Sztejn v. J. Henry Schroder Bank Corp.)

3. **The Issuer's Duties and Rights.** An injunction against payment of an irrevocable letter of credit is properly entered where presentment would facilitate a material fraud by the beneficiary on the issuer or applicant and where comity militates in favor of such an injunction. (Intrinsic Values Corp. v. Superintendencia de Administracion Tributaria)

4. **The Issuer's Duties and Rights.** Equitable subrogation is available to both the issuer and applicant on a standby letter of credit. (Ochoco Lumber Co. v. Fibrex & Shipping Co., Inc.)

VOEST-ALPINE TRADING CO. v. BANK OF CHINA
Beneficiary of credit (P) v. Issuer (D)
167 F. Supp. 2d 940 (S.D. Tex. 2000).

NATURE OF CASE: Action for payment on letter of credit.

FACT SUMMARY: Bank of China (D) issued a letter of credit for the benefit of Voest-Alpine (P). On the basis of several discrepancies between the letter of credit and documents submitted by Voest-Alpine (P), the Bank of China (D) refused to honor the letter of credit. Voest-Alpine (P) claimed that Bank of China (D) had not provided adequate notice of refusal and that the discrepancies were technical and typographical in nature and did not warrant dishonor.

CONCISE RULES OF LAW: (1) A notice of refusal of a letter of credit is deficient where by its own terms it does not plainly state that the issuer is actually rejecting the beneficiary's documents or refusing to honor the letter of credit. (2) Discrepancies between a letter of credit and presentation documents that are technical or typographical in nature do not warrant the rejection of the documents where the whole of the documents obviously relate to the transaction on their face.

FACTS: Voest-Alpine Trading USA Corp. (Voest-Alpine) (P) entered into a contract with Jiangyin Foreign Trade Corp. (JFTC) to sell to JFTC styrene monomer for $1.2 million. JFTC applied for a letter of credit for the benefit of Voest-Alpine (P) from the Bank of China (D). The letter of credit provided for payment once the goods had arrived at Zhangjiagang, China, and Voest-Alpine (P) had presented the documents called for in the letter of credit. The letter of credit had numerous typographical errors in it, including that "Trading USA" in Voest-Alpine's (P) name was inverted and the destination port's name omitted the final "a." The letter of credit clearly stated that it was subject to the 1993 Uniform Customs and Practice, International Chamber of Commerce Publication Number 500 (UCP 500). The goods shipped on July 18, 1995, and on August 1, 1995, Voest-Alpine (P) presented the required documents to Texas Commerce Bank, the presenting bank, which found the discrepancies and alerted Voest-Alpine (P). Voest-Alpine (P) decided the discrepancies did not warrant refusal to pay, and the documents were sent on August 3, 1995, and received by Bank of China (D) on August 9, 1995. On August 11, 1995, Bank of China (D) sent a telex to Texas Commerce Bank that informed of seven discrepancies and that indicated that Bank of China (D) would contact the applicant about the discrepancies. On August 15, 1995, Texas Commerce Bank faxed Bank of China (D) indicating that the discrepancies were not an adequate basis to refuse to pay the letter of credit and requesting honor and payment. Finally, on August 19, 1995, Bank of China (D) sent a telex to Texas Commerce Bank indicating that the discrepancies "may have us refuse to take up the

documents..." Bank of China (D) returned the document and did not honor the letter of credit. Voest-Alpine (P) sued for payment.

ISSUES: (1) Is a notice of refusal of a letter of credit deficient where by its own terms it does not plainly state that the issuer is actually rejecting the beneficiary's documents or refusing to honor the letter of credit? (2) Do discrepancies between a letter of credit and presentation documents that are technical or typographical in nature warrant the rejection of the documents where the whole of the documents obviously relate to the transaction on their face?

HOLDING AND DECISION: (Gilmore, J.) Yes as to issue #1. No as to issue #2. (1) Bank of China (D) claims that under UCP 500, its August 11, 1995, telex to Texas Commerce Bank constituted notice of refusal. Voest-Alpine (P) argues that the telex did not constitute notice of refusal because there was no clear statement of refusal and because the statement in the telex that Bank of China (D) would contact the applicant led to ambiguity. Article 14(d) of the UCP 500 provides that if the issuer elects not to honor the presentation documents, it must provide a notice of refusal within seven banking days of receipt of the documents and must list all discrepancies, the disposition of the rejected documents, and, where it is rejecting the documents, "must give notice to that effect." Here, Bank of China's (D) notice was deficient because nowhere did it state that it was actually rejecting the documents or refusing to honor the letter of credit. Thus, by its own terms, it did not convey refusal. This omission is only compounded by the statement that Bank of China (D) would contact JFTC, because this additional piece of information held open the possibility of acceptance upon waiver of the discrepancies by JFTC. Although Bank of China's (D) August 19, 1995, telex used the word "refuse," this telex, even if it constituted a notice of refusal, came too late, as the expiration of the refusal period would have come on August 18, 1995. Therefore, Bank of China (D) failed to formally refuse the documents before the deadline and is precluded from claiming that the documents were not in compliance with the terms and conditions of the letter of credit. (2) Voest-Alpine (P) claims the discrepancies were technical and typographical in nature that do not warrant the rejection of the documents and urges that a "functional standard" of compliance be used to measure the discrepancies. Although there is a wide range of standards that are used to examine presentation documents for compliance—from strict compliance, to strict compliance where there is risk to the issuer, to strict compliance where there is risk to the applicant, to a mirror image approach—

Continued on next page.

the UCP 500 itself contains a moderate standard that requires "consistency" between the letter of credit and the documents. This standard requires that "the whole of the documents must obviously relate to the same transaction...on its face." This is a common-sense, case-by-case approach that permits minor typographical deviations because the standard is whether the documents bear a rational link to one another. Here, the discrepancies pointed to by Bank of China (D) do not warrant rejection of the documents. Six of the seven discrepancies are at issue. The first, the inversion of "Trading USA" in Voest-Alpine's (P) name, was not a complete misspelling or an omission, and did not signify a different corporate entity, and thus bore an obvious link to the documents. The second, the stamping of the set of originals of the bill of lading as "original," "duplicate," and "triplicate" instead of "original," also did not warrant rejection because it was clear from the face of these documents that they were all originals. Third, the failure to stamp the packing list documents as "original" was also insufficient to reject these documents because they, too, were clearly originals on their face. Fourth, the date of the survey report was after the bill of lading, but it was clear from the plain language of the report that the survey was conducted before the ship departed. Fifth, the letter of credit number had an extra numeral in it on the beneficiary's certified copy of fax. However, adding the letter of credit number to this document was gratuitous and the document checker could have looked to any other document to verify the letter of credit number or looked to the balance of the information in the document and found that, as a whole, it bore an obvious relationship to the transaction. Finally, the fact that the destination port was misspelled by omitting its last "a" also did not warrant rejection of the documents because it was an obvious misspelling (there are no ports in China with the misspelled name) and the other information contained in the document demonstrated linkage to the transaction on its face.

EDITOR'S ANALYSIS: The U.C.C.'s standard for examining presentation documents is strict compliance. This requires an issuer to honor a presentation that "appear on its face strictly to comply with the terms and conditions of the letter of credit." Thus, application of the U.C.C. standard in the instant case could have led to a different result.

NOTES:

SZTEJN v. J. HENRY SCHRODER BANK CORP.

Buyer (P) v. Bank (D)

N.Y. Sup. Ct., 177 Misc. 719, 31 N.Y.S.2d 631 (1941).

NATURE OF CASE: Action to have a letter of credit declared void and enjoin payment of drafts thereunder.

FACT SUMMARY: Sztejn (P) sought to restrain the payment of drafts under a letter of credit on the grounds that the party who was its beneficiary had procured bills of lading and invoices stating he had shipped the bristles Sztejn (P) had contracted to buy when, in fact, only garbage was in the crates.

CONCISE RULE OF LAW: A court can enjoin payment of drafts under a letter of credit where the caller's fraud has been called to the issuing bank's attention before the drafts and documents have been presented for payment.

FACTS: Sztejn (P) was to purchase a quantity of bristles from Transea (D). To pay for them, Sztejn (P) had Henry Schroder (D) issue an irrevocable letter of credit to Transea (D) that provided drafts by Transea (D) for a specified portion of the purchase price would be paid under the letter upon shipment of the merchandise and presentation of an invoice and bill of lading. Transea (D) filled crates with rubbish but procured bills of landing and invoices indicating bristles had been shipped. Transea (D) then presented the documents and drew drafts that were presented to and paid by Chartered Bank. Sztejn (P) sought to have the court declare the letter of credit and drafts null and void and to enjoin the payment or presentment for payment of the drafts. As the party who would be presenting the drafts for payment to Henry Schroder (D), Chartered Bank (D) moved to dismiss the complaint, alleging no cause of action existed because the only requirement was that the documents conform on their face to the requirements of the letter of credit.

ISSUE: If the seller's fraud has been called to the issuing bank's attention before there has been a presentment for payment, can payment of drafts under a letter of credit be enjoined?

HOLDING AND DECISION: (Shientag, J.) Yes. A court can enjoin payment of drafts under a letter of credit where the seller's fraud has been called to the issuing bank's attention before the drafts and documents have been presented for payment. Language to the effect that a letter of credit is independent of the primary contract between the buyer and seller has been used by the courts, but in cases concerning alleged breaches of warranty and not in those involving active fraud on the part of the seller. Motion to dismiss denied.

EDITOR'S ANALYSIS: Had Chartered Bank been deemed a holder in due course, its claim against the issuing bank would not have been defeated despite the seller's fraud. U.C.C. § 5-114(2) has codified the rule of this case by specifying that where there is "fraud in the transaction," the issuer must honor the draft or demand if honor is demanded by a holder in due course but that a court may enjoin honor by the issuer in all other cases.

QUICKNOTES

BILL OF LADING - A receipt or other documentation given to a shipper by a carrier evidencing the contract to transport such goods and that the shipper possessed title to the goods shipped.

FRAUD - A false representation of facts with the intent that another will rely on the misrepresentation to his detriment.

NOTES:

INTRINSIC VALUES CORP. v. SUPERINTENDENCIA DE ADMINISTRACION TRIBUTARIA

Beneficiary of credit (D) v. Applicant of credit (P)
Fla. Ct. App., 806 So. 2d 616 (2002).

NATURE OF CASE: Appeal from denial of motion to dissolve a temporary injunction to stop payment on irrevocable letters of credit.

FACT SUMMARY: Superintendencia De Administracion Tributaria (Superintendencia) (P), the tax administration agency of Guatemala, had irrevocable letters of credit issued by Banco de Guatemela for the benefit of Intrinsic Values Corp. (Intrinsic) (D). First Union National Bank and Barclays Bank, PLC, were the confirming banks. When Intrinsic (D) failed to perform on a contract with Superintendencia (P), Superintendencia (P) obtained an injunction in Guatemala that barred Banco de Guatemala from paying on the letters of credit and sought a similar injunction in Florida against payment by the confirming banks.

CONCISE RULE OF LAW: An injunction against payment of an irrevocable letter of credit is properly entered where presentment would facilitate a material fraud by the beneficiary on the issuer or applicant and where comity militates in favor of such an injunction.

FACTS: Superintendencia (P), the tax administration agency of Guatemala, entered into a contract with Intrinsic Values Corp. (Intrinsic) (D), a Panamanian corporation, for the purchase of various goods. Superintendencia (P) had irrevocable letters of credit issued by Banco de Guatemela for the benefit of Intrinsic, with First Union National Bank and Barclays Bank, PLC, as the confirming banks. When Intrinsic (D) failed to perform on the contract, Superintendencia (P) canceled the contract and obtained an injunction in Guatemala that barred Banco de Guatemala from paying on the letters of credit. Superintendencia (P) then brought an action in Florida to enjoin First Union and Barclays from honoring the letters of credit. The lower court granted a temporary injunction. When Intrinsic presented the letters of credit, it learned of the injunction, intervened, and moved to dissolve it. The lower court denied the motion.

ISSUE: Is an injunction against payment of an irrevocable letter of credit properly entered where presentment would facilitate a material fraud by the beneficiary on the issuer or applicant and where comity militates in favor of such an injunction?

HOLDING AND DECISION: (Shevin, J.) Yes. U.C.C. § 5-109 provides that where honor of a presentation of a letter of credit would facilitate a material fraud by the beneficiary on the issuer or applicant, a court of competent jurisdiction may temporarily or permanently enjoin the issuer from honoring the presentation. Here, Superintendencia (P) demonstrated that honoring a presentation would facilitate such a material fraud by Intrinsic (D), that based on the fact that Intrinsic (D) did not perform on the contract, the contract was canceled, and that Intrinsic (D) had notice of the cancellation. Superintendencia (P) also demonstrated, more likely than not, that it would succeed on a material fraud claim. Under these circumstances, Intrinsic (D) had no basis in fact for making a demand for payment, and permitting it to obtain payment of the money would be unjust. In addition, a foreign decree is entitled to comity where the proceeding that resulted in the decree meets due process and jurisdiction requirements. Here, the Guatemala court's proceedings met those requirements, so the Guatemala injunction is entitled to comity. As a result, the lower court properly enjoined payment by the confirming banks to render effective the Guatemala injunction. Affirmed.

EDITOR'S ANALYSIS: The purpose of the temporary injunction in the instant case was to preserve the status quo pending a final decree by the Guatemala court, presumably on breach of contract or other claims.

NOTES:

OCHOCO LUMBER CO. v. FIBREX & SHIPPING CO., INC.

Applicant on standby letter of credit (P) v. Borrower (D)

Or. App. Ct., 994 P.2d 793 (2000).

NATURE OF CASE: Appeal from dismissal of equitable subrogation claims.

FACT SUMMARY: Ochoco Lumber Co. (Ochoco) (P) was the applicant on a standby letter of credit that was made for the benefit of West One Idaho Bank (West One) and served as security for a loan from West One to Fibrex & Shipping Co., Inc. (Fibrex) (D). When Fibrex (D) defaulted on the loan and refused to reimburse Ochoco (P) on its payment of the standby letter of credit, Ochoco (P) claimed that it was equitably subrogated to West One's rights against Fibrex (D).

CONCISE RULE OF LAW: Equitable subrogation is available to both the issuer and applicant on a standby letter of credit.

FACTS: Fibrex & Shipping, Co., Inc. (Fibrex) (D) obtained a $3,900,000 loan from West One Idaho Bank (West One) for the purchase of timber. Fibrex's (D) sole shareholder and his wife personally guaranteed the loan. As further security, Fibrex (D) obtained a standby letter of credit that was applied for by Ochoco Lumber Co. (Ochoco) (P) and issued by First Interstate Bank (First Interstate). Ochoco (P) had agreed to purchase timber logs from Fibrex (D). When Fibrex defaulted on the loan, West One drew $2 million on the letter of credit from First Interstate. Ochoco (P) reimbursed First Interstate and demanded repayment from Fibrex (D). When Fibrex (D) refused, Ochoco notified West One that it was subrogated to West One's rights against Fibrex (D), but West One refused to acknowledge Ochoco's (P) equitable subrogation rights. The trial court ruled that neither an applicant nor the issuer on a standby letter of credit can be subrogated to the beneficiary's claims, and Ochoco (P) appealed.

ISSUE: Is equitable subrogation available to both the issuer and applicant on a standby letter of credit?

HOLDING AND DECISION: (Kistler, J.) Yes. The defendants argue that equitable subrogation is available only to persons who are secondarily liable for a debt, and that an issuer of a standby letter of credit is primarily liable on the debt. When the standby letter of credit was issued, the statutes that governed letters of credit did not address whether equitable subrogation was available on a standby letter of credit. The fact that a subsequent legislature amended the statute to provide for subrogation for standby letters of credit does not reflect a judgment as to the law that preceded the amendment. Therefore, the court must decide the issue under common-law principles. As a general rule, courts have required that the party seeking subrogation must have paid a debt for which it was secondarily liable. The majority of courts to address this issue have held that although the issuer's obligation on a standby letter of credit is secondary in the sense that it does not arise until the applicant has defaulted, the issuer is not comparable to a guarantor. The minority position is that the issuer is akin to a surety, and that once the issuer has honored the letter of credit, denying subrogation is an insistence on pointless formalism (i.e., the difference between letters of credits and suretyships and guarantees pursuant to the independence principle). The minority view is more persuasive. Here, that view recognizes that First Interstate was a de facto surety for Fibrex's (D) obligations and is consistent with the view that the standby letter of credit issuer's obligation only arises upon default. More importantly, it is consistent with the equitable recognition that having paid the beneficiary, the issuer (or the applicant if it has reimbursed the issuer) should be able to step into the beneficiary's shoes and assert its rights. Reversed and remanded.

EDITOR'S ANALYSIS: The independence principle discussed by the court states that a letter of credit imposes an independent obligation on the issuer to pay. The majority view, based on this principle, is that the issuer is satisfying its own absolute and primary obligation to pay rather than satisfying a secondary obligation, and, therefore, the issuer is primarily liable. In the minority view, once the issuer has honored the letter of credit, the purpose of the independence principle—to ensure prompt payment on the credit—is satisfied and should not be a reason to deny equitable subrogation.

NOTES:

17

CHAPTER 17
INTRODUCTION TO SECURED TRANSACTIONS

QUICK REFERENCE RULES OF LAW

1. **Pre-Code Security Devices.** When a bankrupt gives a lien on accounts to a creditor but retains all indicia of ownership thereof, the lien is voidable in bankruptcy. (Benedict v. Ratner)

BENEDICT v. RATNER

Bankruptcy trustee (P) v. Lender (D)

268 U.S. 353 (1925).

NATURE OF CASE: Appeal from denial of order invalidating a lien.

FACT SUMMARY: Benedict (P), trustee of bankrupt Hub Carpet, sought to invalidate a lien on accounts given by the bankrupt to Ratner (D) wherein all indicia of title to the accounts was retained by the bankrupt.

CONCISE RULE OF LAW: When a bankrupt gives a lien on accounts to a creditor but retains all indicia of ownership thereof, the lien is voidable in bankruptcy.

FACTS: Hub Carpet received certain loan moneys from Ratner (D). In return, Ratner (D) received a lien on all past and future accounts receivable. Unless the lien was foreclosed upon, all indicia of ownership in the accounts was retained by Hub. No recordation of the lien of any sort was made. Hub soon thereafter filed for bankruptcy. Benedict (P), the bankruptcy trustee, filed an action to void the lien as a preferential transfer. The district court upheld the validity of the lien, and the court of appeals affirmed. The Supreme Court granted review.

ISSUE: When a bankrupt gives a lien on accounts to a creditor but retains all indicia of ownership thereof, is the lien voidable in bankruptcy?

HOLDING AND DECISION: (Brandeis, J.) Yes. When a bankrupt gives a lien on accounts to a creditor but retains all indicia of ownership thereof, the lien is voidable in bankruptcy. The Bankruptcy Code allows a trustee to void prefiling fraudulent transfers. What constitutes such a transfer is determined by state law. Here, state law declares as fraudulent a lien on or other security interest in property which is unrecorded, the transferor retaining apparent possession. Ratner (D) contended that this rule should not require delivery, as does transfer of a chattel. However, it is not delivery that matters but rather dominion. When a transferor retains the indicia of dominion over any kind of property, a secret transfer of title can work a fraud on the transferor's future creditors and is, therefore, a fraudulent transfer. Such was the case here. Reversed.

EDITOR'S ANALYSIS: The Bankruptcy Code has long allowed a trustee to void prefiling transfers of interest. These are called "preferential transfers." The fear here is that a soon-to-be bankrupt may attempt to favor certain creditors over others by releasing property prior to filing. Code policy favors equal treatment of creditors, so such transfers are voidable.

NOTES:

18

CHAPTER 18
THE SCOPE OF ARTICLE 9

QUICK REFERENCE RULES OF LAW

1. **Consignments.** A consignor of goods to a bankrupt may be unable to reclaim them upon the consignee's bankruptcy. (In re Fabers, Inc.)

2. **Leases.** A lease agreement is intended as a security agreement where it gives the lessee an option to become the owner of the property for nominal consideration upon completion of the lease term and is intended as a true lease where the consideration is nominal. (In re Architectural Millwork of Virginia, Inc.)

3. **Exclusions from Article 9: Federal Statutes.** One who purchases an airplane but does not record the sale with the FAA will have inferior title to a subsequent purchaser. (Philko Aviation, Inc. v. Shacket)

IN RE FABERS, INC.
Carpet dealer (P) v. Carpet retailer (D)
Bankr. Div., 12 U.C.C. Rep. Serv. 126 (D. Conn. 1972).

NATURE OF CASE: Petition to reclaim goods from a bankrupt estate.

FACT SUMMARY: Mehdi Dilmaghani & Co. (P) delivered certain carpets to be sold on consignment by Fabers, Inc. (D), which subsequently declared bankruptcy.

CONCISE RULE OF LAW: A consignor of goods to a bankrupt may be unable to reclaim them upon the consignee's bankruptcy.

FACTS: Mehdi Dilmaghani & Co. (P) a dealer in Oriental carpets, delivered certain carpets to Fabers, Inc. (D), a carpet retailer in Connecticut. The agreement provided that the carpets remained the property of Mehdi (P) until sale, and that the funds received from any sale remained the property of Mehdi (P). It was essentially a consignment. While the carpets were in Fabers' (D) possession, Fabers (D) filed for bankruptcy. Mehdi (P) then petitioned to reclaim the goods from the bankrupt estate.

ISSUE: May a consignor of goods to a bankrupt be unable to reclaim them upon the consignor's bankruptcy?

HOLDING AND DECISION: (Bankruptcy Referee Seidman) Yes. A consignor of goods to a bankrupt may be unable to reclaim them upon the consignee's bankruptcy. Under U.C.C. § 2-326, adopted in Connecticut, goods delivered for resale are subject to the claims of the possessors creditors unless (1) the seller is generally known by his creditors to sell goods on consignment, or (2) the deliverer of the goods (the consignor) complies with Article 9 filing provisors. Here, Mehdi (P) admittedly did not file any type of Article 9 financing statement. In addition, there is no evidence that Fabers (D) was known by its creditors to sell goods on consignment. Therefore, the carpets were subject to the claims of Fabers' (D) creditors, and therefore beyond the reach of Mehdi (P) to reclaim them. Motion denied.

EDITOR'S ANALYSIS: U.C.C. § 2-326 exists to prevent fraud from being perpetrated upon a consignee's creditors. If goods are in a consignee's possession, the consignee's creditors are entitled to believe that any monies loaned or advanced may be secured by the consignee's inventory. Section 2-326 prevents a secret consignment agreement from defeating this reasonable expectation.

NOTES:

IN RE ARCHITECTURAL MILLWORK OF VIRGINIA, INC.
Creditor (P) v. Debtor (D)
U.S. Bankr. Ct., 226 B.R. 551, 39 U.C.C. Rep. Serv. 2d 36 (W.D. Va. 1998).

NATURE OF CASE: Motion in bankruptcy proceeding to compel assumption or rejection of leases.

FACT SUMMARY: Associates Leasing, Inc. (Associates) (P) moved in bankruptcy proceedings to compel assumption or rejection of leases by Architectural Millwork of Virginia, Inc. (debtor) (D), for agreements involving a Freightliner truck and a Komatsu forklift.

CONCISE RULE OF LAW: A lease agreement is intended as a security agreement where it gives the lessee an option to become the owner of the property for nominal consideration upon completion of the lease term and is intended as a true lease where the consideration is not nominal.

FACTS: Before filing for bankruptcy, Architectural Millwork of Virginia, Inc. (debtor) (D) entered into an agreement with Associates Leasing, Inc. (Associates) (P) for lease of a Freightliner truck (Freightliner agreement). That agreement provided for a final adjustment clause that required the sale of the truck at the end of the lease. The agreement set a residual value of $9,625, and provided that upon sale, any proceeds over the residual value would be credited to the debtor (D), and proceeds less than the residual value would be made up by the debtor (D). The debtor (D) also entered into an agreement regarding a Komatsu forklift (Komatsu agreement) that provided an option to purchase the forklift for one dollar after all scheduled payments were made. The debtor (D) selected the goods without input from Associates (P), and Associates (P) never inspected the goods before or after the agreements.

ISSUE: Is a lease agreement intended as a security agreement where it gives the lessee an option to become the owner of the property for nominal consideration upon completion of the lease term and as a true lease where the consideration is not nominal?

HOLDING AND DECISION: (Anderson, J.) Yes. U.C.C. § 1-207 (37) provides that a security interest is created where the lease provides that upon compliance with the terms of the lease the lessee shall become, or has the option of becoming, the owner of the property for no additional consideration or nominal consideration. Here, the Komatsu agreement falls within the plain language of this section because it provided an option to purchase the forklift for one dollar after all scheduled payments were made. Consequently, that agreement should be characterized as a security agreement. The Freightliner agreement is less clear. Here, the final adjustment clause in that agreement was simply an option for the debtor (D) to purchase the truck at the end of the lease at the price set by the residual value. Again, under the U.C.C., if the debtor (D) could not avoid

paying Associates (P) the value of the payments due under the lease and could become the owner of the truck for nominal or no consideration upon compliance with the lease terms, then the agreement created a security interest. The first of these two conditions is met here—debtor (D) was obligated to pay the full value of the consideration due under the lease, whether at the natural end of the lease or upon earlier termination. As to the second condition, although an option was created to purchase the truck for the residual value ($9,625), this purchase would not be for no consideration or for nominal value—given that the capitalized cost of the truck was $38,500, $9,625 is not nominal. Thus, the transaction fails as one for a security interest. However, that does not necessarily make it a true lease. Looking at other considerations under the Code, such as the debtor's (D) responsibility for taxes, maintenance, fees, or insurance, the court finds that these factors are just as applicable to true leases as they are to security interests. Of greatest importance to the court is whether the vehicle can be purchased for nominal value and whether the lessee will build up any equity in the property. Here, because the option to buy the truck was not for nominal value, and because the parties did not expect the debtor to accrue equity, the Freightliner agreement was a true lease.

EDITOR'S ANALYSIS: As this case demonstrates, determining whether an agreement is a true lease or a security interest is a case-by-case undertaking, with some bright lines for guidance but with a greater emphasis on careful analysis and weighing of all the facts.

NOTES:

PHILKO AVIATION, INC. v. SHACKET
Airplane manufacturer (D) v. Buyer (P)
462 U.S. 406 (1983).

NATURE OF CASE: Review of declaratory relief action adjudicating rights to chattel.

FACT SUMMARY: The Shackets (P), who had purchased an airplane but not recorded the transaction with the FAA, contended that a subsequent sale by their vendor to a third party was void.

CONCISE RULE OF LAW: One who purchases an airplane but does not record the sale with the FAA will have inferior title to a subsequent purchaser.

FACTS: The Shackets (P) purchased an airplane from Smith. On Smith's assurances that he would handle the paperwork, the Shackets (P) did not record their purchase with the FAA. Smith subsequently entered a fraudulent transaction wherein he sold the aircraft to Philko Aviation (D). When the Shackets (P) became aware of Philko's (D) claim on the aircraft, they filed a declaratory relief action, seeking title to the plane. The district court and court of appeals held the plane to belong to the Shackets (P), and the Supreme Court granted review.

ISSUE: Will one who purchases an airplane but does not record the sale with the FAA have inferior title to a subsequent purchaser?

HOLDING AND DECISION: (White, J.) Yes. One who purchases an airplane but does not record the sale with the FAA will have inferior title to a subsequent purchaser. Under 49 U.S.C. § 1403(C), all transfers of aircraft must be registered with the FAA to have priority over subsequent purchasers for value. It is clear, both from the language of the section and from attendant legislative history, that Congress intended that the FAA serve as a central clearing-house for all transactions involving transfers of aircraft and all state regulations to the contrary in this field be preempted. Here, the Shackets (P) did not record their transaction with the FAA. Philko (D), as a subsequent purchaser, therefore had higher title to the aircraft than did the Shackets (P). It, therefore, gained title to the aircraft. Reversed.

CONCURRENCE: (O'Connor, J.) It should be emphasized that a diligent effort to record will be of no use; only actual recordation makes any difference.

EDITOR'S ANALYSIS: As is often the case, § 1403(C) exists to resolve the unhappy situation where both claimants are blameless. Just as with Article 9 of the U.C.C., many situations implicating § 1403(C) will involve wrongdoers long gone. Here, neither the Shackets (P) nor Philko (D) were blameworthy, but someone had to prevail. Section 1403(C) provided a means for resolving such situations.

QUICKNOTES

DECLARATORY JUDGMENT - An adjudication by the courts which grants not relief but is binding over the legal status of the parties involved in the dispute.

RECORDATION - The recording of a document in the public record.

NOTES:

19

CHAPTER 19
THE CREATION OF A SECURITY INTEREST

QUICK REFERENCE RULES OF LAW

1. **Classifying the Collateral.** Under U.C.C. § 9-109, a court should restrict its determination to the buyer's intended use of the collateral at the time of purchase as opposed to the actual use of the collateral after purchase. (In re Morton)

2. **Classifying the Collateral.** Goods in a business are equipment when they are fixed assets or have, as identifiable units, a relatively long period of use. (Morgan County Feeders, Inc. v. McCormick)

3. **Attachment of the Security Interest.** A security interest in after-acquired goods attaches upon the debtor's receipt of autos for resale, even if the vendor has not yet received payment. (Thrift, Inc. v. A.D.E., Inc.)

4. **Attachment of the Security Interest.** A party having a security interest in accounts receivable may not be able to claim an item therein when it is incorrectly entered as such an account. (In re Howell Enterprises, Inc.)

IN RE MORTON
Truck purchaser (D) v. Bank (P)
Bankr. Div., 9 U.C.C. Rep. Serv. 1147 (D. Me. 1971).

NATURE OF CASE: Application by trustee in bankruptcy to invalidate a purchase money security interest.

FACT SUMMARY: The trustee in bankruptcy for Morton (D) asked the court to determine if the purchase money security interest of Maine National Bank (P) was perfected or unperfected.

CONCISE RULE OF LAW: Under U.C.C. § 9-109, a court should restrict its determination to the buyer's intended use of the collateral at the time of purchase as opposed to the actual use of the collateral after purchase.

FACTS: Morton (D) purchased a truck subject to a purchase money security interest held by Maine National Bank (P). He bought the vehicle primarily for personal purposes but after several months began using it for employment purposes. When Morton (D) declared bankruptcy, the Bank's (P) security interest attached by way of a valid security agreement between the seller of the truck and Morton (D). When the security agreement was filed, the seller filed a financing agreement with the town clerk, as required. The trustee in bankruptcy attacked the security interest, contending that because the vehicle was actually used primarily for employment purposes, a second financing statement had to be filed with the secretary of state for the security interest to be perfected.

ISSUE: Under U.C.C. § 9-109, should a court restrict its determination to the buyer's intended use of the collateral at the time of purchase as opposed to the actual use of the collateral after purchase?

HOLDING AND DECISION: (Cyr, Ref. Bankr.) Yes. Under U.C.C. § 9-109 a court should look to the buyer's intended use of the collateral at the time of purchase. To do otherwise would require constant surveillance of collateral after the security interest attaches. The filing of the one financing statement perfected the Bank's (P) purchase money security interest if the collateral constituted consumer goods. However, if the vehicle was neither used nor bought for personal use, a second statement would be required for a perfected interest. Morton (D) intended to use the car for personal use when he purchased it; only later did he use it for work. Accordingly, the purchase money security interest of the Bank (P) was perfected. Application dismissed with prejudice.

EDITOR'S ANALYSIS: How collateral is classified will determine how it will be treated under Article 9 of the U.C.C. To perfect a security interest in a negotiable instrument, a car, or store inventory, each requires completely different steps. It is specifically the debtor's intended use of the collateral that determines how it will be classified.

NOTES:

MORGAN COUNTY FEEDERS, INC. v. McCORMICK
Creditor (P) v. Cattle seller (D)
Colo. Ct. App., 836 P.2d 1051 (1992).

NATURE OF CASE: Appeal from a judgment in an action to determine the classification of collateral.

FACT SUMMARY: After Allen sold some cattle to McCormick (D), but before McCormick (D) took delivery, Morgan County Feeders, Inc. (P), holder of a perfected security interest in the cattle, seized them, alleging that they were equipment and thus were subject to Morgan's (P) security interest.

CONCISE RULE OF LAW: Goods in a business are equipment when they are fixed assets or have, as identifiable units, a relatively long period of use.

FACTS: Allen owned longhorn cattle, which he had acquired to use principally for recreational cattle drives on his recreational business. He entered into an agreement to sell fifty-six head of cattle to McCormick (D). Morgan County Feeders, Inc. (P), holder of a perfected security interest in the cattle, seized them before they were delivered to McCormick (D). In the ensuing trial, the trial court concluded that the cattle purchased by Allen were equipment, rather than inventory, and thus were subject to Morgan County Feeders' (P) security interest. McCormick (D) appealed.

ISSUE: Are goods in a business equipment when they are fixed assets or have, as identifiable units, a relatively long period of use?

HOLDING AND DECISION: (Rothenberg, J.) Yes. Goods in a business are equipment when they are fixed assets or have, as identifiable units, a relatively long period of use. Under the Uniform Commercial Code, "goods" are classified as consumer goods, equipment, farm products, and inventory. The parties agree that the cattle constitute "goods" under the U.C.C. They further agree that the cattle are not "farm products." The remaining issue is whether they are inventory or equipment. Goods are inventory, even though not held for sale, if they are used up or consumed in a short period of time in the production of some end product. Allen did not acquire the cattle for the principal purpose of immediate or ultimate sale or lease but to use for recreational cattle drives. Thus, the trial court was justified in finding that, under these circumstances, the cattle should be classified as "equipment." Affirmed.

EDITOR'S ANALYSIS: The distinction between inventory and equipment is important because buyers of inventory in the ordinary course of business take free of perfected security interests. Under the U.C.C., "goods" are defined as "all things which are movable at the time the security interest attaches." The four major types of goods classifications noted by the court are mutually exclusive.

QUICKNOTES

SECURITY INTEREST - An interest in property that may be sold upon a default in payment of the debt.

NOTES:

THRIFT, INC. v. A.D.E., INC.
Lender (P) v. Car dealer (D)
Ind. Ct. App., 454 N.E.2d 878 (1983).

NATURE OF CASE: Appeal from denial of order of transfer of title and award of recovery on counterclaim for replevin.

FACT SUMMARY: Thrift (P), having a perfected security interest in a dealer's after-acquired inventory, contended that the interest had attached to three vehicles that had been delivered to the dealer without payment to the original seller, A.D.E., Inc. (D).

CONCISE RULE OF LAW: A security interest in after-acquired goods attaches upon the debtor's receipt of autos for resale, even if the vendor has not yet received payment.

FACTS: Thrift, Inc. (P) had made certain loans to Devers, an auto dealer. Securing the loans was a lien on Devers' after-acquired inventory. At one point A.D.E., Inc. (D) agreed to sell three autos to Devers. The autos were given to Devers and taken to his lot, but payment and title transfer were delayed. Thrift (P) then advanced further monies, taking a perfected security interest in the autos. Devers' check to A.D.E. (D) as payment for the cars was dishonored. Thrift (P) obtained possession of the autos upon Devers' default. Thrift (P) sued A.D.E. (D) to obtain title; A.D.E. (D) counterclaimed for replevin. The trial court granted judgment for A.D.E. (D), and Thrift (P) appealed.

ISSUE: Does a security interest in after-acquired goods attach upon the debtor's receipt of autos for resale, even if the vendor has not yet received payment?

HOLDING AND DECISION: (Robertson, J.) Yes. A security interest in after-acquired goods attaches upon the debtor's receipt of autos for resale, even if the vendor has not yet received payment. Section 9-204 of the U.C.C. provides that Article 9 does not apply to autos which are not inventory. However, § 9-109 (i) defines "inventory," and the autos in this case without doubt fell into this definition. A.D.E. (D) argued that Devers merely had possession of the autos, and because he did not have title thereto, he had no right to encumber them. However, § 2-401 (i) of the U.C.C. states that when property is delivered to a buyer, the only interest that can be retained is that of a security nature. Here, A.D.E. (D) delivered the autos but purported to retain title. This it could not do as against a creditor of Devers. For this reason, Thrift's (P) security interest prevailed. Reversed.

EDITOR'S ANALYSIS: One of the prevailing themes of the U.C.C. is openness about interests in goods. Secret liens and other interests which can work frauds upon creditors are disfavored. The Code's provisions usually work in such a manner that a disclosed interest will be superior to a secret lien or interest.

IN RE HOWELL ENTERPRISES, INC.

Parties not identified.

934 F.2d 969 (8th Cir. 1991).

NATURE OF CASE: Appeal from bankruptcy court order establishing priority to an item in a bankrupt estate.

FACT SUMMARY: After Howell Enterprises, Inc. mistakenly listed a letter of credit as an account receivable, a lender having a security interest in such accounts sought to claim it.

CONCISE RULE OF LAW: A party having a security interest in accounts receivable may not be able to claim an item therein when it is incorrectly entered as such an account.

FACTS: Tradax, Inc. and Howell Enterprises devised a plan wherein Tradax would sell rice it milled to a third party in Howell's name. The buyer purchased through a letter of credit made out to Howell but intended to be passed on to Tradax. Through sloppy bookkeeping, the letter of credit was listed on Howell's books as an account receivable. Howell filed for bankruptcy before the letter of credit matured. First National Bank, which had a perfected security interest in Howell's accounts receivable, claimed the right to the letter's proceeds. Tradax made a similar claim. The bankruptcy court held the Bank to have priority, and Tradax appealed.

ISSUE: May a party having a security interest in accounts receivable be able to claim an item therein when it is incorrectly entered as such an account?

HOLDING AND DECISION: (Rosenbaum, J.) No. A party having a security interest in accounts receivable may not be able to claim an item therein when it is incorrectly entered as such an account. A security interest cannot attach unless the debtor giving the interest has rights in the collateral. When the debtor has no such rights, no security interest attaches. When a debtor incorrectly enters an item as an account receivable when in fact it has no interest in such an item, a party having a security interest in such accounts obtains no rights to this item, as the interest never attached. Here, Howell never had any rights in the letter of credit, so no security interest favoring the Bank ever attached to it. Reversed.

EDITOR'S ANALYSIS: A letter of credit is a form of commercial paper that can facilitate a transaction. When a seller is hesitant to extend credit to a buyer, a third party (usually a bank) may guarantee payment through a letter of credit, in which the bank promises to back up the buyer. The bank profits by charging a fee.

NOTES:

20

CHAPTER 20
PERFECTION OF THE SECURITY INTEREST

QUICK REFERENCE RULES OF LAW

1. **Purchase Money Security Interest in Consumer Goods.** A purchase money security interest retains its character when the debt is consolidated with other obligations and thus is not subject to avoidance under Bankruptcy Code § 522(f). (In re Short)

2. **Purchase Money Security Interest in Consumer Goods.** A purchase money security interest may be obtained under UCC § 9-107 even where the debtor first obtains the property and is later reimbursed by the purported purchase money security interest creditor. (General Electric Capital Commercial Automobile Finance, Inc. v. Spartan Motors, Ltd.)

3. **Certain Accounts and Other Intangibles.** That a person is a sophisticated lender does not impact his ability to claim a security interest in accounts receivable. (In re Wood)

IN RE SHORT
Bankrupt householder (P) v. Finance company (D)
U.S. Bankr. Ct., 170 B.R. 128 Bankr., 24 U.C.C. Rep. Serv. 2d 1020
(S.D. Ill. 1994)

NATURE OF CASE: Motion to avoid a lien on household goods in a bankruptcy proceeding.

FACT SUMMARY: Creditor American General Finance (D) argued that its purchase money lien survived after being consolidated with another obligation by debtor Short (P).

CONCISE RULE OF LAW: A purchase money security interest retains its character when the debt is consolidated with other obligations and thus is not subject to avoidance under Bankruptcy Code § 522(f).

FACTS: Short (P) entered into a retail installment contract to buy bedroom furniture. The entire balance was due in one year. The contract to pay the debt, which granted a security interest in the furniture, was assigned to American General Finance (D) on the date of signing. One year later, Short (P) executed a note with American (D) which consolidated the furniture debt with other debts. The note allowed monthly payments, and it listed the collateral as a continued purchase money interest in the bedroom furniture as well as some other household items owned by Short (P). There was no indication that American (D) had a purchase money security interest in these other items. Short (P) then filed bankruptcy and moved to avoid American's (D) lien on all the furniture, contending that the refinancing destroyed the purchase money character of the lien and therefore the lien should be exempt from creditor process pursuant to Bankruptcy Code § 522(f).

ISSUE: Does a purchase money security interest retain its character when the debt is consolidated with other obligations, thereby escaping unavoidability under Bankruptcy Code § 522(f)?

HOLDING AND DECISION: (Meyers, Bankr. J.) Yes. A purchase money security interest retains its character when the debt is consolidated with other obligations and thus is not subject to avoidance under Bankruptcy Code § 522(f). Section 522 (f) allows a debtor to avoid the fixing of a lien on property that would otherwise be exempt if such a lien is a nonpossessory, nonpurchase money security interest. The various circuits have split on whether a purchase money security interest is extinguished when the loan is refinanced through consolidation with other debt. The best approach seems to be the "dual status" approach. In other words, if collateral secures both a purchase money security interest and nonpurchase money security interest, so long as the interests can be separated, a consolidation should not destroy the initial character of the interests. In this case, the consolidated loan was in part a purchase money security interest and in part a nonpurchase

money security interest. Therefore, American's (D) lien remains on the bedroom furniture to the extent that purchase money debt remains, but the motion to avoid is granted for the nonpurchase money lien.

EDITOR'S ANALYSIS: The theory behind automatic perfection of liens on consumer goods is that it is unlikely that the goods will be used to secure other debts. Furthermore, since filing costs money, many consumer purchases would be too small to make filing by the seller financially viable. Under U.C.C. § 9-301 (1)(d), the merchant who sells consumer goods by extending credit holds a superior interest in the collateral as compared to other creditors, without the need to file a financing statement.

NOTES:

132

GENERAL ELECTRIC CAPITAL COMMERCIAL AUTOMOTIVE FINANCE, INC. v. SPARTAN MOTORS, LTD.

Secured creditor (P) v. Debtor (D)

N.Y. Sup. Ct. App. Div., 246 App. Div. 2d 41 (1998).

NATURE OF CASE: Suit to enforce security interest in collateral.

FACT SUMMARY: GECC (P) sought to enforce its security interest in Spartan's (D) collateral against GMAC and others.

CONCISE RULE OF LAW: A purchase money security interest may be obtained under UCC § 9-107 even where the debtor first obtains the property and is later reimbursed by the purported purchase money security interest creditor.

FACTS: A predecessor of GECC (P) entered into an "Inventory Security Agreement" with Spartan (D) in connection with its floor plan financing of the dealership's inventory. By assignment of the agreement, GECC (P) obtained a blanket or "dragnet" lien on Spartan's inventory to secure a debt in excess of $1 million. The security agreement was filed with the county clerk and Secretary of State. Spartan (D) subsequently signed a new wholesale security agreement with GMAC in which GMAC agreed to finance Spartan's (D) inventory, which was duly filed. GMAC notified GECC (P) of its competing security interest. GECC (P) commenced suit against Spartan (D) seeking $1,180,999.98, representing money then due to GECC (P) under its agreement with Spartan (D). Spartan (D) subsequently filed a bankruptcy petition and ceased doing business. GECC (P), GMAC and MBNA took possession of and liquidated their respective collateral. GECC (P) settled all of its claims against all the defendants except GMAC, which it accused of converting two Mercedes Benz vehicles in violation of its security interest. The court granted GECC's (P) motion for summary judgment. GMAC appealed.

ISSUE: May a purchase money security interest be obtained under UCC § 9-107 even where the debtor first obtains the property and is later reimbursed by the purported purchase money security interest creditor?

HOLDING AND DECISION: (Friedmann, J.) Yes. A purchase money security interest may be obtained under UCC § 9-107 even where the debtor first obtains the property and is later reimbursed by the purported purchase money security interest creditor. A perfected purchase money security interest is an exception to the general first-in-time, first-in-right rule of competing security interests and has priority over a prior security interest in the same property. The purchase money security interest must meet the UCC's definition found in § 9-107 of a security interest: "(a) taken or retained by the seller of the collateral to secure all or part of its price; or (b) taken by a person who by making advances or incurring an obligation gives value to enable the debtor to acquire rights in or the use of such collateral if such value is in fact so used." The issue here is whether GMAC's payment to Spartan as reimbursement after it had acquired two Mercedes Benz automobiles constituted an "advance" or "obligation" granting GMAC a purchase money security interest in the cars. There are two arguments against such a finding: (1) courts have been reluctant to find a purchase money security interest where, as in this case, title to and possession of the merchandise has already passed to the debtor before the loan was advanced; and (2) the express wording of the agreement between GMAC and Spartan (D) seems to accord GMAC purchase money secured status only if GMAC pays the manufacturer, distributor or other seller directly. Prior to the enactment of the UCC, the sequence of such transfers was dispositive. The UCC § 9-107 was intended to liberalize the rigid transactional rules. The courts have since considered temporal proximity between the debtor's acquisition of the property and value given as one factor to be considered in the determination. The critical inquiry, however, is the intent of the parties, as evidenced by the language of the agreement and the attendant circumstances. Here GMAC's reimbursements to Spartan (D) were made six and two days after the respective purchases, and such post-purchase reimbursement was common both in the trade and in Spartan's (D) dealings with its financers. With respect to the express language of the agreement between GMAC and Spartan (D), the express terms of an agreement and a different course of performance should be construed as consistent whenever reasonable. When such construction is unreasonable, the express terms of the agreement control. Moreover, a written contract may be modified by the parties' post-agreement course of performance. Here there was no dispute that it was the custom in the trade and in Spartan's (D) dealings with its financers to reimburse the debtor following delivery of the merchandise and title. The supreme court erred when it found that GMAC did not acquire a purchase money security interest in the vehicles under § 9-107. GMAC is entitled to retain the proceeds of the sale and to summary judgment. Reversed.

EDITOR'S ANALYSIS: Courts have also considered passage of title to be an important factor in determining whether a purchase money security interest exists. The court rejects this rule on the basis that there are many circumstances in which passing of title would be irrelevant to the intentions of the parties.

IN RE WOOD
Lending attorney (P) v. Borrowing attorney (D)
67 Bankr. 321, 2 U.C.C. Rep. Serv. 2d 1098 (W.D.N.Y. 1986).

NATURE OF CASE: Appeal from order holding security interest invalid.

FACT SUMMARY: Larkin (P), who had loaned money to Wood (D) and taken a security interest in certain accounts receivable but had filed no financing statement, was denied secured-creditor status on account of his alleged status as a sophisticated lender.

CONCISE RULE OF LAW: That a person is a sophisticated lender does not impact his ability to claim a security interest in accounts receivable.

FACTS: Larkin (P), an attorney, loaned Wood (D), another attorney, $10,000. Larkin (P) later took as security a lien on Wood's (D) contingency interest in two cases Wood (D) was handling. Larkin (P) had otherwise no experience in using accounts receivable as security interests. Wood (D) later filed for bankruptcy. Larkin (P) brought an action seeking to enforce his security interest. The bankruptcy court held the lien invalid, and Larkin (P) appealed.

ISSUE: Will the fact that a person is a sophisticated lender impact his ability to claim a security interest in accounts receivable?

HOLDING AND DECISION: (Telesca, J.) No. That a person is a sophisticated lender does not impact his ability to claim a security interest in accounts receivable. U.C.C. § 9-302, exempts from the general requirement of the filing of financing statements to perfect security interests in accounts receivable those situations where the assignment of such accounts do not constitute a significant part of the accounts of the assignor. This is meant to cover isolated or casual assignments, where neither party may be aware of or have reason to suspect the applicability of Article 9. The tests which have been developed in this area look to the percentage of the assignor's accounts that are given for security and the regularity, or lack thereof, of such assignments. Here, the Bankruptcy Court found, quite properly, that the assignment fell within § 302's exemption. However, the court concluded that, because Larkin (P) was an attorney and therefore a sophisticated lender, he was not entitled to invoke the exception. This was incorrect; as the section makes no reference to lender sophistication, this should not be considered in assessing the section's applicability. Reversed.

EDITOR'S ANALYSIS: The test announced here is subjective in nature. The factors are whether a "significant part" of the assignor's accounts are secured, or whether the transaction is "casual or isolated." It is foreseeable that one situation can exist without the other. The courts are split on which is the more determinative criterion.

NOTES:

CHAPTER 22*
PRIORITY

QUICK REFERENCE RULES OF LAW

1. **Simple Disputes.** To be enforceable, a dragnet provision in a consumer loan must meet a strict "same class" test for subsequent loans and must specifically reference antecedent loans. (In re Wollin)

2. **Purchase Money Security Interests: The Basic Rule.** A seller who mistakenly delivers a product to a buyer prior to payment and does not file a financing statement may lose priority to a subsequent creditor who takes a security interest. (Galleon Industries, Inc. v. Lewyn Machinery Co.)

3. **Inventory and Livestock.** A purchase money security interest (PMSI) has superiority over an earlier perfected interest where: (a) the PMSI is perfected at the time the debtor receives possession of the inventory; (b) the PMSI creditor gives written notification to all holders of competing interests that had U.C.C.-1 financing statements on file when the PMSI creditor filed its U.C.C.-1; (c) the competing secured creditor receives notification within five years before the debtor receives possession of the inventory; and (d) the notification state that the person expects to acquire a PMSI in the inventory of the debtor and describing such inventory. (Kunkel v. Sprague National Bank)

4. **Buyers.** A vendee does not purchase in the ordinary course of business if he is aware of improprieties in the transaction. (International Harvester Co. v. Glendenning)

5. **Buyers.** A lender issuing credit secured by inventory does not have priority over a creditor with a purchase-money interest in the inventory. (First National Bank and Trust Co. of El Dorado v. Ford Motors Credit Co.)

6. **Buyers.** When a chattel mortgagee of livestock allows the debtor to possess the stock for sale, the sales broker will not be liable if the mortgagee loses his security. (Clovis National Bank v. Thomas)

7. **Buyers.** A buyer of farm products takes them subject to a security interest created by the seller where he receives written notice of this interest from the secured party within one year before the sale of the products. (Farm Credit Bank of St. Paul v. F & A Dairy)

8. **Article 2 Claimants.** A seller's reclamation claim to goods it has sold to a debtor in bankruptcy is subject to the claim of a holder of a perfected security interest in the debtor's assets and is rendered valueless upon sale of the goods where the secured claim exceeds the value of the reclamation claim. (In re Alrco, Inc.)

9. **Fixtures.** Where personalty takes on the nature of real property, it becomes a fixture. (George v. Commercial Credit Corp.)

10. **Fixtures.** A party with a security interest in after-acquired fixtures has priority over one supplying purchase-money credit on such fixtures, who had not complied with Article 9's financing statement rules. (Lewiston Bottled Gas Co. v. Key Bank of Maine)

11. **Fixtures.** A first mortgagee is entitled to priority over a fixture financier in the funds realized from a foreclosure sale of the mortgaged premises. (Maplewood Bank & Trust v. Sears, Roebuck & Co.)

* There are no cases in Chapter 21.

12. **Tax Liens—Basic Priority.** The federal priority statute does not require that a federal tax claim be given preference over a judgment creditor's perfected lien on real property even though such preference is not authorized by the Federal Tax Lien Act of 1966. (United States v. Estate of Romani)

13. **Tax Liens and After-Acquired Property.** For purposes of the Federal Tax Lien Act's § 6323(c) safe harbor provision for after-acquired property, a security interest in qualified contract rights covers the proceeds of those rights, even where such proceeds are an account receivable, and the proceeds fall within the scope of the safe harbor's protection. (Plymouth Savings Bank, v. U.S. I.R.S.)

IN RE WOLLIN
Creditor (P) v. Debtor (D)
249 B.R. 555, 41 U.C.C. Rep. Serv. 2d 1257 (Bankr. D. Oregon 2000).

NATURE OF CASE: Objections to confirmation and to proofs of claim in consolidated bankruptcy proceeding.

FACT SUMMARY: Oregon Federal Credit Union (OFCU) (P) claimed that "dragnet" clauses in credit agreements that provided for cross-collateralization on other loans should be enforced.

CONCISE RULE OF LAW: To be enforceable, a dragnet provision in a consumer loan must meet a strict "same class" test for subsequent loans and must specifically reference antecedent loans.

FACTS: Prior to the Moodys and Wollin (collectively "debtors") (D) filing for bankruptcy under Chapter 13, Oregon Federal Credit Union (OFCU) (P) had extended lines of credit and issued credit cards to the debtors (D). Advances against the lines of credit were secured by vehicles that were to be purchased by the loans, and all the loans had identical "dragnet" clauses that provided for cross-collateralization on other loans. OFCU (P) claimed that these dragnet provisions should be enforced, and, in each case, objected to confirmation. The debtors (D), in turn, objected to OFCU's (P) proofs of claim. The Chapter 13 Trustee recommended confirmation and the court took the matter under advisement.

ISSUE: To be enforceable, must a dragnet provision in a consumer loan meet a strict "same class" test for subsequent loans and specifically reference antecedent loans?

HOLDING AND DECISION: (Radcliffe, C. J.) Yes. With regard to subsequent loans (Moodys' VISA charges), OFCU (P) argues that the dragnet clause should be enforced according to its plain meaning. Thus, in the case of the Moodys (D), OFCU (P) argues that their Ford Bronco and Ford pickup truck should secure their VISA charges because the charges are either "any other amount" owed "in the future" or because they are the "same class" of debt, namely consumer debt. Both arguments based on "plain meaning" are rejected. First, for all future advances to be covered by a dragnet clause, they must be of the same class as the primary obligation and must be very closely related. This is true in the commercial setting. Accordingly, at least as strict an interpretation of the "same class" test should apply in the consumer context. Thus, all consumer debts would not meet this test, but those debts that are incurred for the same subject as covered by the primary loan (e.g., vehicles loans for vehicles purposes) would be. Here, the VISA charges are not sufficiently related to the loan for the pickup truck, because a loan to purchase a vehicle "differs both in scope and solemnity" from the miscellaneous charges typical of a VISA account. As to

antecedent loans (earlier lines of credit for both the Moodys and Wollin (D), and VISA charges for Wollin), OFCU (P) again argues that the plain meaning of the dragnet clauses should be applied. The majority of courts seem to apply a "plain meaning" test, whereas a minority require that the clause specifically reference antecedent debt. Because a standard that is stricter than "plain meaning" is applied for future debts, no less strict a test should be applied for prior debts, especially in the consumer context. Therefore, the "specific reference" standard is adopted. Here, the antecedent debts were not specifically referenced. Accordingly, the vehicles do not secure them. Objections to confirmation are overruled and objections to claims are sustained.

EDITOR'S ANALYSIS: When an individual debtor files a Chapter 13 bankruptcy petition, typically creditors vie for priority with respect to the debtor's remaining assets.

NOTES:

GALLEON INDUSTRIES, INC. v. LEWYN MACHINERY CO.

Buyer (D) v. Seller (P)

Ala. Ct. Civ. App., 50 Ala. App. 334, 279 So. 2d 137 (1973).

NATURE OF CASE: Appeal from order of replevin.

FACT SUMMARY: Lewyn Machinery (P), which mistakenly had delivered equipment to buyer Galleon (D) prior to payment, contended that it had priority over a creditor of Galleon (D) who had taken a security interest.

CONCISE RULE OF LAW: A seller who mistakenly delivers a product to a buyer prior to payment and does not file a financing statement may lose priority to a subsequent creditor who takes a security interest.

FACTS: Lewyn Machinery Co. (P) entered into a sales transaction with buyer Galleon Industries (D) for a piece of equipment. Delivery was to occur upon payment. By accident, the machine was delivered prior to payment. Lewyn (P) then sent an invoice, requesting payment within 30 days. A week after delivery, Central Bank and Trust (D) had entered into a security arrangement with Galleon (D), and perfected a security interest in the equipment. Upon Galleon's (D) default, Lewyn (P) sued to recover the machine. The trial court ordered the machine returned, and Galleon (D) and Central Bank (D) appealed.

ISSUE: May a seller who mistakenly delivers a product to a buyer prior to payment and does not file a financing statement lose priority to a subsequent creditor who takes a security interest?

HOLDING AND DECISION: (Wright, J.) Yes. A seller who mistakenly delivers a product to a buyer prior to payment and does not file a financing statement may lose priority to a subsequent creditor who takes a security interest. A seller who delivers goods to a buyer whom he then bills is a credit seller, the legal equivalent of a purchase-money lender. Under U.C.C. § 9-312(4), a purchase-money lender will have priority over all other secured creditors if he files a financing statement within ten days of the debtor's receipt of the monies or goods purchased therewith. If he fails to do so, he may lose priority. Here, Lewyn (P) did not file a financing statement. Therefore, as a credit seller, it lost priority to Central Bank (D), which did file a financing statement. Therefore, Lewyn (P) is not entitled to the equipment. Reversed.

EDITOR'S ANALYSIS: Purchase-money creditors are given special treatment under the U.C.C, as embodied in § 9-312(4). A prior creditor's lien on after-acquired property will not attach to a purchase-money lien on such property if the purchase-money lender properly perfects. If this were not the case, the availability of purchase money would be greatly diminished, with negative economic consequences.

NOTES:

KUNKEL v. SPRAGUE NATIONAL BANK

Bankruptcy trustee (P) v. Secured creditor (D)

128 F.3d 636 (8th Cir. 1997).

NATURE OF CASE: Adversarial proceeding in a bankruptcy case.

FACT SUMMARY: The trustee in bankruptcy (P) filed an adversarial proceeding to determine the superiority between competing interests of Hoxie, a purchase money secured creditor, and Sprague (D), in the net proceeds from the sale of the Morkens' livestock inventory.

CONCISE RULE OF LAW: A purchase money security interest (PMSI) has superiority over an earlier perfected interest where: (a) the PMSI is perfected at the time the debtor receives possession of the inventory; (b) the PMSI creditor gives written notification to all holders of competing interests that had U.C.C.-1 financing statements on file when the PMSI creditor filed its U.C.C.-1; (c) the competing secured creditor receives notification within five years before the debtor receives possession of the inventory; and (d) the notification state that the person expects to acquire a PMSI in the inventory of the debtor and describing such inventory.

FACTS: Sprague (D) made several loans to the Morkens pursuant to certain loan agreements and promissory notes. The Morkens executed a security agreement in favor of Sprague (D) in their inventory, farm products, equipment and accounts receivable. Hoxie finances and sells cattle. The Morkens purchased interests in approximately 1900 head of cattle from Hoxie. For each transaction, Morken executed a loan agreement and promissory note granting Hoxie a purchase money security interest (PMSI) in the cattle. Hoxie did not file a U.C.C.-1 financing statement but instead perfected its security interest by taking possession of the cattle pursuant to feedlot agreements. The Morkens filed a Chapter 11 bankruptcy case. Hoxie then sold the cattle and, after deducting the amounts owed Hoxie for care and feeding, $550,000 remained. The bankruptcy trustee (P) commenced a proceeding to determine whether Sprague (D) or Hoxie were entitled to the sale proceeds. Hoxie and the trustee reached a settlement. Hoxie and Sprague (D) filed cross-motions for summary judgment and the district court affirmed the bankruptcy court's summary judgment for Hoxie holding that Hoxie had priority over Sprague's earlier security interest in the collateral. The district court also held that Sprague (D) did not have a security interest in the cattle under the U.C.C. because the debtor "lacked rights in the collateral." Sprague (D) appealed.

ISSUE: Does a purchase money security interest have superiority over an earlier perfected interest?

HOLDING AND DECISION: (Gibson, J.) Yes. A purchase money security interest has superiority over an earlier perfected interest where: (a) the PMSI is perfected at the time the debtor receives possession of the inventory; (b) the PMSI creditor gives written notification to all holders of competing interests that had U.C.C.-1 financing statements on file when the PMSI creditor filed its U.C.C.-1; (c) the competing secured creditor receives notification within five years before the debtor receives possession of the inventory; and (d) the notification state that the person expects to acquire a PMSI in the inventory of the debtor and describing such inventory. Under the U.C.C., a security interest attaches where: (a) either the secured party has possession of the collateral by agreement with the debtor or the debtor has signed a security agreement; (b) value has been given; and (c) the debtor has rights in the collateral. The U.C.C. fails to define the term "rights in the collateral." Courts consider such factors as the extent of the debtor's control over the property and whether the debtor bears the risk of ownership. Article 2 principles may also be considered. The district court erred in its interpretation of Article 2, since the sale and delivery of the cattle by Hoxie to Morken granted Morken "rights in the collateral." This was based on the fact that a sale has transpired, Hoxie had constructively delivered the cattle to Morken and had possession of the cattle on Morken's behalf, Morken had title to and owned the cattle, Hoxie merely retained a security interest in the cattle as bailee, Hoxie's U.C.C. Article remedy of refusing to deliver the cattle had been cut off, and Morken had rights in the collateral sufficient for Sprague's (D) security interest to attach. Thus Sprague (D) had a perfected security interest in the cattle and the district court is reversed as to that issue. However, Hoxie's PMSI has superiority over Sprague's (D) interest under the Kansas U.C.C. § 84-9-312(3). The general rule is that the first creditor to perfect its security interest beats later perfected security interests. However, the PMSI provides an exception to the general rule and has superiority over an earlier perfected interest where: (a) the PMSI is perfected at the time the debtor receives possession of the inventory; (b) the PMSI creditor gives written notification to all holders of competing interests that had U.C.C.-1 financing statements on file when the PMSI creditor filed its U.C.C.-1; (c) the competing secured creditor receives notification within five years before the debtor receives possession of the inventory; and (d) the notification state that the person expects to acquire a PMSI in the inventory of the debtor and describing such inventory. Sprague (D) argued that superiority status could not be obtained

Continued on next page.

by a PMSI creditor who perfected its security interest by possession rather than filing. There is no support for this in the U.C.C. Next it must be determined whether Hoxie fulfilled the statutory requirements to obtain superiority. The only issue here is the timing of Hoxie's PMSI notice, which was received after the cattle were sold and this suit commenced. The notification requirement here is triggered by actual and not constructive possession of the inventory; thus, notification was timely. Sprague (D) also argued that the purpose of the statute is frustrated by granting superiority to as PMSI without requiring pre-perfection notification to prior filed secured creditors. The notification is required to state that the person expects or has a PMSI in the particular inventory; thus, the PMSI can wait to notify competing secured creditors until after it has acquired and perfected its security interest. Reversed as to the district court's holding that Sprague (D) did not have a security interest in the cattle and affirmed as to its judgment that Hoxie's security interest has priority.

EDITOR'S ANALYSIS: Note that the 1999 revision of the U.C.C. elaborates the procedure for obtaining a PMSI in a debtor's livestock.

NOTES:

INTERNATIONAL HARVESTER CO. v. GLENDENNING
Corporation (P) v. Farmer (D)
Tx. Sup. Ct., 505 S.W.2d 320 (1974).

NATURE OF CASE: Appeal from denial of award of damages for conversion.

NOTES:

FACT SUMMARY: Glendenning (D) contended that he had purchased certain equipment in the ordinary course of business, even though he had been aware that the vendor had misrepresented certain aspects of the transaction.

CONCISE RULE OF LAW: A vendee does not purchase in the ordinary course of business if he is aware of improprieties in the transaction.

FACTS: Barnes, an International Harvester Co. (P) dealer, sold to Glendenning (D), a farmer and occasional farm equipment dealer, three tractors for $16,000. Glendenning (D) knew the tractors were worth about $22,500. When filling out the paper work, Barnes stated that the tractors had been sold for $24,700, $16,000 in cash and $9,700 worth of trade-in equipment. Glendenning (D), who had once been an International Harvester (P) dealer himself, knew that Barnes had done this to placate International Harvester (P), which had a purchase-money security interest in the tractors he bought. Glendenning (D) later sold the tractors. International Harvester (P) brought a conversion action. The jury held Glendenning (D) to have been a purchaser in the ordinary course of business who took free of International Harvester's (P) lien. International Harvester (P) appealed.

ISSUE: Does a vendee purchase in the ordinary course of business if he is aware of improprieties in the transaction?

HOLDING AND DECISION: (Williams, C.J.) No. A vendee does not purchase in the ordinary course of business if he is aware of improprieties in the transaction. To be a buyer in the ordinary course of business within the meaning of U.C.C. § 9-307 requires that the buyer act in good faith without knowledge that the sale to him is in violation of the rights of a third party. Here, Glendenning (D), an experienced seller of International Harvester (P) products, had ample reason to suspect that the reason for Barnes' falsification of the record of sale was to deceive International Harvester (P) into thinking that its security interest had not been impaired. This hardly constituted good faith. For that reason the jury was demonstrably wrong in its finding that Glendenning (D) had been a buyer in the ordinary course of business. Reversed.

EDITOR'S ANALYSIS: Section 9-307 does not define a buyer in the ordinary course of business. However, the section does refer to § 1-201(9). There, it is provided that such a buyer must purchase without knowledge that he is impairing the rights of a third party.

FIRST NATIONAL BANK AND TRUST CO. OF EL DORADO v. FORD MOTOR CREDIT CO.

Corporation (P) v. Corporation (D)

Kan. Sup. Ct., 231 Kan. 431, 646 P.2d 1057 (1982).

NATURE OF CASE: Appeal from order mandating delivery of certain collateral.

FACT SUMMARY: First National (P) took as collateral for a loan two vehicles belonging to a dealer, over which Ford Motor Credit (D) had a perfected security interest.

CONCISE RULE OF LAW: A lender issuing credit secured by inventory does not have priority over a creditor with a purchase-money interest in the inventory.

FACTS: Heritage Ford obtained its inventory from Ford Motor Co. It financed its inventory from Ford Motor Credit Co. (D), which took a security interest in the vehicles sold to Heritage. Seeking additional funds, officers of Heritage took out two loans from First National Bank and Trust Co. of El Dorado (P), secured by two vehicles which the officers had signed over to themselves. Heritage went out of business and defaulted on the loans. Ford Motor Credit (D) repossessed the vehicles. First National (P) filed an action to assert its interest in the two vehicles. The trial court held that First National (P) had priority, and Ford Motor Credit (D) appealed.

ISSUE: Does a lender issuing credit secured by inventory have priority over a creditor with a purchase-money interest in the inventory?

HOLDING AND DECISION: (Fromme, J.) No. A lender issuing credit secured by inventory does not have priority over a creditor with a purchase-money interest in the inventory. U.C.C. § 9-312(3) provides that a purchase-money creditor has priority over all conflicting secured creditors if he perfects at the time of receipt of the inventory by the debtor. U.C.C. § 9-307 provides that a purchaser in the ordinary course of business will take the inventory free of the lien that the vendor had previously given. However, under the facts of this case, this rule does no good for the Bank (P). The officers of Heritage were not buyers in the ordinary course of business, so their signing over the vehicles to themselves did not extinguish Ford Motor Credit's (D) lien. This being the case, Ford Motor Credit's (D) perfected security interest took priority. Reversed.

EDITOR'S ANALYSIS: Section 9-307 exists for obvious reasons. One buying a product from a vendor has a right to expect that the vendor has the legal right to convey good title. For the protections of the section to come into effect, however, the buyer must pay something approximating fair market value. If he does not, he is not a buyer in the ordinary course of business.

QUICKNOTES

FAIR MARKET VALUE - The price of particular property or goods that a buyer would offer and a seller accept in the open market, following full disclosure.

SECURITY INTEREST - An interest in property that may be sold upon a default in payment of the debt.

NOTES:

CLOVIS NATIONAL BANK v. THOMAS
Bank (P) v. Cattle broker (D)
N.M. Sup. Ct., 77 N.M. 554, 425 P.2d 726 (1967).

NATURE OF CASE: Appeal from denial of award of damages for conversion.

FACT SUMMARY: Clovis National (P), having a security interest in certain cattle, allowed the debtor to retain possession thereof for sale.

CONCISE RULE OF LAW: When a chattel mortgagee of livestock allows the debtor to possess the stock for sale, the sales broker will not be liable if the mortgagee loses his security.

FACTS: W.D. Bunch had a continuing relationship with Clovis National Bank (P) wherein the Bank (P) would advance monies to Bunch, to buy young cattle which he would raise and then sell, usually at auction. The Bank (P) would take a security interest in the cattle to secure the loans. The security agreement provided that Bunch would not dispose of the cattle without first obtaining the Bank's (P) approval. Nonetheless, Bunch regularly sold the cattle without notifying the Bank (P), a practice which the Bank (P) knew about without raising an objection. At one point certain cattle purchased by Bunch received the brand of his son, and, when they were sold, the proceeds were paid to the son, who refused to turn any monies over to the Bank (P). The Bank (P) sued Thomas (D), the cattle broker/auctioneer, for conversion. The trial court found for Thomas (D), and the Bank (P) appealed.

ISSUE: When a chattel mortgagee of livestock allows the debtor to possess the stock for sale, will the sales broker be liable if the mortgagee loses his security?

HOLDING AND DECISION: (Oman, J.) No. When a chattel mortgagee of livestock allows the debtor to possess the stock for sale, the sales broker will not be liable if the mortgagee loses his security. The general rule is that when an auctioneer sells property on behalf of a principal who was not in fact legally authorized to convey title, the auctioneer is liable to any true owner or mortgagee, whether or not he had actual or constructive knowledge of that person's interest. However, it is also the rule that when a mortgagee under a chattel mortgage allows the mortgagor to retain possession of the property and sell the same at will, the mortgagee waives his lien as against third parties. This is precisely the case here. The Bank (P) was admittedly aware of Bunch's habit of selling the cattle without its consent. Consequently, it waived any rights it might have had against third parties, such as Thomas (D). Affirmed.

EDITOR'S ANALYSIS: The significance of the farmer's role in American society is the basis for the U.C.C.'s deference shown farmers as debtors. Unlike with purchase of other kinds of goods, a buyer in the ordinary course who purchases farm products does not take free of the interest of another's secured interest in the goods purchased. The drafters of the code sought to encourage financial institutions to lend to farmers; in turn, their encouragement comes from the knowledge that this interest in the goods will not be lost if they are sold to a third party. In Clovis, only because the lender knew of the circumstances was the rule not applied, as that knowledge was deemed a valid waiver.

QUICKNOTES

CHATTEL - An article of personal property, as distinguished from real property; a thing personal and moveable.

CONVERSION - The act of depriving an owner of his property without permission or justification.

SECURITY INTEREST - An interest in property that may be sold upon a default in payment of the debt.

NOTES:

FARM CREDIT BANK OF ST. PAUL v. F & A DAIRY

Bank (P) v. Dairy farm (D)

Wis. App. Ct., 165 Wis. 2d 360, 477 N.W. 2d 357 (1991).

NATURE OF CASE: Appeal from award of restitution for conversion.

FACT SUMMARY: In the Bank's (P) action in conversion against F & A Dairy (D), the district court awarded the Bank (P) restitution for certain payments due it under a security-interest-satisfying payment obligation, even though F & A (D) was not privy to the agreement creating the interest.

CONCISE RULE OF LAW: A buyer of farm products takes them subject to a security interest created by the seller where he receives written notice of this interest from the secured party within one year before the sale of the products.

FACTS: As collateral for a loan, Farm Credit Bank (P) obtained and perfected a security interest from the Bonneprises, covering all accounts arising from the sale or other disposition of their milk and milk products. The Bonneprises were selling milk to Land O' Lakes Dairy. In return for waiver of its lien, the Bank (P) executed an assignment with Land O' Lakes and the Bonneprises whereby Land O' Lakes would pay the Bank (P) $4,333 per month from the Bonneprises' milk proceeds. After the Bonneprises switched dairies and began selling their milk to F. & A. Dairy (D) in August 1988, the Bank (P) notified F & A (D) on and four days after August 22, 1988, of its assignment and security interest and demanded payments in accordance with the assignment. When F & A (D) refused to pay the Bank (P) for the months of August through November, the Bank (P) brought an action in conversion against F& A (D) to recover the amount due. The district court awarded restitution in that amount plus 5% interest. F & A (D) appealed.

ISSUE: Does a buyer of farm products take them subject to a security interest created by the seller where he receives written notice of this interest from the secured party within one year before the sale of the products?

HOLDING AND DECISION: (Cane, J.) Yes. A buyer of farm products takes them subject to a security interest created by the seller where he receives written notice of this interest from the secured party within one year before the sale of the products. This rule merely restates the principle articulated in 7 U.S.C. § 1631 of the Food Security Act. Where the buyer receives proper notice, including notice of any payment obligation, but fails to perform this obligation, he purchases the products subject to the security interest. Here, F & A (D) received notice of the Bank's (P) security interest in the milk it purchased from the Bonneprises, including notice of the $4,333 per month payment obligation but failed to comply with the obligation. Thus, the trial court did not err in

requiring it to perform the obligation for the months it had adequate notice with interest. Affirmed in part; reversed in part; remanded.

EDITOR'S ANALYSIS: The financing statement a buyer files with the central filing office under the Food Security Act must be more detailed than the usual one filed under the U.C.C. See § 1631(c)(4) for the definition of an "effective financing statement," which must include, among other things, the Social Security number of the debtor, the amount of farm products covered, and their location. See also Sanford, The Reborn Farm Products Exception Under the Food Security Act of 1985, 20 U.C.C. L.J. 3 (1987). Assuming the proper guidelines are followed, if the buyer obtains either a release or waiver from the secured party (or follows his instructions as to payments), the buyer takes free of the security interest in the farm products.

QUICKNOTES

ASSIGNMENT - A transaction in which a party conveys his or her entire interest in property to another.

CONVERSION - The act of depriving an owner of his property without permission or justification.

RESTITUTION - The return or restoration of what the defendant has gained in a transaction to prevent the unjust enrichment of the defendant.

SECURITY INTEREST - An interest in property that may be sold upon a default in payment of the debt.

NOTES:

IN RE ARLCO, INC.
Creditor (P) v. Debtor (D)
239 B.R. 261, 39 U.C.C. Rep. Serv. 2d (Bankr. S.D.N.Y. 1999).

NATURE OF CASE: Motion in bankruptcy proceeding for summary judgment for reclamation.

FACT SUMMARY: Galey & Lord, Inc. (Galey) (P) sought to reclaim goods it had sold on credit to Arley Corp. (Arley) (debtor) (D), but CIT Group/Business Credit Inc. (CIT) held a perfected security interest in substantially all of Arley's (D) assets.

CONCISE RULE OF LAW: A seller's reclamation claim to goods it has sold to a debtor in bankruptcy is subject to the claim of a holder of a perfected security interest in the debtor's assets and is rendered valueless upon sale of the goods where the secured claim exceeds the value of the reclamation claim.

FACTS: Galey & Lord, Inc. (Galey) (P) sold goods on credit to Arley Corp. (Arley) (debtor) (D). Before Arley (D) filed for bankruptcy under Chapter 11, Galey (P) sought to reclaim goods it had shipped to Arley (D). CIT Group/Business Credit Inc. (CIT) held a perfected security interest in substantially all of Arley's (D) assets, including inventory. After Arley (D) filed for bankruptcy, all of Arley's (D) assets as a going concern were sold under an asset purchase agreement. Galey (P) moved for summary judgment on its reclamation claim, which the bankruptcy Trustee opposed on several grounds, including that Galey's (P) right to reclamation was subject to CIT's perfected security interest.

ISSUE: Is a seller's reclamation claim to goods it has sold to a debtor in bankruptcy subject to the claim of a holder of a perfected security interest in the debtor's assets and rendered valueless upon sale of the goods where the secured claim exceeds the value of the reclamation claim?

HOLDING AND DECISION: (Gonzalez, J.) Yes. The bankruptcy statute in § 546(c) recognizes any right of a seller to reclaim under applicable nonbankruptcy law. U.C.C. § 2-702 forms the non-bankruptcy statutory right upon which sellers base their reclamation demand. In addition to providing that the seller must establish that statute's requirements, § 2-702 provides in sub-section 3 that the seller's right to reclamation is subject to the rights of a good faith purchaser from the buyer. Most courts hold that a holder of a prior perfected, floating lien on inventory, like CIT here, is a good faith purchaser with rights superior to those of a reclaiming seller. Galey (P) argues that the language in § 2-702 ("under this Article") is applicable only to purchasers who acquire their interest under Article 2 of the U.C.C. An analysis of the Code, however, shows that the definition of purchaser is broad enough to include an Article 9 secured party. Thus, if CIT qualifies as a good faith purchaser for value, even if Arley (D) had voidable title

to the goods, it could transfer good title to CIT, and Galey's reclamation claim would be subject to CIT's interest. Notwithstanding debate by legal scholars as to whether reclaiming sellers should get priority against a prior secured lender with an after-acquired property interest, the court's task is to enforce the plain meaning of the statute. Under that plain meaning, a creditor with a security interest in after-acquired property who acted in good faith and for value, which includes acquiring rights as security for or in total or partial satisfaction of a pre-existing claim, is a good faith purchaser, and a reclaiming seller's claim is subject to the purchaser's claim. Here, CIT acted in good faith. Galey (D) argues that CIT's actions were not in good faith because it knew of Arley's (P) troubles and stopped funding Arley (P) without informing Arley's (P) other creditors. However, the U.C.C.'s good faith element does not require a secured creditor to continue to fund a business with enormous debt and losses. Such a decision is "clearly reasonable" and, therefore, there is no genuine issue as to CIT's good faith. There also is no issue that CIT gave value. Therefore, CIT qualifies as a good faith purchaser for value. Although Galey's (P) reclamation right is subject to CIT's rights, it is not automatically extinguished. Accordingly, Galey (P) argues that Galey is entitled to an administrative claim or lien in lieu of its right to reclamation if there is any surplus collateral. The Trustee, however, argues that when the goods subject to the reclamation demand are liquidated and the proceeds are used to pay the secured creditor' claim, the reclaiming seller's subordinated right is rendered valueless, as opposed to being automatically extinguished. The majority approach is to give the reclaiming seller the right to reclaim, or an administrative claim or lien in lieu thereof, only when the goods or proceeds from those goods exceeds the value of the secured party's claim. Here, all the goods Galey (P) sought to reclaim were sold and the proceeds were used to pay CIT—and even then a balance was due to CIT. Therefore, Galey's claim was rendered valueless, as was any administrative claim or lien based on the reclamation claim.

EDITOR'S ANALYSIS: Some legal scholars argue that § 2-702 gives a seller the rights of a purchase-money security holder for 10 days (the time period during which a seller may reclaim), and that a purchase-money lender "undoubtedly beats" a creditor with a security interest in after-acquired property. That view holds that a party with a security interest should only be considered a good faith purchaser for value if it has suffered detrimental reliance by extending new value (which CIT did not do here).

GEORGE v. COMMERCIAL CREDIT CORP.

Mobile home owner (D) v. Bank (P)

440 F. 2d 551 (7th Cir. 1971).

NATURE OF CASE: Appeal from judgment upholding secured creditor's interest in a fixture.

FACT SUMMARY: In Commercial's (P) action against George (D), the district court ruled that despite George's (D) arguments that a mobile home, which he as trustee in bankruptcy had an interest in, was personalty, Commercial's (P) interest as mortgage was superior because the mobile home had become a fixture.

CONCISE RULE OF LAW: Where personalty takes on the nature of real property, it becomes a fixture.

FACTS: After Foskett contracted to purchase a large mobile home, he executed a real estate mortgage to Highway Mobile Home Sales, Inc., which assigned the mortgage to Commercial Credit Corp. (P). Once the mobile home was delivered to Foskett's property, he applied for a homeowner's insurance policy, asked the seller to remove the home's wheels, and adapted it as his permanent residence. Moreover, the home was never again operated on or over the highways, and it was occupied by now-bankrupt Foskett continuously, until he was forced to vacate by order of George (D), trustee in bankruptcy. Commercial (P), however challenged George's (D) interest in the mobile home, arguing that it had become a fixture under Wisconsin law. This, Commercial (P) asserted, made it a secured creditor with an interest superior to that of George (D) in the home. The district court, rejecting George's (D) arguments that the mobile home was personalty, ruled in Commercial's (P) favor. George (D) appealed.

ISSUE: Where personalty takes on the nature of real property, does it become a fixture?

HOLDING AND DECISION: (Duffy, J.) Yes. Where personalty takes on the nature of real property, it becomes a fixture. This rule follows from examining applicable common law cases determining when personalty becomes affixed to real property. In Auto Acceptance and Loan Corp. v. Keln, 18 Wis. 2d 178 (1962), the court reaffirmed an earlier decision which stated the three tests for determining in a given case whether facilities remain personalty or have become fixtures. These tests are: (1) actual physical annexation to the realty; (2) application or adoption to the use or purpose to which the realty is devoted, and (3) the intention of the person making annexation to make a permanent accession to the freehold. In the instant case, since Foskett purchased a homeowner's insurance policy for his mobile home intent,

requested the seller to have its wheels removed (permanence), and adapted it as his permanent residence (application), the district court did not err in determining that it had become a fixture under Wisconsin law. Affirmed.

EDITOR'S ANALYSIS: The U.C.C. has only the most limited definition of fixtures. Read §§ 9-313 (1)(a) and 9-313 (2) and official Comment 2. Obviously pre-Code state law defining fixtures is very important. State law tests ranged from a pure annexation test (measured by the difficulty of removal) to an "intention of the parties" test (for which the leading case is Teaff v. Hewitt, 1 Ohio St. 511 (1853)).

QUICKNOTES

FIXTURE - An item of personal property that has become so attached to the real property that it is considered a part of the real property.

NOTES:

LEWISTON BOTTLED GAS CO. v. KEY BANK OF MAINE
Seller of air conditioning (P) v. Bank (D)
Me. Sup. Jud. Ct., 601 A.2d 91 (1992).

NATURE OF CASE: Appeal from declaratory judgment setting creditor priority to certain equipment.

FACT SUMMARY: Key Bank (D) contended that its security interest in after-acquired fixtures of a debtor had priority over one having a purchase-money security interest.

CONCISE RULE OF LAW: A party with a security interest in after-acquired fixtures has priority over one supplying purchase-money credit on such fixtures, who had not complied with Article 9's financing statement rules.

FACTS: Key Bank of Maine (D) loaned certain moneys to Grand Beach Inn, Inc. The loan was secured by liens attaching to the property, including after-acquired fixtures. Subsequent to this, Grand Beach contracted to purchase some 90 air-conditioning units from Lewiston Bottled Gas Co. (P). These units were purchased on credit. Grand Beach gave a purchase-money security interest to Lewiston (P). The air conditioners were installed in the various units of the inn. The record owner of the property was DiBiase, Grand Beach's owner. Lewiston's (P) financing statement made no mention of DiBiase, only Grand Beach. Grand Beach defaulted, and Lewiston (P) brought a declaratory relief action to assert its lien. The trial court held Key Bank's (D) interest to have priority, and Lewiston (P) appealed.

ISSUE: Does a party with a security interest in after-acquired fixtures have priority over one supplying purchase-money credit on such fixtures, who had not complied with Article 9's financing statement rules?

HOLDING AND DECISION: (Clifford, J.) Yes. A party with a security interest in after-acquired fixtures has priority over one supplying purchase-money credit on such fixtures, who had not complied with Article 9's financing statement rules. One having a purchase-money security interest in fixtures will have priority over one having a preexisting security interest in after-acquired fixtures. However, § 9-402(5) requires that the financing statement perfecting the interest list the name of the record owner of the property. Here, the units were undoubtedly fixtures. Fixtures, per U.C.C. § 9-313(a), are goods physically annexed to real property, adapted to the use to which the real property is put, and intended to become part of the realty. The units in question fall within this definition. However, Lewiston's (P) financing statement did not mention DiBiase, the true owner of record. This being so, Lewiston (P) failed to comply with Article 9 and, thus, had no priority here. Affirmed.

EDITOR'S ANALYSIS: The factors making personal property into fixtures enunciated in U.C.C. § 9-313(1) were taken from the common law. Of the three factors, intent is probably the most determinative. The code looks to "objective" intent (intent that can reasonably be inferred from the parties' conduct), not any subjective intent the parties may have had.

QUICKNOTES

DECLARATORY JUDGMENT - An adjudication by the courts which grants not relief but is binding over the legal status of the parties involved in the dispute.

FIXTURE - An item of personal property that has become so attached to the real property that it is considered a part of the real property.

LIEN - A claim against the property of another in order to secure the payment of a debt.

SECURITY INTEREST - An interest in property that may be sold upon a default in payment of the debt.

NOTES:

MAPLEWOOD BANK & TRUST
v. SEARS, ROEBUCK & CO.
Bank (P) v. Department store (D)
Sup. Ct. N.J., 265 N.J.Super. 25, 625 A.2d 537; cert. granted, 134 N.J. 483,
634 A.2d 529 (1993).

NATURE OF CASE: Appeal from the dismissal of a counterclaim in an action to determine priority interests in a foreclosure sale.

FACT SUMMARY: Sears (D) took a security interest in certain kitchen fixtures it installed on the Capers' (D) property on which Maplewood (P) had previously taken a purchase-money mortgage.

CONCISE RULE OF LAW: A first mortgagee is entitled to priority over a fixture financier in the funds realized from a foreclosure sale of the mortgaged premises.

FACTS: Maplewood Bank and Trust (P) was the holder of a first purchase-money mortgage dated September 20, 1988, and recorded on October 5, 1988, on the Capers' (D) property. On May 31, 1989, Sears, Roebuck and Company (D) filed a financing statement covering kitchen fixtures it installed on the mortgaged premises. When the Capers (D) defaulted on their loans, Maplewood (P) filed a complaint for foreclosure. Sears (D) filed an answer and counterclaim stating that it was entitled to priority over Maplewood (P) for the sums received in the foreclosure sale because of its fixture filing pursuant to U.C.C. § 9-313, and that it was entitled to the difference between the price of the home with and without the new kitchen. Sears' (D) answer and counterclaim were stricken and an unopposed foreclosure sale ensued. Sears (D) appealed the dismissal of the counterclaim.

ISSUE: Is a first mortgagee entitled to priority over a fixture financier in the funds realized from a foreclosure sale of the mortgaged premises?

HOLDING AND DECISION: (Coleman, J.) Yes. A first mortgagee is entitled to priority over a fixture financier in the funds realized from a foreclosure sale of the mortgaged premises. Here, U.C.C. § 9-313 does not give Sears (D) priority over Maplewood (P) on the proceeds from the foreclosure sale. Sears' (D) perfected security interest was in the goods and chattels that became fixtures, and such interest attached to those goods before they became fixtures. Therefore, Sears' (D) superiority pursuant to U.C.C. § 9-313 applies only to those goods that became fixtures, and not the premises at large. Pursuant to U.C.C. § 9-313(8) as adopted in New Jersey, Sears' (D) remedy is to remove the goods from the premises and reimburse Maplewood (P) for any damage caused by the removal. In entering into this security agreement, Sears (D) knew of the risk it was taking and the remedy offered by state law. If the law is to be changed to allow creditors such as Sears (D) to have priority in similar foreclosure sale funds, that is

to be determined by the state legislature. Summary judgment in favor of Maplewood (P) is affirmed.

EDITOR'S ANALYSIS: Draft § 9-604(b), formerly § 9-501(g), states that "If a security agreement covers goods that are or become fixtures, a secured party, subject to subsection (c), may proceed under this part or in accordance with the rights and remedies with respect to real [estate] [property], in which case the other provisions of this part do not apply." This subsection is intended to clarify the notion that a security interest in fixtures may be enforced under any of the applicable provisions of Part 5. The subsection also serves to overrule cases holding that a secured party's only remedy after default is the removal of the fixtures from the real estate.

QUICKNOTES

COUNTERCLAIM - An independent cause of action brought by a defendant to a lawsuit in order to oppose or deduct from the plaintiff's claim.

FIXTURE - An item of personal property that has become so attached to the real property that it is considered a part of the real property.

NOTES:

UNITED STATES v. ESTATE OF ROMANI
Federal government (P) v. Debtor (D)
523 U.S. 517 (1998).

NATURE OF CASE: Estate administration.

FACT SUMMARY: The federal government (P) sought to prohibit the transfer of Romani's (D) estate to a judgment creditor on the basis that it had first priority for payment under the federal priority statute.

CONCISE RULE OF LAW: The federal priority statute does not require that a federal tax claim be given preference over a judgment creditor's perfected lien on real property even though such preference is not authorized by the Federal Tax Lien Act of 1966.

FACTS: A judgment of $400,000 was entered in favor of Romani Industries against Francis Romani (D), and became a lien against all Romani's (D) real property in the county. Subsequently, the IRS filed a series of tax liens on Romani's (D) property totaling $490,000. When Romani (D) died, his estate consisted of property worth $53,001. The estate's administrator sought permission to transfer the property to the judgment creditor, Romani Industries, in lieu of execution. The government (P) opposed the transaction on the basis that the federal priority statute, 31 U.S.C. § 3713(a), gave it the right to be paid first. The court authorized the conveyance. The superior court affirmed and the Pennsylvania Supreme Court also affirmed. The government (P) appealed.

ISSUE: Does the federal priority statute require that a federal tax claim be given preference over a judgment creditor's perfected lien on real property even though such preference is not authorized by the Federal Tax Lien Act of 1966?

HOLDING AND DECISION: (Stevens, J.) No. The federal priority statute does not require that a federal tax claim be given preference over a judgment creditor's perfected lien on real property even though such preference is not authorized by the Federal Tax Lien Act of 1966. State law provides that a judgment creates a lien against real property when it is recorded in the county where the property is located. Here the judgment creditor obtained a valid lien on real property in Cambria County before the debtor's death and before the government (P) served notice of its tax liens. Congress has continually ameliorated the harsh impact of the Federal Tax Lien Act with respect to secured creditors. Thus the government's (P) liens are not valid against the earlier lien created by the recording of Romani Industries' judgment. The government (P) contends, however, that the federal priority statute should be read as giving the United States (P) a preference over other unsecured creditors. Courts are divided as to this issue and the federal priority statute does not address it. The question becomes how to reconcile these two statutes. Justice Jackson, in a dissent from a harsh application of the federal priority statute, emphasized the importance of considering other relevant federal policies when applying the statute. He stated that while the priority statute asserts federal supremacy over contrary state policy, it is not a limitation on the federal government (P) nor does it prevail over all other federal policies. In several situations, the Court has concluded that a specific policy embodied in a later enacted statute should control the construction of the federal priority statute. Here the bankruptcy law provides an additional context in which the federal policy should be given effect despite the language of the priority statute. Here the Tax Lien Act is the later, more specific and comprehensive statute reflecting strong policy objections to the enforcement of secret liens. Nothing in the legislative history of the federal priorty statute supports the conclusion that Congress authorized the equivalent of a secret lien when it has already stated that the liens expressly authorized by the priority statute are not valid in such cases. Affirmed.

EDITOR'S ANALYSIS: The federal priority statute provides that a claim of the federal government "shall be paid first" from a decedent's estate when that estate is not sufficient to pay all of the decedent's debts. The federal priority statute, which has virtually been unchanged since its enactment, provides a broad grant of priority for all federal claims without exception. The courts, however, have given priority over federal claims to earlier perfected liens if such liens are "choate." The Supreme Court has failed to identify this term.

NOTES:

PLYMOUTH SAVINGS BANK v. U.S. I.R.S.

Lienor (P) v. Lienor (D)

187 F.3d 203 (1st Cir. 1999).

NATURE OF CASE: Appeal from summary judgment on the priority of liens.

FACT SUMMARY: Plymouth Savings Bank (Bank) (P) and the Internal Revenue Service (I.R.S.) both held valid liens on money owed by Jordan Hospital (Hospital) to Shirley Dionne (Dionne) pursuant to a personal service contract, and each lienor claimed priority.

CONCISE RULE OF LAW: For purposes of the Federal Tax Lien Act's § 6323(c) safe harbor provisions for after-acquired property, a security interest in qualified contract rights covers the proceeds of those rights, even where such proceeds are an account receivable, and the proceeds fall within the scope of the safe harbor's protection.

FACTS: Shirley Dionne (Dionne) owed Plymouth Savings Bank (Bank) (P) $64,465 on a loan. The Bank (P) had a security interest in all of Dionne's personal property, including contract rights and all cash and non-cash proceeds resulting from the rendering of services by Dionne. Dionne had executed a $85,000 promissory note in favor of the Bank (P) on April 13, 1994. Dionne also owed money to the I.R.S. (D), which filed tax liens against Dionne's property on December 19, 1994, and February 14, 1995. On March 31, 1995, Dionne entered into a personal services contract with Jordan Hospital (Hospital). The Hospital owed Dionne a $75,000 balance on the contract, and the Bank (P) sued the Hospital in state court to recover this unpaid balance. The state court held that the Bank (P) had a secured interest in the money because it was a "proceed" of services, but instead of awarding the Bank (P) the money, it directed the Bank (P) to bring a declaratory judgment to determine whether its interest had priority over other lien-holders. The Bank (P) brought such an action. The IRS (D) claimed that its liens had priority, and the federal district court granted summary judgment in its favor. The Bank (P) appealed.

ISSUE: For purposes of the Federal Tax Lien Act's safe harbor provisions for after-acquired property, does a security interest in qualified contract rights cover the proceeds of those rights, even when such proceeds are an account receivable, and the proceeds fall within the scope of the safe harbor's protections?

HOLDING AND DECISION: (Cudahy, J.) The Federal Tax Lien Act (FTLA) grants the U.S. a lien on all the property of a person who fails to pay taxes, whether acquired before or after the lien is filed. Section 6323, however, gives certain commercial liens priority over federal tax liens, including security interests in a taxpayer's property that are "in existence" before filing of the notice of the tax lien. Section 6323(c) extends the priority of these prior security interests to certain "qualified property" (the 6323(c) safe harbor) that is acquired after the notice of the tax lien. To fall within the safe harbor, a security interest must be in property covered by a "commercial transactions financing agreement." A commercial transactions financing agreement is secured by "commercial financing security," which can include paper of a kind arising in commercial transactions—which includes "contract rights"—and accounts receivable. A commercial financing security must be acquired before the 46th day after the date of the tax lien filing. Here, Dionne entered the contract with the Hospital exactly 45 days after the tax lien was filed. Thus, the issue is whether she "acquired" the right to the money owed her by the Hospital; if she did, then Bank's (P) lien trumps the I.R.S.'s (D) lien because the Dionne-Bank agreement is a commercial transactions financing agreement, the Dionne-Hospital contract is a commercial financing security, the Bank's (P) security is in qualified property, and the money is after-acquired property that falls within the safe harbor. If, conversely, Dionne did not acquire rights to the money when she signed the contract, the I.R.S.'s lien takes priority. Under I.R.S. regulations, what Dionne acquired when she signed the contract with the Hospital was a "contract right" to be paid in the future because she had not as yet performed, and, therefore, the contract, and the rights under it, is qualified property covered by the Bank's (P) security interest and protected by the safe harbor. The next issue is whether the money itself is such qualified property. Under the tax regulations, "proceeds" are whatever is received when collateral is "exchanged." Proceeds are considered acquired at the time that the qualified property is acquired. Here, therefore, the proceeds of the contract rights are considered to have been acquired by Dionne at the time she made the contract. However, the proceeds are an account receivable—the right to payment of the money upon performance. The I.R.S. (D) correctly argues that Dionne did not earn the right to payment before the 45 days from the tax lien filing. Nonetheless, it is the contract and the contract rights under it, not the account receivable, that constitutes the qualified property, and the proceeds under that qualified property are deemed acquired at the time the qualified property was acquired. This results because the regulations do not distinguish between forms of proceeds. Moreover, the account receivable is proceeds because Dionnes' performance "exchanged" her contract right into an account receivable. Here, the regulations make it clear that as long as the contract was entered into within 45 days of the tax lien filing, the rights under that contract and all the proceeds of those rights come within the protection of § 6323's safe harbor. This result is supported by the U.C.C., the principles of which

Continued on next page.

Congress intended to incorporate into the tax lien provisions. Accordingly, the Bank's (P) lien trumps the I.R.S.'s (D). Reversed and remanded.

EDITOR'S ANALYSIS: The I.R.S. argued that Dionne did not enter the contract in the "ordinary" course of her trade or business, as required by § 6323. The subject of the contract was the transfer of Dionne's business license, which, the I.R.S. argued, was not in the ordinary course of her business. However, the contract was a personal services contract, and such contracts were normally entered into in Dionne's business. The court left this issue of "ordinariness" for remand because it is a very fact-sensitive issue on which few facts had been developed, but it did note that if the I.R.S. characterized the transaction as a sale or transfer of a license, the proceeds from that transaction would clearly have entitled the Bank (P) to the money without having to "navigate § 6323(c)'s maze of definitions."

NOTES:

23

CHAPTER 23
BANKRUPTCY AND ARTICLE NINE

QUICK REFERENCE RULES OF LAW

1. **The Floating Lien in Bankruptcy.** Payments made to a creditor by a debtor during 90 days before the debtor files for bankruptcy will not be avoided as preferential transfers where the creditor has a floating lien and it cannot be shown that the creditor received a greater amount by virtue of the payments than it would have received in a hypothetical bankruptcy liquidation. (In re Smith's Home Furnishings, Inc.)

IN RE SMITH'S HOME FURNISHINGS, INC.
Bankruptcy trustee (P) v. Creditor (D)
254 F.3d 959 (9th Cir. 2001).

NATURE OF CASE: Appeal from affirmance of judgment in bankruptcy proceeding holding that transfer is not preferential.

FACT SUMMARY: Transamerica Commercial Finance Corp. (TCFC) (D) had a floating lien in the inventory of Smith's Home Furnishings, Inc. (Smith's). During the 90 days before Smith's filed for bankruptcy, Smith's paid TCFC (D) over $12 million in 36 payments. The bankruptcy trustee (P) sought to avoid these payments as preferences.

CONCISE RULE OF LAW: Payments made to a creditor by a debtor during 90 days before the debtor files for bankruptcy will not be avoided as preferential transfers where the creditor has a floating lien and it cannot be shown that the creditor received a greater amount by virtue of the payments than it would have received in a hypothetical bankruptcy liquidation.

FACTS: Transamerica Commercial Finance Corp. (TCFC) (D) was one of the primary lenders for Smith's Home Furnishings, Inc. (Smith's). TCFC's (D) loans were secured by a first-priority floating lien on Smith's prime inventory and proceeds from it, with the inventory serving as collateral. When Smith's started to experience substantial losses, TCFC reduced its line of credit, and Smith's made substantial paydowns of Smith's debt in 36 payments totaling over $12 million between May and August 22, 1995. On August 18, 1995, TCFC (D) declared a final default. For the first time, TCFC (D) also sought to require Smith's to segregate the proceeds from its collateral. On August 22, 1995, Smith's voluntarily filed for bankruptcy under Chapter 11, and TCFC (D) took possession of its collateral and liquidated it for $10,823,010.58, or $94,200.62 more than the amount Smith's still owed it. The case was converted to a Chapter 7 liquidation and the Chapter 7 trustee (P) discovered the over-$12 million in payments that Smith's had made to TCFC (D) during the 90 days before the petition date ("preference period"). When TCFC (D) refused to return the payments, the trustee (P) sought to avoid the payments as preferential transfers. The bankruptcy court ruled that the trustee (P) had failed to meet his burden of proof. On appeal, the district court affirmed. The trustee (P) appealed to the Court of Appeals.

ISSUE: Will payments made to a creditor by a debtor during 90 days before the debtor files for bankruptcy be avoided as preferential transfers where the creditor has a floating lien and it cannot be shown that the creditor received a greater amount by virtue of the payments than it would have received in a hypothetical bankruptcy liquidation?

HOLDING AND DECISION: (Hall, J.) No. The Bankruptcy Code permits a trustee to avoid a transfer from a debtor to a creditor where such transfer enables the creditor to receive a "greater amount" than it would have received under a Chapter 7 proceeding if the transfer had not occurred. The parties dispute whether the over-$12 million in payments made during the preference period enabled TCFC to receive a "greater amount" than it would have if the transfer had not occurred and TCFC received payments only pursuant to a Chapter 7 liquidation. The trustee (P), who had the burden of proof on this issue, made two arguments: first, that the over-$12 million payments plus the amount that TCFC (D) received from the sale of its collateral was greater than the amount it received from the sale of the collateral alone (the "add-back" method); second, that TCFC (D) had not traced the source of the allegedly preferential payments to sales of its collateral. (A) With regard to the add-back method, the trustee (P) did not meet his burden. Pre-petition transfers to a creditor who is fully secured on the petition date are generally not preferential. Here, TCFC (D) was never undersecured at any time during the preference period because the value of the collateral exceeded Smith's indebtedness to TCFC (D). If TCFC (D) was never undercollateralized, then TCFC (D) could not have received more by virtue of the over-$12 million payments than it would have received in a hypothetical liquidation without the payments. Because TCFC (D) had a floating lien, the collateral and indebtedness changed throughout the preference period, and, therefore, the trustee (P) could not prove that the amount of indebtedness was greater than the amount of collateral at some point during the preference period. Moreover, a floating lien does not shift the burden of proof on this issue to the creditor. The trustee (P) urges that the burden be shifted, but he is using § 547(c)(5), which is an affirmative defense provision. Here, TCFC (D) does not have to use an affirmative defense until the trustee (P) has initially proved that the creditor was undersecured as of the petition date. Because the trustee (P) failed to carry its burden, there is no shift of burden. (B) As to the trustee's (P) argument that TCFC (D) had not traced the source of the allegedly preferential payments to sales of its collateral, the payments in the instant case came from commingled funds that were not all from the sales of goods subject to TCFC's (D) lien. Thus, the challenged payments were not made directly from the proceeds of the sales of TCFC's collateral. Conversely, there was no evidence that Smith's did not sell off enough of TCFC' (D) collateral to account for all the challenged payments—but it is the trustee's (P) burden to prove whether or not the alleged preferential payments came from the proceeds of the sale of its

Continued on next page.

own collateral. Here, the trustee (P) did not meet that burden. Affirmed.

EDITOR'S ANALYSIS: The paramount policy behind § 547 of the Bankruptcy Code is to ensure equality of distribution among creditors of the debtor. If a floating lien creditor truly does not profit from a transfer made during the preference period, then the creditor should not be forced to repay the transferred payments. This section also attempts to discourage creditors from rushing to extract payments from the debtor shortly before the petition of bankruptcy is filed.

NOTES:

CHAPTER 24
PROCEEDS

QUICK REFERENCE RULES OF LAW

1. **The Meaning of Proceeds.** A purchase money security interest in collateral has priority over a conflicting security interest in the same collateral or its proceeds if it is perfected before the latter interest. (Farmers Cooperative Elevator Co. v. UnionState Bank)

2. **Priorities in Proceeds.** A recipient of a payment made "in the ordinary course" by a debtor takes that payment free and clear of any claim that a secured party may have in the payment as proceeds, absent collusion intended to defraud the secured party. (HCC Credit Corp. v. Spring Valley Bank & Trust Co.)

FARMERS COOPERATIVE ELEVATOR CO.
v. UNION STATE BANK
Feed supplier (P) v. Bank (D)
Iowa Sup. Ct., 409 N.W. 2d 178 (1987).

NATURE OF CASE: Appeal from ruling on motion denying priority to plaintiff's security interest.

FACT SUMMARY: In Co-op's (P) action against Union State (D), the district court ruled that Union State's (D) security interest in certain livestock and their supplies was superior to Co-op's (P) competing interest since it was perfected prior to Co-op's (P).

CONCISE RULE OF LAW: A purchase money security interest in collateral has priority over a conflicting security interest in the same collateral or its proceeds if it is perfected before the latter interest.

FACTS: After Cockrum formed a security agreement with Union State Bank (D) covering his livestock and their supplies and Union State (D) perfected its interest, he entered into several purchase money agreements with Farmers Cooperative Elevator Co. (P) (Co-op) for livestock feed. When he subsequently defaulted on both obligations, Co-op (P) sued Cockrum, seeking possession of the hogs on the grounds that they were the proceeds of the feed. As a result, Union State (D) filed a statement of indebtedness and requested that its security interests be established as a first security lien on Cockrum's hog inventory. On Co-op's (P) motion to adjudicate law points, the district court ruled that Union State's (D) security interest in the hogs was prior and superior to Co-op's (P). Co-op (P) appealed.

ISSUE: Does a purchase money security interest in collateral have priority over a conflicting security interest in the same collateral or its proceeds if it is perfected before the latter interest?

HOLDING AND DECISION: (Larson, J.) Yes. A purchase money security interest in collateral has priority over a conflicting security interest in the same collateral or its proceeds if it is perfected before the latter interest. This rule merely restates the principle outlined in § 554.9312(4) of the Iowa Commercial Code. Section 554.9306 defines "proceeds" to include "whatever is received upon the sale, exchange, collection, or other disposition of collateral or proceeds." The "other disposition of collateral" language found in this section has been found not to include the consumption of feed since "there are no traceable proceeds to which the security interest may be said to have attached" once the feed is consumed. (See First Nat'l. Bank of Brush v. Bostron, 564 P.2d 965, 966 (Colo. App. 1977).) Moreover, Bostron points out that feed eaten by cattle does not become commingled with them as contemplated by U.C.C. § 9-315, the companion statute to Iowa's § 554.9315(1). In the instant case, the district court did not err in finding that the hogs were not the proceeds of their feed, and therefore, Union State's (D) security interest in them was superior to Co-op's (P). Affirmed.

EDITOR'S ANALYSIS: In a related area concerning proceeds, Article 9 does not usually apply to security interests taken in either insurance policies or bank accounts as collateral. This is because the common law or other statutes regulate these transactions. However insurance payments or bank account moneys that qualify as "proceeds" are regulated by the Code.

QUICKNOTES
SECURITY INTEREST - An interest in property that may be sold upon a default in payment of the debt.

NOTES:

HCC CREDIT CORP. v. SPRINGS VALLEY BANK & TRUST CO.

Secured creditor (P) v. Bank (D)
Ind. Sup. Ct., 712 N.E.2d 952 (1999).

NATURE OF CASE: Suit to recover proceeds of sale.

FACT SUMMARY: HCC (P) brought suit against Springs Valley Bank (D) to recover payment due pursuant to its perfected security interest in Hesston tractors which were sold by Lindsey and the proceeds of which were paid to the bank (D).

CONCISE RULE OF LAW: A recipient of a payment made "in the ordinary course" by a debtor takes that payment free and clear of any claim that a secured party may have in the payment as proceeds, absent collusion intended to defraud the secured party.

FACTS: Lindsey purchased wholesale tractor equipment from Hesston for resale in its farm machinery sales and service business. HCC (P) provided financing for the purchases. Written contracts governed the relationship between the parties, including a security agreement. In the security agreement Lindsey granted HCC (P) a security interest in all equipment purchased from Hesston and in the proceeds from the sale of the equipment. Lindsey also agreed to pay HCC (P) immediately for equipment sold from the proceeds of the sale. The Indiana State Department of Transportation agreed to purchase 14 Hesston tractors from Lindsey. Lindsey received payment from the state and wrote a check payable to Springs Valley Bank (D) for $212,104.75 to pay for debts owed by Lindsey to the bank (D). Lindsey filed a bankruptcy liquidation proceeding and dissolved. HCC (P) sought to recover the $199,122 in proceeds from the sale of the Hesston tractors that the bank (D) received from Lindsey. Both parties moved for summary judgment, which was granted in favor of the bank (D). The court of appeals affirmed and HCC (P) appealed.

ISSUE: Does a recipient of a payment made "in the ordinary course" by a debtor take that payment free and clear of any claim that a secured party may have in the payment as proceeds, absent collusion intended to defraud the secured party?

HOLDING AND DECISION: (Sullivan, J.) Yes. A recipient of a payment made "in the ordinary course" by a debtor takes that payment free and clear of any claim that a secured party may have in the payment as proceeds, absent collusion intended to defraud the secured party. Under both the security agreement and Article 9 of the U.C.C., HCC (P) had a valid and perfected security interest in the $199,122 proceeds from the sale of the tractors. The general rule is that the secured party, upon a debtor's default, has priority over all others except as otherwise provided by the U.C.C. priority rules. However, Comment 2(c) to

Article 9 provides an exception to the general rule for "payments and transfers in the ordinary course" without any collusion on the part of the debtor. Thus, when "cash proceeds are covered into the debtor's checking account and paid out in the operation of the debtor's business, recipients of the funds of course take free of any claim which the secured party may have in them as proceeds." This was the rule followed by the trial court and the court of appeals. HCC (P) now argues that its perfected security interest entitles it to the proceeds. Commercial policy considerations support both the rights of the secured party and the rights of the transferee in the present situation. In Citizens National Bank, the court set forth commercial policy considerations supporting the rights of a secured party against a bank's right of set-off. There the court stated that a secured creditor should be able to rely on its compliance with U.C.C.'s perfection requirements as against the unrecorded interest of the setting-off bank, otherwise the secured creditor could not rely on recording. Conversely, there are also sound policy reasons for allowing third party transferees to retain the proceeds of another's collateral. In Harley Davidson Motor Co., the court recognized that if "ordinary course" of business is defined too narrowly, the ordinary suppliers will find themselves called upon to return ordinary payments. Furthermore, these suppliers will have the burden of contacting secured creditors to obtain permission to take payment from the debtor's commingled bank account. Comment 2(c) was intended to resolve this conflict in competing interests. Whether a payment was made in the ordinary course will be a function of the extent to which the payment was made in the routine operation of the debtor's business and the extent to which the recipient was aware that it was acting to the prejudice of the secured party. Since imposing liability too readily on payees could impede the free flow of goods and services, the transfer will be free of any claim that a secured party may have in the proceeds, unless the payment would constitute windfall to the recipient. A windfall occurs when the recipient has no reasonable expectation of being paid ahead of a secured creditor because of the extent to which the payment was made outside the ordinary routine of the debtor's business or because the recipient was aware it was acting to the prejudice of the secured party or both. Lindsey's payment to the bank (D) here was not a payment in the ordinary course of the operation of Lindsey's business. The bank (D) was aware that HCC (P) had a valid and perfected security interest in Lindsey's inventory. This was an extremely large payment, which Lindsey had never made before and was not in the ordinary course of its business. For the bank (D) to prevail

Continued on next page.

would result in a windfall since the bank (D) had no reasonable expectation that Lindsey would liquidate its debt to the bank (D) in advance of payment to HCC (P). Reversed and remanded.

EDITOR'S ANALYSIS: The court lists several factors to be taken into consideration in determining whether a payment is routine, including its size, frequency, whether the debtor received any consideration in return, and whether the obligation was due. With respect to the awareness of prejudice prong, the nature of the relationship between the transferee and debtor may give rise to a presumption of awareness of prejudice, particularly if the transferee is a secondary lender whose debt is subordinated to the secured creditor. In such cases the secondary lender will be presumed to have actual knowledge of the prejudice to the secured creditor, since typically the secondary lender will have made the loan with the knowledge that the secured creditor has priority.

NOTES:

CHAPTER 25
DEFAULT

QUICK REFERENCE RULES OF LAW

1. **Default.** An action to recover on a note does not preclude a subsequent action to foreclose upon collateral securing the note. (State Bank of Piper City v. A-Way, Inc.)

2. **Default.** A creditor may accelerate the maturity of a debt when he deems himself insecure, but he must make demand or give notice to purchaser before he repossesses the collateral. (Klingbiel v. Commercial Credit Corp.)

3. **Repossession and Resale.** Oklahoma law creates a nondelegable duty on the part of a creditor to refrain from breaching the peace when repossessing secured collateral, and therefore the creditor is liable for trespass and any resulting damages caused by an independent contractor employed by the creditor to repossess such collateral. (Williamson v. Fowler Toyota, Inc.)

4. **Repossession and Resale.** One having a security interest in chattel may not foreclose thereon in a confrontational manner. (Hillman v. Cobado)

5. **Redemption and Strict Foreclosure.** A secured party who intends to sell the collateral in the normal course of his business must account to the debtor for any surplus, even if strict foreclosure has occurred. (Reeves v. Foutz & Tanner, Inc.)

STATE BANK OF PIPER CITY v. A-WAY, INC.

Bank (P) v. Grain storage facility (D)

115 Ill. 2d 401, 504 N.E.2d 737 (1987).

NATURE OF CASE: Review of order reversing dismissal of debt collection action.

FACT SUMMARY: State Bank of Piper City (P), after receiving partial satisfaction of a judgment on a note, brought an action to foreclose collateral securing the note.

CONCISE RULE OF LAW: An action to recover on a note does not preclude a subsequent action to foreclose upon collateral securing the note.

FACTS: State Bank of Piper City (P) obtained a judgment against Brenner in the amount of $131,083.91. Learning that Brenner had stored certain grain with A-way, Inc. (D), upon which First Bank (P) had a security interest, the Bank (P) demanded that A-way (D) make an accounting. A-way (D) listed 5,141.20 bushels, which were valued at $11,310.64. Mistakenly equating the volume with the value, State Bank (P) obtained an order mandating that A-way (D) pay it $5,141.20, which it did. Realizing its mistake eight months later, the Bank (P) brought an action to enforce its security interest. The trial court dismissed, holding the foreclosure action barred by the prior judgment. The court of appeal reversed, and the Illinois Supreme Court granted review.

ISSUE: Does an action to recover on a note preclude a subsequent action to foreclose upon collateral securing the note?

HOLDING AND DECISION: (Ward, J.) No. An action to recover on a note does not preclude a subsequent action to foreclose upon collateral securing the note. U.C.C. § 9-501(1) permits a secured creditor either to reduce a claim to judgment or to foreclose upon or otherwise proceed against the collateral. The section specifically states that the remedies are cumulative. The effect of this language is to permit a creditor to proceed against an obligation or any security thereon, at the creditor's option, without any fear of the subsequent suit being barred by the doctrine of merger. Here, the Bank (P) went first against the obligation and then against the balance owing through an action against collateral. This it was entitled to do. Affirmed.

EDITOR'S ANALYSIS: Merger (a subset of the doctrine of res judicata) is an old common law concept. Essentially, it provides that a judgment will bar any claim which could have been brought along with the suit underlying the judgment. The rule still has much vitality; unless a statutory exception to it exists, it will be applied in an appropriate situation.

QUICKNOTES

MERGER - The acquisition of one company by another, after which the acquired company ceases to exist as an independent entity.

DOCTRINE OF RES JUDICATA - The rule of law that a final judgment by a court precludes subsequent litigation between the parties regarding the same cause of action.

NOTES:

KLINGBIEL v. COMMERCIAL CREDIT CORP.

Car buyer (P) v. Car repossessor (D)

439 F.2d 1303 (10th Cir., 1971).

NATURE OF CASE: Appeal from award of damages for conversion.

FACT SUMMARY: Commercial Credit Corp. (D) repossessed Klingbiel's (P) car without notice or demand for performance even though he was not behind in his payments.

CONCISE RULE OF LAW: A creditor may accelerate the maturity of a debt when he deems himself insecure, but he must make demand or give notice to purchaser before he repossesses the collateral.

FACTS: Klingbiel (P) entered into an installment contract with a dealer for the purchase of a new car. The contract provided that, if the purchaser defaulted or the dealer felt itself or the vehicle insecure, the unpaid balance would, without notice, become due. Furthermore, the contract permitted the mortgage to be foreclosed in any lawful manner and allowed the dealer, without notice or demand for performance, to lawfully take possession of the vehicle. The dealer assigned the contract to Commercial (D). Before Klingbiel's (P) first monthly installment was due, Commercial (D) felt itself insecure and repossessed the car without notice to Klingbiel (P). Klingbiel (P) sued Commercial (D) for unlawful conversion. The jury found for Klingbiel (P) and awarded actual and punitive damages. Commercial (D) appealed, contending that no notice or demand was necessary prior to repossession.

ISSUE: Must a creditor who accelerates the maturity of a debt make demand or give notice to the purchaser before he repossesses the collateral?

HOLDING AND DECISION: (Brown, J.) Yes. A creditor may accelerate the maturity of a debt when he deems himself insecure but must make demand or give notice to the purchaser before he repossesses the collateral. In the contract in this case, the clause that allowed the seller to take possession of the car without notice or demand followed the clause that required notice/demand before seller could act on a declared acceleration. According to the sequential language of the contract, Commercial (D) could have entered Klingbiel's (P) premises and taken possession of his car without notice, i.e., stealthily, in the dead of night, but only upon default, that is, only after Klingbiel (P) had either failed or refused to perform after receiving notice and demand for performance. Here, Klingbiel (P) was not given a chance to do either; his car simply disappeared without any contact from Commercial (D) before or after the repossession. Failure of notice/demand made Commercial's (D) repossession an unlawful conversion. Affirmed.

EDITOR'S ANALYSIS: "Insecurity clauses" like the one in this case are expressly authorized by U.C.C. § 1-208. Some jurisdictions interpret the clauses to permit acceleration at the whim of the creditor, while others allow acceleration only if a reasonable, prudent creditor would consider himself insecure. U.C.C. § 1-208 simply requires that the secured party act in "good faith."

QUICKNOTES

COLLATERAL - Property that secures the payment of a debt.

CONVERSION - The act of depriving an owner of his property without permission or justification.

NOTES:

WILLIAMSON v. FOWLER TOYOTA, INC.

Automobile shop (P) v. Creditor (D)

Okla. Sup. Ct., 1998 Okla. 14, 956 P.2d 858 (1998).

NATURE OF CASE: Suit for trespass and damages.

FACT SUMMARY: Williamson Auto (P) brought suit against Fowler (D) for damages sustained when one of its cars was repossessed from its locked premises.

CONCISE RULE OF LAW: Oklahoma law creates a nondelegable duty on the part of a creditor to refrain from breaching the peace when repossessing secured collateral, and therefore the creditor is liable for trespass and any resulting damages caused by an independent contractor employed by the creditor to repossess such collateral.

FACTS: Fowler (D) sold a Chevette to Gilmore for approximately $3,000. When Gilmore defaulted on the payments Fowler (D) declared Gilmore in default and hired McGregor to repossess the car. In the meanwhile, Gilmore had become sick and donated the car to Camp Hudgens. The caretaker of the camp took the car to Williamson (P) for inspection. Williamson (P) had no knowledge of any lien on the car nor that Gilmore was in default. McGregor discovered the location of the car from one of Gilmore's relatives. He cut the chain to Williamson Auto (P) with bolt cutters, entered the lot, pushed the car out and towed it. Williamson (P) brought suit alleging his losses at $15 for the lock, and $30 for billable time. He was awarded $45 in actual damages and $15,000 in punitive damages. The court of appeals reversed and this court granted review.

ISSUE: Is a creditor liable for trespass and any resulting damages caused by an independent contractor employed by the creditor to repossess secured collateral?

HOLDING AND DECISION: (Wilson, J.) Yes. Oklahoma law creates a nondelegable duty on the part of a creditor to refrain from breaching the peace when repossessing secured collateral, and therefore the creditor is liable for trespass and any resulting damages caused by an independent contractor employed by the creditor to repossess such collateral. Fowler (D) claimed that it was not liable for the torts of its independent contractors, and that it did not fall within an exception to that general rule for work that is inherently dangerous or unlawful. Other courts, however, have held that repossession work is inherently dangerous and that one who is about to cause something to occur that will probably be injurious to third parties is liable if he does not take all reasonable precautions to anticipate, obviate, and prevent their probable consequences. The issue of whether injury might reasonably have been anticipated as a probable consequence is a question of fact for the jury. A number of courts have also held that the duty of a secured party to repossess peaceably is nondelegable; thus, a secured creditor may be held liable for the torts of its repossessor

even if the repossessor was acting as an independent contractor. Oklahoma law provides for self-help repossession by a secured party so long as the repossession does not constitute a breach of the peace. In construing what constitutes a breach of the peace, the Supreme Court of Alabama has stated that the creditor's privilege is severely restricted where repossession can only be accomplished by the destruction of barriers intended to keep out intruders. Here McGregor cut the chain locking the gate to Williamson Auto (P) and entered without permission of the owner. Fowler (D) is liable for McGregor's trespass and breach of the peace. Judgment of trial court affirmed.

EDITOR'S ANALYSIS: Trespass occurs when there is an actual physical invasion of the real property of another without such owner's permission.

NOTES:

HILLIMAN v. COBADO

Cattle raiser (P) v. Cattle seller (D)

N.Y. Sup. Ct., 499 N.Y.S. 2d 610 (1986).

NATURE OF CASE: Action seeking replevin of repossessed chattel.

FACT SUMMARY: Cobado (D) repossessed certain cattle belonging to Szata (P) in a highly confrontational manner.

CONCISE RULE OF LAW: One having a security interest in chattel may not foreclose thereon in a confrontational manner.

FACTS: Cobado (D) sold Szata (P) certain cattle. He took a purchase-money security interest. Later, believing Szata (P) to be impairing his security by selling some of the cattle, Cobado (D) elected to repossess, as his security instrument permitted him to do. He showed up at Szata's (P) ranch unannounced and began rounding up the cattle. Szata (P) protested that he was not in default. A police officer appeared and ordered Cobado (D) to desist, but he continued anyway. Szata (P) later brought a replevin action, seeking return of the repossessed cattle.

ISSUE: May one having a security interest in chattel foreclose thereon in an confrontational manner?

HOLDING AND DECISION: (Horey, J.) No. One having a security interest in chattel may not foreclosure thereon in a confrontational manner. Under § 9-504 of the U.C.C., one having a security interest in chattel may use self-help and repossess the security when the debtor defaults or impairs the security. However, the U.C.C. clearly states that such repossession must be effected without a breach of the peace. Such breach of the peace means not only actual violence but any act likely to produce violent reaction. In this case, Cobado (D) without doubt did effect his repossession in a manner likely to produce violence, particularly by ignoring Szata's (P) demands that he leave the property and his failure to obey a policeman's orders. Since the repossession was effected in an illegal manner, it was invalid, and the cattle must be returned. So ordered.

EDITOR'S ANALYSIS: For the most part, self-help is looked upon with disfavor in all areas of the law. Repossession is the most notable exception to general rules against self-help. Generally, the requirement that repossession be effected peaceably is strictly enforced.

QUICKNOTES

CHATTEL - An article of personal property, as distinguished from real property; a thing personal and moveable.

REPLEVIN - An action to recover personal property wrongfully taken.

SECURITY INTEREST - An interest in property that may be sold upon a default in payment of the debt.

NOTES:

REEVES v. FOUTZ & TANNER, INC.
Erstwhile owners of jewelry (P) v. Pawnshop (D)
N.M. Sup. Ct., 94 N.M. 760, 617 P.2d 149 (1980).

NATURE OF CASE: Appeal from reversal of award of surplus proceeds from a foreclosure sale.

FACT SUMMARY: After sending Reeves (P) and Begay (P) a notice of intent to retain the jewelry they had pawned, Foutz & Tanner, Inc. (D) sold it in the regular course of its business.

CONCISE RULE OF LAW: A secured party who intends to sell the collateral in the normal course of his business must account to the debtor for any surplus, even if strict foreclosure has occurred.

FACTS: Reeves (P) and Begay (P) left their Navaho jewelry as collateral with Foutz & Tanner, Inc. (D), a pawnshop, in return for a loan, which they promised to repay in 30 days. The jewelry was worth several times the amount they borrowed. When Reeves (P) and Begay (P) defaulted on the loan, Foutz (D) sent each of them a notice of intent to retain the collateral. When neither Reeves (P) nor Begay (P) objected to the retention, Foutz (D), in accordance with its normal business practice, sold the jewelry. Foutz (D) did not account to Reeves (P) or Begay (P) for any surplus. Reeves (P) and Begay (P) brought suit against Foutz (D). The trial court applied U.C.C. § 9-504, requiring that Foutz (D) return any surplus from the sale of the jewelry to Reeves (P) and Begay (P). The appellate court reversed, and Reeves (P) and Begay (P) appealed.

ISSUE: Must a secured party who intends to sell the collateral in the normal course of his business account to the debtor for any surplus, even if strict foreclosure has occurred?

HOLDING AND DECISION: (Sosa, C.J.) Yes. A secured party who intends to sell the collateral in the normal course of his business must account to the debtor for any surplus, even if strict foreclosure has occurred. A secured party in possession of collateral may choose one of two courses of action upon default by the debtor: (1) pursuant to U.C.C. § 9-504, he may sell the collateral, but he must account to the debtor for any surplus, or (2) pursuant to U.C.C. § 9-505(2), he may strictly foreclose by retaining the collateral for his own use in satisfaction of the obligation. However, waiver of surplus rights under § 9-505(2) is appropriate only when prompt resale of repossessed collateral in the ordinary course of business is not contemplated by the creditor. Since, in this case, Foutz (D) did intend to sell the jewelry in its normal course of business, he must comply with § 9-504 and account for any surplus. Reversed.

EDITOR'S ANALYSIS: One of the advantages of strict foreclosure over resale of the collateral is that the secured party need not worry about later challenges regarding the fairness of a resale price, as sometimes occurs under § 9-504. Reeves appears to eliminate this advantage, at least in those cases where the intention of the secured party to resell the collateral can be shown.

QUICKNOTES
COLLATERAL - Property that secures the payment of a debt.

NOTES:

CHAPTER SA
SALES, LEASES, AND LICENSES

QUICK REFERENCE RULES OF LAW

1. **Contract Formation: The Statute of Frauds.** Annotated purchase order forms signed by the buyer, sent to the seller, and retained without objection fall within the merchant's exception, satisfying the statutory requirement of a writing even without the seller's signature. (Bazak International Corp. v. Mast Industries, Inc.)

2. **Contract Formation: Offer and Acceptance.** A provision disclaiming consequential damages materially alters the contract and therefore is not an additional term under U.C.C. § 2-207(2). (Dale R. Horning Co. v. Falconer Glass Industries, Inc.)

3. **Warranties of Quality: Burden of Proof.** (1) A customer may not recover damages under an implied warranty theory unless he can show that the product or good that injured him was unfit for the ordinary purposes for which such goods are used. (2) A customer may not recover damages under a strict tort liability theory unless he shows that the product or good that injured him was defective. (Flippo v. Mode O'Day Frock Shops of Hollywood)

4. **Warranties of Quality: Disclaimers and Limitations.** Where a new car express warranty limits a buyer's remedy to repair and replacement of defective parts but the new car is so riddled with defects that the limited remedy of repair and replacement fails its essential purpose, the buyer may institute an action to recover damages for breach of warranty and, in a proper case, incidental and consequential damages. (Goddard v. General Motors Corp.)

5. **Contract Terms: Risk of Loss—No Breach.** Where goods are held by a bailee to be delivered without being moved, the risk of loss passes to the buyer on acknowledgment by the bailee of the buyer's right to possession of the goods. (Jason's Foods, Inc. v. Peter Eckrich & Sons, Inc.)

6. **Remedies: The Statute of Limitations.** Accrual of a cause of action for breach of an express auto warranty occurs upon discovery of the defect. (Nationwide Insurance Co. v. General Motors Corp./Chevrolet Motor Division)

7. **Remedies: The Statute of Limitations.** A buyer of goods may bring an indemnity action against the seller for liability incurred to a third party for a defect in the goods, and the statute of limitations begins to run when the buyer pays damages to the third party or the third party obtains judgment against the buyer, whichever occurs first. (Central Washington Refrigeration, Inc. v. Barbee)

8. **Letters of Credit: Duties and Rights of the Issuer.** Attachment of invoices to a demand on a letter of credit will constitute compliance with such a letter's proof requirements. (U.S. Industries, Inc. v. Second New Haven Bank)

9. **Letters of Credit: Duties and Rights of the Issuer.** Equitable subrogation is unavailable when a letter of credit satisfies a party's liability. (Tudor Development Group, Inc. v. United States Fidelity & Guaranty Co.)

10. **Licenses.** A buyer accepts goods when, after an opportunity to inspect, he fails to make an effective rejection. (ProCD, Inc. v. Zeidenberg)

BAZAK INTERNATIONAL CORP. v. MAST INDUSTRIES, INC.

Corporation (P) v. Corporation (D)
73 N.Y.2d 113, 535 N.E.2d 633 (1989).

NATURE OF CASE: Appeal from reversal of denial of motion to dismiss an action for breach of contract and fraud.

FACT SUMMARY: When Mast (D) failed to send textiles which Bazak (P) had agreed to purchase, Bazak (P) filed suit for breach of contract and fraud, but Mast (D) moved to dismiss, contending that the purchase order forms which allegedly confirmed the parties' oral agreement could not be considered confirmatory documents within the U.C.C. and failed to satisfy the Statute of Frauds.

CONCISE RULE OF LAW: Annotated purchase order forms signed by the buyer, sent to the seller, and retained without objection fall within the merchant's exception, satisfying the statutory requirement of a writing even without the seller's signature.

FACTS: After Mast's (D) marketing director, Fedorko, met with Bazak's (P) president, Feldman, offering to sell Feldman certain textiles that Mast (D) was closing out, the parties negotiated all the terms of an oral agreement except price. The following day, they agreed on a price, and Fedorko told Feldman that Bazak (P) would receive written invoices for the goods the next day and that the textiles would be delivered shortly. When Bazak (P) had still not received any invoices a week later, Feldman went to the New York City offices of Mast's (D) parent company, where, following Fedorko's instructions, Feldman sent five purchase orders by telecopier to Mast's (D) Massachusetts office. Small type at the bottom of each form read in pertinent part: "This is only an offer and not a contract unless accepted in writing by the seller, and subject to prior sale." Bazak (P) signed each form, but Mast (D) did not. That same day, Feldman received written confirmation of Mast's (D) receipt of the orders. Mast (D) made no objection to the terms set forth in the telecopied purchase orders but never delivered the textiles, despite Bazak's (P) demands. Bazak (P) filed suit, alleging breach of contract and fraud. Mast (D) moved to dismiss, contending that the purchase orders were insufficient under U.C.C. § 2-201 to satisfy the Statute of Frauds. The trial court denied the motion to dismiss, but the appellate division reversed. Bazak (P) appealed.

ISSUE: Do annotated purchase order forms signed by the buyer, sent to the seller, and retained without objection fall within the merchant's exception, satisfying the statutory requirement of a writing even without the seller's signature?

HOLDING AND DECISION: (Kaye, J.) Yes. Annotated purchase order forms signed by the buyer, sent to the seller, and retained without objection fall within the merchant's exception, satisfying

the statutory requirement of a writing even without the seller's signature. U.C.C. § 2-201(1) requires that the writing be "sufficient to indicate" a contract, while § 2-201(2) calls for a writing "in confirmation of the contract." While explicit words of confirmation are not required, the writing still must satisfy the test articulated in U.C.C. § 2-201(1). In determining whether writings are confirmatory documents within U.C.C. § 2-201(2), neither explicit words of confirmation nor express references to the prior agreement are required; the writings are sufficient so long as they afford a basis for believing that they reflect a real transaction between the parties. Taken as a whole, there was sufficient evidence that the writings rest on a real transaction and therefore satisfy the Statute of Frauds. The handwritten notations on the purchase order forms provided a basis for believing that the documents were in furtherance of a previous agreement. The terms set forth were highly specific, with precise quantities, descriptions, prices per unit, and payment terms stated. Finally, Mast (D) itself relayed Bazak's (P) forms. These factors, considered together, adequately indicated confirmation of a preexisting agreement so as to permit Bazak (P) to go forward and prove its allegations. In addition, the fraud count may be read to assert that Mast's (D) persistent promises to send invoices induced Bazak (P) to undertake an obligation to a third person for which it now stands responsible. It has long been recognized that "the circumstances constituting a fraud are peculiarly within the knowledge of the party against whom the fraud is being asserted," and such an assertion is plainly sufficient to survive a motion to dismiss. Reversed (order of the trial court affirmed).

DISSENT: (Alexander, J.) The purchase orders, which described themselves as offers and did not otherwise indicate the existence of a completed agreement, were not "sufficient against the sender" because they failed to "indicate that a contract for sale has been made between the parties." Consequently, they were not confirmatory memoranda sufficient to satisfy the Statute of Frauds.

EDITOR'S ANALYSIS: Special merchant rules are sprinkled throughout Article 2 of the U.C.C., distinguishing the obligations of businesspeople from others. Among the suggested motivations was to state clear, sensible rules better adjusted to the reality of what commercial transactions were, thereby promoting predictable, dependable, decent business practices. Section 2-201(2) recognized the common practice among merchants, particularly small businesses, to enter into oral sales agreements later confirmed in writing by one of the parties.

DALE R. HORNING CO. v.
FALCONER GLASS INDUSTRIES, INC.
Plaintiff (P) v. Manufacturer (D)
730 F. Supp. 962 (S.D. Ind. 1990).

NATURE OF CASE: Action for damages for breach of warranty.

FACT SUMMARY: Falconer (D) claimed that a provision disclaiming consequential damages did not materially alter its agreement with AGM (P) and was therefore a permissible additional term under U.C.C. § 2-207(2).

CONCISE RULE OF LAW: A provision disclaiming consequential damages materially alters the contract and therefore is not an additional term under U.C.C. § 2-207(2).

FACTS: AGM (P) purchased glass product from Falconer (D) for use on an office building that AGM (P) was constructing. The parties orally agreed to the sale, and Falconer (D) was made aware that AGM (P) would suffer damages if the glass was not received by the date contracted for. AGM (P) and Falconer (D) each sent confirming forms of the oral agreement. AGM's (P) purchase order contained no provision for warranty. Falconer's (D) form contained a provision that disclaimed consequential damages. In the commercial glass industry, suppliers usually disclaim consequential damages but often cover part or all of the expenses incurred by defective glass. The glass delivered by Falconer (D) was defective and although eventually conforming goods were sent, AGM (P) suffered damages and expenses due to the delay. AGM (P) filed suit for breach of warranty. Falconer (D) contended that the provision disclaiming consequential damages was effective since it was an additional term which did not materially alter the contract, and because AGM (P) failed to object to it, it was bound by the disclaimer. [The casebook excerpt did not explain the significance of Horning Co., a title party.]

ISSUE: Does a provision disclaiming consequential damages materially alter the terms of contract for purposes of U.C.C. § 2-207(2)?

HOLDING AND DECISION: (McKinney, J.) Yes. A provision which disclaims consequential damages materially alters the contract and pursuant to U.C.C. § 2-207(2) is not an additional term governing the agreement. When an offeree's acceptance form contains provisions not included in the offer, the provisions become part of the contract unless the offeror objects, or the terms materially alter the agreement. Material alteration focuses on the surprise and hardship to the offeror. Where the offeror suffers surprise or hardship due to the additional term, it will be considered a material alteration and will not be controlling on the contract. The provision disclaiming consequential damages in Falconer's (D) acceptance was not a surprise to AGM (P) because the practice was common in the industry. However, the

provision would shift the responsibility and liability for the delay due to defective products to AGM (P), which thus would impose a hardship on AGM (P). As such, it is a material alteration of the contract. Therefore, under § 2-207(2), it is an additional term which is dropped from the agreement. Judgment for AGM (P).

EDITOR'S ANALYSIS: The first clause of U.C.C. § 2-207, discussing conditional assent, is often referred to as the proviso clause. If acceptance is made conditional on assent to additional terms, the contract is only created by the party's performance and U.C.C. § 2-207(3) supplies the terms. If acceptance is not made conditional, then § 2-207(2) determines the validity of the additional terms.

QUICKNOTES
CONSEQUENTIAL DAMAGES - Monetary compensation that may be recovered in order to compensate for injuries or losses sustained as a result of damages that are not the direct or foreseeable result of the act of a party, but that nevertheless are the consequence of such act and which must be specifically pled and demonstrated.

NOTES:

FLIPPO v. MODE O'DAY FROCK SHOPS OF HOLLYWOOD

Customer (P) v. Clothing store (D)

Ark. Sup. Ct., 248 Ark. 1, 449 S.W.2d 692 (1970).

NATURE OF CASE: Appeal from denial of damages for negligence, breach of implied warranty, and strict liability in tort.

FACT SUMMARY: Flippo (P) sought damages for injury sustained when she was bitten by a spider while trying on a pair of pants at Mode O'Day Frock Shops (D).

CONCISE RULE OF LAW: (1) A customer may not recover damages under an implied warranty theory unless he can show that the product or good that injured him was unfit for the ordinary purposes for which such goods are used. (2) A customer may not recover damages under a strict tort liability theory unless he shows that the product or good that injured him was defective.

FACTS: Flippo (P), a customer in Mode O'Day (D) ladies' clothing store, was bitten on the leg by a spider while trying on a pair of stretch pants. Flippo (P) was subsequently hospitalized for approximately 30 days. A suit for damages was instituted against Mode O'Day Frock Shops (D) and Goforth (D), the shop owner, for negligence, breach of implied warranty, and strict tort liability. At trial, the court refused requested instructions offered by Flippo (P) on theories of implied warranty and strict tort liability. The jury returned a verdict for Mode O'Day (D) and Goforth (D). Flippo (P) appealed, based entirely on the court's refusal to submit the case upon implied warranty and strict tort liability theories.

ISSUE: (1) Can a customer recover damages on theories of implied warranty where the customer cannot prove that the goods which injured him were unfit for the ordinary purposes for which such goods were used? (2) Can a customer recover damages in strict tort liability where he cannot prove that the goods that caused the injury were defective in any manner?

HOLDING AND DECISION: (Harris, J.) (1) No. A customer may not recover damages under an implied warranty theory unless he can show that the product or good that injured him was unfit for the ordinary purposes for which such goods are used. (2) No. A customer may not recover damages under a strict tort liability theory unless he shows that the product or good that injured him was defective. In this case, the court found that the pair of pants itself was fit for ordinary purposes for which stretch pants are used; there was nothing wrong from a manufacturing standpoint. There was also no evidence that the goods were defective in any manner. The spider was the cause of the injury, and it was apparent that the spider was not part of the product. Affirmed.

EDITOR'S ANALYSIS: In a warranty suit, the plaintiff has the burden of proving (1) the creation of the warranty, (2) its breach, (3) its causal connection to the plaintiff's injury (proximate cause), and (4) the fact and extent of the injury. In this case, Flippo (P) failed to prove that the warranty was breached. The implied warranty of merchantability assures the user that the product is fit for the ordinary purposes for which such goods are used, and the pair of pants met this standard.

NOTES:

GODDARD v. GENERAL MOTORS CORP.
Car owner (P) v. Car manufacturer (D)
Ohio Sup. Ct., 60 Ohio St. 2d 41, 396 N.E.2d 761 (1979).

NATURE OF CASE: Appeal from reversal of award of damages for breach of warranty.

FACT SUMMARY: When his new Chevrolet Vega station wagon developed numerous mechanical problems shortly after purchase, which General Motors (D) and its dealers failed to properly repair, Goddard (P) filed this action for breach of the express 12-month or 12,000-mile warranty.

CONCISE RULE OF LAW: Where a new car express warranty limits a buyer's remedy to repair and replacement of defective parts but the new car is so riddled with defects that the limited remedy of repair and replacement fails its essential purpose, the buyer may institute an action to recover damages for breach of warranty and, in a proper case, incidental and consequential damages.

FACTS: Goddard (P) received delivery of a new Chevrolet Vega station wagon on October 2, 1972, for $3,180. The purchase contract contained a warranty for a period of 12 months or 12,000 miles, whichever first occurred, during which General Motors (D) would repair any defective or malfunctioning part of the vehicle, with certain stated exceptions. The contract expressly stated that loss of time, inconvenience, loss of use of the vehicle, or consequential damages were not covered by the warranty. Beginning on or about October 29, 1972, Goddard's (P) Vega experienced numerous mechanical problems, including a persistent vibration which was so bad that it caused certain bolts on the car to fall off and be lost. After numerous repairs, some of which were done adequately and some of which were done inadequately, the car still did not function properly, causing Goddard (P) to give up on his Vega in June 1973, when he ordered a new Chevrolet from the same dealer. In August, with approximately 18,000 miles on the Vega, it was "wholesaled" for $2,200. Goddard (P) filed this action for breach of warranty. The jury awarded him damages in the amount of $7,500. The trial court overruled General Motors' (D) motion for a new trial but ordered a remittitur of the jury award to $5,000, the amount requested in the complaint. The court of appeals reversed, remanding for additional proceedings on the question of damages. Goddard (P) appealed.

ISSUE: Where a new car express warranty limits a buyer's remedy to repair and replacement of defective parts, but the new car is so riddled with defects that the limited remedy of repair and replacement fails its essential purpose, may the buyer institute an action to recover damages for breach of warranty and, in a proper case, incidental and consequential damages?

HOLDING AND DECISION: (Herbert, J.) Yes. Where a new car express warranty limits a buyer's remedy to repair and replacement of defective parts, but the new car is so riddled with defects that the limited remedy of repair and replacement fails its essential purpose, the buyer may institute an action to recover damages for breach of warranty and, in a proper case, incidental and consequential damages. As authorized by U.C.C. § 2-719(1)(a), General Motors (D) attempted to limit its liability under the express warranty to the repair and replacement of defective parts. Pursuant to § 2-719(3), General Motors (D) purported to exclude any liability for consequential damages. A significant number of authorities have held that language similar to that in the instant case is an adequate expression of the seller's intent to limit the buyer's remedy to the repair and replacement of defective parts. However, whether in fact such a provision is effective to preclude recourse to the other remedial provisions of the U.C.C. depends in part on whether the limitation of remedy provision complies with § 2-719, the enabling statute. Although, in most cases, a limited remedy may be fair and reasonable and satisfy the reasonable expectations of a new car purchaser, other courts and some commentators have generally recognized that when a seller is unable to fulfill its warranted obligation to effectively repair or replace defects in goods which are the subject matter of the sale, such as in the instant case, the buyer is deprived of the benefits of the limited remedy, and it therefore fails its essential purpose. Reversed in part and remanded [to the trial court for the purpose of adducing evidence upon the amount of direct and consequential damages properly recoverable] in part.

EDITOR'S ANALYSIS: In declining to enforce the disclaimer of consequential damages expressed by General Motors (D) in its warranty, the court took note of the stated purpose of the remedial provisions of U.C.C. § 1-106(1), which provides that the remedies expressed in the U.C.C. should be liberally administered with the view of placing the aggrieved party in as good a position as if the other party had fully performed. Furthermore, the court noted that the U.C.C. indicates that parties who conclude a contract for sale "must accept the legal consequence that there be at least a fair quantum of remedy for breach of the obligations or duties outlined in the contract." However, where the buyer is not a consumer, courts are less likely to invalidate a disclaimer of liability for consequential damages, even where the limited remedy "fails its essential purpose."

QUICKNOTES

EXPRESS WARRANTY - An express promise made by one party to a contract that the other party may rely on a fact, relieving that party from the obligation of determining whether the fact is true and indemnifying the other party from liability if that fact is shown to be false.

JASON'S FOODS, INC. v. PETER ECKRICH & SONS, INC.
Pork rib seller (P) v. Pork rib buyer (D)
774 F.2d 214 (7th Cir. 1985).

NATURE OF CASE: Appeal from summary judgment denying damages for breach of contract.

FACT SUMMARY: Jason's Foods (P) sought to recover the contract price for 38,000 pounds of "St. Louis style" pork ribs when Peter Eckrich & Sons (D) backed out of a purchase agreement on the grounds that the ribs had been destroyed in a fire before they had acknowledged possession, and, thus, they had not accepted the risk of loss.

CONCISE RULE OF LAW: Where goods are held by a bailee to be delivered without being moved, the risk of loss passes to the buyer on acknowledgment by the bailee of the buyer's right to possession of the goods.

FACTS: On December 30, 1982, Jason's Foods (P) contracted to sell 38,000 pounds of "St. Louis style" pork ribs to Peter Eckrich & Sons (D). The delivery was to be effected by a transfer of the ribs from Jason's (P) account in an independent warehouse to Eckrich's (D) account in the same warehouse, without the ribs actually being moved. In its confirmation of the deal, Jason's Foods (P) notified Eckrich (D) that the transfer in storage would be made between January 10 and 14. On January 13, Jason's (P) phoned the warehouse and requested that the ribs be transferred to Eckrich's (D) account. A clerk at the warehouse noted the transfer immediately but did not mail a warehouse receipt until January 17 or January 18, and it was not until Eckrich (D) received the receipt on January 24 that they knew the transfer had taken place. However, on January 17 the ribs had been destroyed by a fire in the warehouse. Jason's (P) sued Eckrich (D) for the price. The district judge ruled that the risk of loss had not passed to Eckrich (D) and granted their summary judgment motion. Jason's (P) appealed.

ISSUE: Does the risk of loss pass from the seller to the buyer upon acknowledgment by the bailee of the transfer to the seller where the goods are held by a bailee to be delivered without actually being moved?

HOLDING AND DECISION: (Posner, J.) No. Where goods are held by a bailee to be delivered without being moved, the risk of loss passes to the buyer on acknowledgment by the bailee of the buyer's right to possession of the goods. This means that the acknowledgment must be made to the buyer, not the seller. Here, the bailee notified the seller that the goods had been transferred to the buyer, but the bailee did not notify the buyer. Jason's (P) tried to argue that Eckrich (D) received acknowledgment of their right to possession on the day that the title was actually transferred in the bailee's books (January 13), but this argument was rejected by the court. Nothing was presented demonstrating

that the trial court's decision was unsupported by the evidence. Affirmed.

EDITOR'S ANALYSIS: Under the old Uniform Sales Act, the risk of loss stayed with the person having technical title to the goods and passed to the buyer only when title to the goods switched to the buyer. The U.C.C. expressly states that its rules as to who bears the risk of loss have nothing to do with technical title (§ 2-401(1)). U.C.C. § 2-509(3) sets out the general rule on the transfer of risk of loss: "absent contrary agreement, (1) where the seller is a merchant, the risk of loss passes to the buyer on buyer's actual receipt of the goods, and (2) where the seller is not a merchant, risk of loss passes to the buyer when the seller tenders delivery." Section 2-509(3), however, only applies when § 2-509(2) does not.

QUICKNOTES

BAILEE - Person holding property in trust for another party.

RISK OF LOSS - Liability for damage to or loss of property that is the subject matter of a contract for sale.

NOTES:

NATIONWIDE INSURANCE CO. v. GENERAL MOTORS CORP./ CHEVROLET MOTOR DIVISION

Insurance company (P) v. Car manufacturer (D)

625 A.2d 1172, 21 U.C.C. Rep. Serv. 2d 277 (1993).

NATURE OF CASE: Appeal from dismissal of action seeking damages for breach of express and implied warranty.

FACT SUMMARY: Nationwide Insurance Co. (P) contended that a twelve-month/12,000-mile warranty on a car explicitly extended to "future performance" of the car so that the cause of action accrued when the breach of warranty was discovered rather than when the car was delivered.

CONCISE RULE OF LAW: Accrual of a cause of action for breach of an express auto warranty occurs upon discovery of the defect.

FACTS: Nationwide's (P) insured purchased a vehicle from General Motors Corp. (D). The vehicle contained a one-year/12,000-mile warranty covering parts and labor for defects. Within this period the auto was destroyed, allegedly due to a defect. Nationwide (P), the purchaser's insurer, brought an action based on the express warranty, as well as implied warranties. The suit was brought more than four years after delivery of the vehicle but less than four years after its loss. The trial court dismissed on statute of limitations grounds, and Nationwide (P) appealed.

ISSUE: Does accrual of a cause of action for breach of an express auto warranty occur upon discovery of the defect?

HOLDING AND DECISION: (Cappy, J.) Yes. Accrual of a cause of action for breach of an express auto warranty occurs upon discovery of the defect. Section 2725 of the U.C.C. provides a four-year statute of limitations for breach of a warranty, with the cause to accrue upon delivery. However, an exception is made when an express warranty extends to "future performance." In that situation, accrual occurs upon discovery of the breach. A warranty covering parts and labor for a specified period, while not exactly dealing with "future performance," deals with, at the time of purchase, a contingency that may occur in the future. This is sufficiently like a warranty dealing with future performance that it should fall within the ambit of the exception found in § 2725. This being so, the count based on the express warranty was timely filed and should not have been dismissed. However, the implied warranties of merchantability and fitness do not extend to future performance of the car and were filed too late. Affirmed in part; reversed in part.

DISSENT: (Larsen, J.) The implied warranties also extend to future performance.

DISSENT: (Zappala, J.) A promise for repair is not the same thing as a promise against freedom from defects. The warranty here was a promise to repair and did not promise any specific future performance.

EDITOR'S ANALYSIS: Section 2725 provides that most warranty breach causes of action accrue as of delivery. This is based on the notion that a vendor can only warrant goods as of the time he surrenders possession. After this point, it would be unfair to let the statute fail to commence running. Buyers and seller may contract for a shorter statute of limitations but may not increase the period beyond four years.

QUICKNOTES

EXPRESS WARRANTY - An express promise made by one party to a contract that the other party may rely on a fact, relieving that party from the obligation of determining whether the fact is true and indemnifying the other party from liability if that fact is shown to be false.

IMPLIED WARRANTY - An implied promise made by one party to a contract that the other party may rely on a fact, relieving that party from the obligation of determining whether the fact is true and indemnifying the other party from liability if that fact is shown to be false.

NOTES:

CENTRAL WASHINGTON REFRIGERATION, INC.
v. BARBEE
Refrigeration company (P) v. Orchard (D)
Wash. Sup. Ct., 133 Wash. 2d 509 (1997).

NATURE OF CASE: Suit seeking indemnity and/or contribution for damages.

FACT SUMMARY: Central (P) brought suit against McCormack (D), a third party, seeking contribution and/or indemnification for damages paid as a result of a defect in the refrigeration coils supplied by McCormack (D).

CONCISE RULE OF LAW: A buyer of goods may bring an indemnity action against the seller for liability incurred to a third party for a defect in the goods, and the statute of limitations begins to run when the buyer pays damages to the third party or the third party obtains judgment against the buyer, whichever occurs first.

FACTS: In 1987 Central (P) contracted with a Yakima orchard to install a set of cold storage rooms to store fruit. Central (P) then contracted with McCormack (D) to purchase the refrigeration coils which Central (P) was to install. The orchard experienced problems with the storage rooms and ultimately defaulted on its payments. Central (P) sued for payment and the orchard counterclaimed for damages asserting Central (P) responsible for the failure of the system. In 1992 Central (P) filed a third party complaint against McCormack (D) alleging the coils were defective and seeking contribution and/or indemnity. The court dismissed McCormack on (D) summary judgment. Central (P) settled with the orchard for $220,000 and appealed the summary judgment. The court of appeals affirmed and this court granted review.

ISSUE: May a buyer of goods bring an indemnity action against the seller for liability incurred to a third party for a defect in the goods, and does the statute of limitations begin to run when the buyer pays damages to the third party or the third party obtains judgment against the buyer, whichever occurs first?

HOLDING AND DECISION: (Sanders, J.) Yes. A buyer of goods may bring an indemnity action against the seller for liability incurred to a third party for a defect in the goods, and the statute of limitations begins to run when the buyer pays damages to the third party or the third party obtains judgment against the buyer, whichever occurs first. Indemnity means reimbursement and may lie when one party discharges a liability that another party should rightfully have assumed. Indemnity is an equitable cause of action and may be implied in fact. This occurs when one party incurs a liability the other party should discharge by virtue of the nature of the relationship between them and gives rise to the right of implied indemnity. Here the issue is whether the contractual relationship between buyer and seller under the U.C.C. is

sufficient to give rise to the implied right when a defect in the goods causes damage to a third-party consumer. The majority rule set forth in Bellevue South Assocs. v. HRH Constr. Corp. holds that the contractual relationship and the U.C.C.'s implied warranties provide sufficient basis for an indemnification claim. This court adopts the majority rule and holds a contractual relationship under the U.C.C. with its implied warranties provides sufficient basis for an implied indemnity claim when the buyer incurs liability to a third party as a result of a defect in the goods that would constitute a breach of the seller's express or implied warranties. The statute of limitations accrues when the party seeking indemnity pays or is legally obligated to pay damages to the third party. Reversed and remanded.

DISSENT: (Guy, J.) By holding contract-based indemnity claims outside the U.C.C.'s four-year statute of repose, commercial retailers are left susceptible to indemnity claims indefinitely. Here Central's (P) claim was governed by U.C.C. § 2-725 requiring a claim to be made within four years after the breach occurred, *i.e.* when delivery is made, and was properly dismissed.

EDITOR'S ANALYSIS: A statute of repose, found in U.C.C. § 2-725, differs from a statute of limitations in that the latter prohibits plaintiffs from commencing an already accrued claim after a specified period, while the former terminate the right of action after the prescribed period whether or not he injury has been sustained.

NOTES:

U.S. INDUSTRIES, INC.
v. SECOND NEW HAVEN BANK

Corporation (P) v. Bank (D)

462 F. Supp. 662 (D. Conn. 1978).

NATURE OF CASE: Action seeking payment on a letter of credit.

FACT SUMMARY: Rather than sending a certified statement along with a demand on a letter of credit, U.S. Industries (P) submitted invoices.

CONCISE RULE OF LAW: Attachment of invoices to a demand on a letter of credit will constitute compliance with such a letter's proof requirements.

FACTS: On instructions from Railroad Salvage, Inc., Second New Haven Bank (D) issued a letter of credit to U.S. Industries, Inc. (P). The letter specified that any demand on the letter contain a certified statement that the goods in question had been shipped to Railroad Salvage. U.S. Industries (P) shipped the goods contemplated by the letter. The demand on the letter was accompanied by two invoices but no statement. The Bank (D) refused payment. U.S. Industries (P) sued to recover on the letter.

ISSUE: Will attachment of invoices to a demand on a letter of credit constitute compliance with such a letter's proof requirements?

HOLDING AND DECISION: (Daly, J.) Yes. Attachment of invoices to a demand on a letter of credit will constitute compliance with such a letter's proof requirements. Under U.C.C. § 5-114, an issuer is obligated to honor a demand for payment which complies with the terms of the letter of credit. The requirements of a letter must be given strict compliance for the issuer's obligation to arise. However, the purpose of the certification requirement in the letter at issue here was to ensure that the goods in question had been delivered; it was to serve an evidentiary function. The submission of invoices, as was done in this case, served the same function. Consequently, strict compliance requirements do not preclude the validity of the demand made in this case. Judgment for U.S. Industries (P) in the amount of $28,044.

EDITOR'S ANALYSIS: Generally speaking, the profit margin for banks is fairly small with respect to letters of credit. Hence, courts do not tend to construe them broadly. The strict compliance rule cited above is an example of this. A smart bank officer, however, will not try to take undue advantage of this judicial deference, as the Bank (D) here arguably did.

TUDOR DEVELOPMENT GROUP, INC. v. UNITED STATES FIDELITY & GUARANTY CO.

(Parties not identified.)
968 F.2d 357 (3rd Cir. 1992).

NATURE OF CASE: Appeal in action for breach of contract.

FACT SUMMARY: Dauphin Deposit Bank ("Dauphin") (P) honored a standby letter of credit made on behalf of Associates (D) with the Township as beneficiary, and then sought the funds of USF&G's performance bonds on a theory of equitable subrogation.

CONCISE RULE OF LAW: Equitable subrogation is unavailable when a letter of credit satisfies a party's liability.

FACTS: Associates (D) was the developer of a subdivision construction project. Associates (D) contracted with SCC to construct buildings and ECU to construct roadways and improvements. SCC's performance was guarantied by performance bonds supplied by USF&G, and ECU's performance was guarantied by performance bonds supplied by Wausau. The Township in which the subdivision existed required Associates (D) to provide it with a bond or standby letter of credit guarantying the improvements to the area. Dauphin (P) supplied Associates (D) with an irrevocable standby letter of credit payable upon Township's certification that the improvements had not been completed. Associates (D) agreed to reimburse Dauphin (P) if Dauphin (P) had to pay and assigned to Dauphin (P) the Wausau performance bonds as security, but not the USF&G performance bonds. SCC defaulted in its contract with Associates (D) and caused to Associates (D) default in its contract with Township. Township drew on its letter of credit from Dauphin (P) and Associates (D) sought a settlement with USF&G for SCC's breach of contract. USF&G provided $594,000 as settlement for SCC's breach held by the court for determination of competing claims. Associates (D) claimed an interest in the funds as the obligee of the agreement, and Dauphin (P) claimed it had an interest in those funds in that it was equitably subrogated to Associates's (D) position due to its payment of the letter of credit to Township. The court ruled for Associates (D) and Dauphin (P) appealed.

ISSUE: Is equitable subrogation available to situations involving letters of credit?

HOLDING AND DECISION: (Cowen, J.) No. Equitable subrogation is unavailable when a letter of credit satisfies a party's liability. Equitable subrogation is allowed only when a party secondarily liable, like a guarantor, pays the debt of a party primarily liable. Here, Dauphin (P) was fulfilling its primary obligation to Township under its letter of credit. The most important feature of letters of credit is the independent nature of the instruments. Allowing Dauphin (P) to claim secondary liability, thereby allowing equitable subrogation, would diminish the independent nature of the instrument. Therefore the decision of the lower court is affirmed.

DISSENT: (Becker, J.) Standby letters of credit may in some circumstances obtain equitable subrogation to the rights of the customer. The independence principle should guaranty that the issuer pays first, without regard to any litigation. However, once the issuer has paid, allowing equitable subrogation would not affect the independent nature of the letter of credit. If no equitable subrogation is allowed, fewer banks will be willing to issue letters of credit and this may hurt the efficiency of commerce. Equitable subrogation for letters of credit, while a close issue, should be decided on a case-by-case basis, thereby leaving courts with the ability to avoid unfair windfalls.

EDITOR'S ANALYSIS: The subrogation issue is litigated mostly in the context of Bankruptcy Code § 509(a), which states that ". . . an entity that is liable with the debtor on, or that has secured, a claim of a creditor against the debtor, and that pays such claim, is subrogated to the rights of the creditor to the extent of such payment." Courts have held that with respect to letters of credit, the independence principle ensures that an issuer is not "liable with the debtor" and is therefore precluded from subrogation. And while revised U.C.C. § 5-117 provides an issuer with a subrogation remedy, many courts feel that the U.C.C. section is inapplicable in bankruptcy, as subrogation rights in bankruptcy are governed by Bankruptcy Code § 509.

QUICKNOTES

GUARANTOR - A party who agrees to be liable for the debt or default of another.

SUBROGATION - The substitution of one party for another in assuming the first party's rights or obligations.

NOTES:

ProCD, INC. v. ZEIDENBERG
Software manufacturer (P) v. Purchaser (D).
86 F.3d 1477 (7th Cir. 1996).

NATURE OF CASE: Appeal from an order in favor of defendant in a case alleging breach of the terms of a shrinkwrap or end-user license.

FACT SUMMARY: When Zeidenberg (D), a customer, bought and then resold the data compiled on its CD-ROM software disk, ProCD (P) sued for breach of contract.

CONCISE RULE OF LAW: A buyer accepts goods when, after an opportunity to inspect, he fails to make an effective rejection.

FACTS: ProCD (P) compiled information from over 3,000 telephone directories into a computer database which it sold on CD-ROM disks. Every box containing the disks declared that the software came with restrictions stated in an enclosed license. This license, which was encoded on the CD-ROM disks as well as printed in the manual, and which appeared on a user's screen every time the software ran, limited use of the application program and listings to non-commercial purposes. Zeidenberg bought a ProCD (P) software package but decided to ignore the license and to resell the information in the database. Zeidenberg (D) also made the information from ProCD's (P) database available over the Internet for a price, through his corporation. ProCD (P) sued for breach of contract. The district court found that placing the package of software on the shelf was an "offer," which the customer "accepted" by paying the asking price and leaving the store with the goods. A contract includes only those terms which the parties have agreed to and one cannot agree to secret terms. Thus, the district court held that buyers of computer software need not obey the terms of shrinkwrap licenses. Such licenses were found to be ineffectual because their terms did not appear on the outsides of the packages. ProCD (P) appealed.

ISSUE: Does a buyer accept goods when, after an opportunity to inspect, he fails to make an effective rejection?

HOLDING AND DECISION: (Easterbrook, J.) Yes. A buyer accepts goods when, after an opportunity to inspect, he fails to make an effective rejection under §2-602 of the Uniform Commercial Code. A vendor, as master of the offer, may invite acceptance by conduct, and may propose limitations on the kind of conduct that constitutes acceptance. ProCD (P) proposed a contract that a buyer would accept by using the software after having an opportunity to read the license at leisure. Zeidenberg (D) did this, since he had no choice when the software splashed the license across his computer screen and would not let him proceed without indicating acceptance. The license was an ordinary contract accompanying the sale of products and was therefore governed by the common law of contracts and the

Uniform Commercial Code. Transactions in which the exchange of money precedes the communication of detailed terms are common. Buying insurance or buying a plane ticket are two common examples. ProCD (P) extended an opportunity to reject if a buyer should find the license terms unsatisfactory. Zeidenberg (D) inspected the package, tried out the software, learned of the license, and did not reject the goods. Reversed and remanded.

EDITOR'S ANALYSIS: The sale of information contained in computer databases presented new challenges to courts. Some courts found that the sale of software was the sale of services, rather than of goods. This case treated the sale of software as a sale of goods governed by Article 2 of the U.C.C.

QUICKNOTES
CD-ROM - Compact disc - read only memory.

INSPECTION OF GOODS - The examination of goods, which are the subject matter of a contract for sale, for the purpose of determining whether they are satisfactory.

REJECTION - The refusal to accept the terms of an offer.

SHRINKWRAP LICENSE - Terms of restriction packaged inside a product.

U.C.C. § 2-602 - Provides that a rejection after an opportunity to inspect may be effective unless the buyer manifests acceptance in the manner invited by the offeror.

NOTES:

P

CHAPTER P
PAYMENT LAW

QUICK REFERENCE RULES OF LAW

1. **Negotiation: Special and Blank Endorsement.** An assignee may not recover the proceeds of a promissory note unless the payee or owner of the note has a right to transfer it. (McCrackin v. Hayes)

McCRACKIN v. HAYES
Assignee (P) v. Executor of note (D)
Ga. Ct. App., 118 Ga. App. 267, 163 S.E.2d 246 (1968).

NATURE OF CASE: Appeal from denial of damages for breach of payment of a promissory note.

FACT SUMMARY: In McCrackin's (P) action against Hayes (D) on a promissory note, the district court ruled that McCrackin (P), as assignee, could not recover the proceeds on the note because the assignor had no right to transfer it to him.

CONCISE RULE OF LAW: An assignee may not recover the proceeds of a promissory note unless the payee or owner of the note has a right to transfer it.

FACTS: McCrackin (P) brought an action against Hayes (D) in district court, alleging that Hayes (D) had executed a promissory note "to Richard P. Baker, d/b/a Baker Construction Company" and that Baker, for a valuable consideration, transferred and assigned the note to McCrackin (P). The note and assignment (by a separate writing) attached to the petition showed that the payee on the note was "Baker Construction Co.," and the assignment was executed by "Richard P. Baker." Hayes (D) denied that he was indebted to McCrackin (P), arguing that Baker was not the payee and, thus, without power to make an assignment. The district court, agreeing with Hayes (D), reached a judgment in his favor. McCrackin (P) appealed.

ISSUE: If the payee or owner of a promissory note did not have a right to transfer it, may an assignee recover the proceeds from it?

HOLDING AND DECISION: (Hall, J.) No. An assignee may not recover the proceeds of a promissory note unless the payee or owner of the note has a right to transfer it. This rule is consistent with relevant statutory provisions in the Georgia code dealing with commercial practice. In the instant case, since the readily discernible facts indicate that any chose of action or property right in the note was in Baker Construction, Baker had no right individually to assign it to McCrackin (P). Accordingly, the district court did not err in reaching a judgment in Hayes' (D) favor, denying the validity of this assignment. Affirmed.

EDITOR'S ANALYSIS: In the original version of Article 3, only a holder has the right to sue on an instrument to enforce payment according to § 3-301, but § 3R-301 would allow owners who were nonholders to sue in some circumstances, replacing the original word "holder" with the more-inclusive "person entitled to enforce the instrument." To qualify as a holder under § 1-201(20), a person must meet two requirements: (1) possession of the instrument and (2) good title (through valid negotiation) all the way from the drawer through the various transferees to the current processor. Failure to establish holder status because of defects in negotiation can be legally fatal.

NOTES:

180

CHAPTER ST
SECURED TRANSACTIONS

QUICK REFERENCE RULES OF LAW

1. **Default.** That the result to the debtor will be harsh is not a sufficient basis for refusing to foreclose a mortgage upon real estate given as supplemental security for a debt. (Foster v. Knutson)

2. **Default: Repossession and Resale.** A creditor may not recover the costs of repossession if so doing would be unfair. (Imperial Discount Corp. v. Aiken)

FOSTER v. KNUTSON
Sellers (P) v. Buyers (D)
Wash. Sup. Ct., 527 P.2d 1108 (1974).

NATURE OF CASE: Appeal from order denying judicial foreclosure upon real estate mortgage.

FACT SUMMARY: A trial court refused to foreclose a mortgage on real estate given as supplemental security for a debt due to the harshness of the result to the debtors, the Knutsons (D).

CONCISE RULE OF LAW: That the result to the debtor will be harsh is not a sufficient basis for refusing to foreclose a mortgage upon real estate given as supplemental security for a debt.

FACTS: Ronald and Jack Knutson (buyers) (D) contracted to purchase stock in Hesperian Orchards, Inc. from Myron and Earl Foster and an associate (sellers) (P). The sale was secured by a lien upon the shares of stock. Due to inclement weather, the orchard's crop was far below expectations. The buyers (D) could not make payments on the purchase. The parties agreed to a modification of the purchase agreement which involved, among other things, a supplemental mortgage on certain real estate of buyers (D) and an express declaration that, in event of default, all U.C.C. remedies were available. The buyers (D) defaulted. A foreclosure sale was held of the subject stock. The sellers (P) purchased the stock at a public auction, at a price well below that agreed upon in the defaulted-upon contract. The sellers (P) sought to foreclose upon the mortgage in buyers' (D) real estate. The trial court denied this, holding that it would be inequitable. The sellers (P) appealed.

ISSUE: Is the fact that the result to the debtor will be harsh a sufficient basis for refusing to foreclose a mortgage upon real estate given as supplemental security for a debt?

HOLDING AND DECISION: (Utter, J.) No. That the result to the debtor will be harsh is not a sufficient basis for refusing to foreclose a mortgage upon real estate given as supplemental security for a debt. In considering an action based on contract, a court must first determine whether the contract was lawfully formed. The court here agreed that the contract in question had so been, and this was an appropriate ruling. This having been done, the court must next determine, by reference to law and the contract itself, what the rights and obligations of the parties are. When the parties have created a specific right or obligation, and this is not contrary to law, it must be enforced; the court has no right to refuse to enforce it on the court's perceived view of the fairness of the result. Under the U.C.C., which was specifically referred to in the contract, a creditor may sell goods subject to security, keep the proceeds, and seek a deficiency from the debtor. U.C.C. § 9-504(2). This is what the sellers (P) sought to do

here. The fact that they sold the stock to themselves is immaterial, as long as the sale was fair, which it was. Consequently, the sellers (P) were entitled to seek a deficiency, and the trial court was in error for denying this to them. Reversed.

EDITOR'S ANALYSIS: The U.C.C. provides for two basic procedures for a creditor of a defaulting debtor. The creditor may levy on his security, then sue for any deficiency. Alternatively, he may sue first and then levy on either the secured property or any unsecured property. Per the U.C.C., the choice of procedure is with the creditor.

NOTES:

IMPERIAL DISCOUNT CORP. v. AIKEN
Seller/creditor (P) v. Purchaser (D)
38 Misc. 2d 187, 238 N.Y.S. 2d 269 (1963).

NATURE OF CASE: Action seeking damages for expenses incurred in the repossession and sale of an auto.

FACT SUMMARY: An unpaid debt of $11.75 on a car battery led to the repossession and sale of the auto, and the creditor also sought to recover the expenses involved in the repossession.

CONCISE RULE OF LAW: A creditor may not recover the costs of repossession if so doing would be unfair.

FACTS: Aiken (D) purchased an auto battery for $35. It was to be paid in installments. The debt instrument created a security interest in the auto as well as the battery. Aiken (D) defaulted on a balance of $11.75. Imperial Discount Corp. (P), the seller/creditor, repossessed the auto and sold it at an auction. It then brought an action for damages against Aiken (D) for $128, the total of the auctioneer's fees and storage charges, less the amount realized at the sale of the auto.

ISSUE: May a creditor recover the costs of repossession if so doing would be unfair?

HOLDING AND DECISION: (Composto, J.) No. A creditor may not recover the costs of repossession if so doing would be unfair. Under the literal terms of New York's retail installment sales act, a creditor can recover such costs any time. However, when the circumstances of a repossession were sufficiently oppressive to the debtor, this court will not infer a legislative intent that further obligations be heaped upon the debtor. Here, a default of $11.75 led to the loss of Aiken's (D) vehicle. To further burden him with a judgment of $128 would shock the conscience of this court and will not be done. Judgment for Aiken (D).

EDITOR'S ANALYSIS: Although the dollar amounts at issue here were quite small, this case is illustrative of a significant issue in legal philosophy. Apparently Imperial (P) had a right to collect, under a literal reading of the law in question. The court chose not to obey the letter of the law in question but rather to infer certain legislative intents not found in the law in question. Whether it is proper for a court to do this is a hotly debated legal issue.

NOTES:

GLOSSARY
COMMON LATIN WORDS AND PHRASES ENCOUNTERED IN THE LAW

A FORTIORI: Because one fact exists or has been proven, therefore a second fact that is related to the first fact must also exist.

A PRIORI: From the cause to the effect. A term of logic used to denote that when one generally accepted truth is shown to be a cause, another particular effect must necessarily follow.

AB INITIO: From the beginning; a condition which has existed throughout, as in a marriage which was void ab initio.

ACTUS REUS: The wrongful act; in criminal law, such action sufficient to trigger criminal liability.

AD VALOREM: According to value; an ad valorem tax is imposed upon an item located within the taxing jurisdiction calculated by the value of such item.

AMICUS CURIAE: Friend of the court. Its most common usage takes the form of an amicus curiae brief, filed by a person who is not a party to an action but is nonetheless allowed to offer an argument supporting his legal interests.

ARGUENDO: In arguing. A statement, possibly hypothetical, made for the purpose of argument, is one made arguendo.

BILL QUIA TIMET: A bill to quiet title (establish ownership) to real property.

BONA FIDE: True, honest, or genuine. May refer to a person's legal position based on good faith or lacking notice of fraud (such as a bona fide purchaser for value) or to the authenticity of a particular document (such as a bona fide last will and testament).

CAUSA MORTIS: With approaching death in mind. A gift causa mortis is a gift given by a party who feels certain that death is imminent.

CAVEAT EMPTOR: Let the buyer beware. This maxim is reflected in the rule of law that a buyer purchases at his own risk because it is his responsibility to examine, judge, test, and otherwise inspect what he is buying.

CERTIORARI: A writ of review. Petitions for review of a case by the United States Supreme Court are most often done by means of a writ of certiorari.

CONTRA: On the other hand. Opposite. Contrary to.

CORAM NOBIS: Before us; writs of error directed to the court that originally rendered the judgment.

CORAM VOBIS: Before you; writs of error directed by an appellate court to a lower court to correct a factual error.

CORPUS DELICTI: The body of the crime; the requisite elements of a crime amounting to objective proof that a crime has been committed.

CUM TESTAMENTO ANNEXO, ADMINISTRATOR (ADMINISTRATOR C.T.A.): With will annexed; an administrator c.t.a. settles an estate pursuant to a will in which he is not appointed.

DE BONIS NON, ADMINISTRATOR (ADMINISTRATOR D.B.N.): Of goods not administered; an administrator d.b.n. settles a partially settled estate.

DE FACTO: In fact; in reality; actually. Existing in fact but not officially approved or engendered.

DE JURE: By right; lawful. Describes a condition that is legitimate "as a matter of law," in contrast to the term "de facto," which connotes something existing in fact but not legally sanctioned or authorized. For example, de facto segregation refers to segregation brought about by housing patterns, etc., whereas de jure segregation refers to segregation created by law.

DE MINIMUS: Of minimal importance; insignificant; a trifle; not worth bothering about.

DE NOVO: Anew; a second time; afresh. A trial de novo is a new trial held at the appellate level as if the case originated there and the trial at a lower level had not taken place.

DICTA: Generally used as an abbreviated form of obiter dicta, a term describing those portions of a judicial opinion incidental or not necessary to resolution of the specific question before the court. Such nonessential statements and remarks are not considered to be binding precedent.

DUCES TECUM: Refers to a particular type of writ or subpoena requesting a party or organization to produce certain documents in their possession.

EN BANC: Full bench. Where a court sits with all justices present rather than the usual quorum.

EX PARTE: For one side or one party only. An ex parte proceeding is one undertaken for the benefit of only one party, without notice to, or an appearance by, an adverse party.

EX POST FACTO: After the fact. An ex post facto law is a law that retroactively changes the consequences of a prior act.

EX REL.: Abbreviated form of the term ex relatione, meaning, upon relation or information. When the state brings an action in which it has no interest against an individual at the instigation of one who has a private interest in the matter.

FORUM NON CONVENIENS: Inconvenient forum. Although a court may have jurisdiction over the case, the action should be tried in a more conveniently located court, one to which parties and witnesses may more easily travel, for example.

GUARDIAN AD LITEM: A guardian of an infant as to litigation, appointed to represent the infant and pursue his/her rights.

HABEAS CORPUS: You have the body. The modern writ of habeas corpus is a writ directing that a person (body) being detained (such as a prisoner) be brought before the court so that the legality of his detention can be judicially ascertained.

IN CAMERA: In private, in chambers. When a hearing is held before a judge in his chambers or when all spectators are excluded from the courtroom.

IN FORMA PAUPERIS: In the manner of a pauper. A party who proceeds in forma pauperis because of his poverty is one who is allowed to bring suit without liability for costs.

INFRA: Below, under. A word referring the reader to a later part of a book. (The opposite of supra.)

IN LOCO PARENTIS: In the place of a parent.

IN PARI DELICTO: Equally wrong; a court of equity will not grant requested relief to an applicant who is in pari delicto, or as much at fault in the transactions giving rise to the controversy as is the opponent of the applicant.

IN PARI MATERIA: On like subject matter or upon the same matter. Statutes relating to the same person or things are said to be in pari materia. It is a general rule of statutory construction that such statutes should be construed together, i.e., looked at as if they together constituted one law.

IN PERSONAM: Against the person. Jurisdiction over the person of an individual.

IN RE: In the matter of. Used to designate a proceeding involving an estate or other property.

IN REM: A term that signifies an action against the res, or thing. An action in rem is basically one that is taken directly against property, as distinguished from an action in personam, i.e., against the person.

INTER ALIA: Among other things. Used to show that the whole of a statement, pleading, list, statute, etc., has not been set forth in its entirety.

INTER PARTES: Between the parties. May refer to contracts, conveyances or other transactions having legal significance.

INTER VIVOS: Between the living. An inter vivos gift is a gift made by a living grantor, as distinguished from bequests contained in a will, which pass upon the death of the testator.

IPSO FACTO: By the mere fact itself.

JUS: Law or the entire body of law.

LEX LOCI: The law of the place; the notion that the rights of parties to a legal proceeding are governed by the law of the place where those rights arose.

MALUM IN SE: Evil or wrong in and of itself; inherently wrong. This term describes an act that is wrong by its very nature, as opposed to one which would not be wrong but for the fact that there is a specific legal prohibition against it (malum prohibitum).

MALUM PROHIBITUM: Wrong because prohibited, but not inherently evil. Used to describe something that is wrong because it is expressly forbidden by law but that is not in and of itself evil, e.g., speeding.

MANDAMUS: We command. A writ directing an official to take a certain action.

MENS REA: A guilty mind; a criminal intent. A term used to signify the mental state that accompanies a crime or other prohibited act. Some crimes require only a general mens rea (general intent to do the prohibited act), but others, like assault with intent to murder, require the existence of a specific mens rea.

MODUS OPERANDI: Method of operating; generally refers to the manner or style of a criminal in committing crimes, admissible in appropriate cases as evidence of the identity of a defendant.

NEXUS: A connection to.

NISI PRIUS: A court of first impression. A nisi prius court is one where issues of fact are tried before a judge or jury.

N.O.V. (NON OBSTANTE VEREDICTO): Notwithstanding the verdict. A judgment n.o.v. is a judgment given in favor of one party despite the fact that a verdict was returned in favor of the other party, the justification being that the verdict either had no reasonable support in fact or was contrary to law.

NUNC PRO TUNC: Now for then. This phrase refers to actions that may be taken and will then have full retroactive effect.

PENDENTE LITE: Pending the suit; pending litigation underway.

PER CAPITA: By head; beneficiaries of an estate, if they take in equal shares, take per capita.

PER CURIAM: By the court; signifies an opinion ostensibly written "by the whole court" and with no identified author.

PER SE: By itself, in itself; inherently.

PER STIRPES: By representation. Used primarily in the law of wills to describe the method of distribution where a person, generally because of death, is unable to take that which is left to him by the will of another, and therefore his heirs divide such property between them rather than take under the will individually.

PRIMA FACIE: On its face, at first sight. A prima facie case is one that is sufficient on its face, meaning that the evidence supporting it is adequate to establish the case until contradicted or overcome by other evidence.

PRO TANTO: For so much; as far as it goes. Often used in eminent domain cases when a property owner receives partial payment for his land without prejudice to his right to bring suit for the full amount he claims his land to be worth.

QUANTUM MERUIT: As much as he deserves. Refers to recovery based on the doctrine of unjust enrichment in those cases in which a party has rendered valuable services or furnished materials that were accepted and enjoyed by another under circumstances that would reasonably notify the recipient that the rendering party expected to be paid. In essence, the law implies a contract to pay the reasonable value of the services or materials furnished.

QUASI: Almost like; as if; nearly. This term is essentially used to signify that one subject or thing is almost analogous to another but that material differences between them do exist. For example, a quasi-criminal proceeding is one that is not strictly criminal but shares enough of the same characteristics to require some of the same safeguards (e.g., procedural due process must be followed in a parol hearing).

QUID PRO QUO: Something for something. In contract law, the consideration, something of value, passed between the parties to render the contract binding.

RES GESTAE: Things done; in evidence law, this principle justifies the admission of a statement that would otherwise be hearsay when it is made so closely to the event in question as to be said to be a part of it, or with such spontaneity as not to have the possibility of falsehood.

RES IPSA LOQUITUR: The thing speaks for itself. This doctrine gives rise to a rebuttable presumption of negligence when the instrumentality causing the injury was within the exclusive control of the defendant, and the injury was one that does not normally occur unless a person has been negligent.

RES JUDICATA: A matter adjudged. Doctrine which provides that once a court of competent jurisdiction has rendered a final judgment or decree on the merits, that judgment or decree is conclusive upon the parties to the case and prevents them from engaging in any other litigation on the points and issues determined therein.

RESPONDEAT SUPERIOR: Let the master reply. This doctrine holds the master liable for the wrongful acts of his servant (or the principal for his agent) in those cases in which the servant (or agent) was acting within the scope of his authority at the time of the injury.

STARE DECISIS: To stand by or adhere to that which has been decided. The common law doctrine of stare decisis attempts to give security and certainty to the law by following the policy that once a principle of law as applicable to a certain set of facts has been set forth in a decision, it forms a precedent which will subsequently be followed, even though a different decision might be made were it the first time the question had arisen. Of course, stare decisis is not an inviolable principle and is departed from in instances where there is good cause (e.g., considerations of public policy led the Supreme Court to disregard prior decisions sanctioning segregation).

SUPRA: Above. A word referring a reader to an earlier part of a book.

ULTRA VIRES: Beyond the power. This phrase is most commonly used to refer to actions taken by a corporation that are beyond the power or legal authority of the corporation.

ADDENDUM OF FRENCH DERIVATIVES

IN PAIS: Not pursuant to legal proceedings.

CHATTEL: Tangible personal property.

CY PRES: Doctrine permitting courts to apply trust funds to purposes not expressed in the trust but necessary to carry out the settlor's intent.

PER AUTRE VIE: For another's life; in property law, an estate may be granted that will terminate upon the death of someone other than the grantee.

PROFIT A PRENDRE: A license to remove minerals or other produce from land.

VOIR DIRE: Process of questioning jurors as to their predispositions about the case or parties to a proceeding in order to identify those jurors displaying bias or prejudice.

CASENOTE LEGAL BRIEFS